THE
POLITICAL THEORY
OF
John C. Calhoun

J C Calhoun

THE
POLITICAL THEORY
OF
John C. Calhoun

August O. Spain

1968
OCTAGON BOOKS, INC.
New York

Reprinted 1968
by special arrangement with Twayne Publishers, Inc.

OCTAGON BOOKS, INC.
175 FIFTH AVENUE
NEW YORK, N. Y. 10010

Printed in U.S.A. by
NOBLE OFFSET PRINTERS, INC.
NEW YORK 3, N. Y.

TO

Margaret Eliza Spain, *née* Roberts

indomitable rebel

Preface

This study was originally undertaken as a doctoral dissertation at Yale University under the tutelage of Professor Francis W. Coker, and was completed there in 1937. Since then a few minor changes have been made; for them, as well as for the initial performance, the author, of course, assumes full responsibility. Thanks are due to the generosity of the late Professor Ulrich B. Phillips for the use of his private library, which this writer found rich in source materials not generally available. The study offers, it is believed, a comprehensive exposition of the political theory of John C. Calhoun. Other studies of this subject have been considerably abbreviated, and have made, it appears, errors of analysis and of interpretation, which this work seeks to correct. Considerable attention is devoted here to the historical origins of Calhoun's political ideas. An attempt has been made to relate the nature of Calhoun's theory to the historical events of his life-time; and it readily appears that his thought on government arose in part out of rationalization for the political defense of Southern civilization. But he also strove, with more historical insight and philosophical perspective than later critics have credited to him, to base his political doctrines upon concepts of universal and enduring validity. This study gives a more favorable estimate of Calhoun as a thinker, it is recognized, than that heretofore accepted. This new appraisal can be maintained, however, without any loss of objectivity.

The chief deficiency in Calhoun's thought, according to Merriam, Parrington, and others, was his failure to appreciate the social and economic forces that were impelling the country toward nationalistic unification during the middle period of American history. This is a mistaken view. Calhoun was acutely conscious of the trend to political centralization and of the moving forces in the process. Only an extremely mechanistic determinism would justify characterizing his opposition to the trend as blind or entirely futile. An effort is made to show how certain political facts of the time supported Calhoun's view of sovereignty as located in the States. Also this study offers an appreciation of the pioneering character of Calhoun's adaptation and use of the organic Greek view of the relation between the state and the individual; a more logical exposition of his doctrine of nullification as related to his theory of the concurrent majority; a reconsideration, in the light of successful decentralization elsewhere, especially in the British Commonwealth of Nations, of the charges of impracticality and impossibility directed against the theory of the concurrent majority; and a clearer treatment of the influence of Calhoun on Von Seydel in Germany.

An effort has been made to point out some possible significance in Calhoun's thought for present-day political problems. Especial attention is given to his belief in the efficacy of political decentralization. A suggestion is offered for the application of the theory of the concurrent majority to the solution of the modern American urban-rural problem. Finally a comparison is made between the position of Calhoun and that of modern Southern agrarians.

AUGUST O. SPAIN

Fort Worth
December, 1950

Contents

Part I

Life of Calhoun

I

Life of Calhoun

A. HIS PUBLIC CAREER

JOHN CALDWELL CALHOUN, planter, lawyer, statesman, and philosopher, was one of the most significant figures in the middle period of American history. He was one of the political giants whose struggles during most of this time involved issues of gravest importance for the destiny of the country. For more than forty years of an active public life, years which covered two foreign wars, vigorous westward expansion, rapid growth of population, unprecedented industrial and commercial development, and the spread of political democracy—all entailing in the sphere of practical politics problems of the most difficult and complicated sort—Calhoun worked hard, long and ably to approach his chosen ideal of "the perfect statesman."[1] He served as a member of the legislature of South Carolina, member of the U. S. House of Representatives, Secretary of War, Vice-President, Secretary of State, and Senator. At times his hopes were high for attaining the Presidency, but this he never achieved. In the political warfare of the epoch, which was marked by a gradual but steady growth of sectional antagonisms, Calhoun became the chief representative of the planter aristocracy of the South. The "sweep of economic forces," the social and political concomitants of the industrial revolution, brought a new force into power in the North. It was Calhoun's part to oppose this industrial capitalism in its efforts to win dominance in the federal government, to forestall its wooing of the free but agrarian West,[2] and to protect the South against its aggressions. His efforts to achieve these ends were various. But what is of primary interest in this study, and what constitutes probably his most enduring claim to fame, is his work as the theoretical and practical exponent of nullification and State rights.[3] These he used as powerful weapons in the defense of slavery and of the sectional interests of the South.

Calhoun was born on March 18, 1782[4], near Abbeville, South Carolina, of Scotch-Irish parentage. Both his father and his mother were of immigrant stock that had moved Southward by stages from Pennsylvania to settle finally in the uplands of South Carolina, where they lived hardily as frontier farmers. Calhoun's boyhood was spent for the most part on the family farm. He worked in the fields along with the slaves, and after his father's death he shouldered some of the burdens of management. Prepared with some smattering of learning by the famous schoolmaster, Moses Waddel, Calhoun attended Yale for two years and Reeve's law school at Litchfield, Connecticut, for almost as long. Then, after some study in a law office at Charleston, he began to practice in Abbeville. Although his work proved quite profitable, his early "aversion to law"[5] persisted; and he gave it up entirely as soon as he had fairly begun his career in politics. He was elected to the United States House of Representatives in 1810, after having served for two years in the State legislature where he distinguished himself chiefly by his aggressive denunciations of British depredations of American ships on the high seas. It appears that it was largely his attitude on this subject, together, of course, with some recognition of his ability, that secured him political preferment at this time. Then, in January, 1811, on the verge of his work in the larger sphere, Calhoun married his cousin, Floride Bon-

neau Calhoun, of Charleston. Their joint means, coupled
with his careful administration of their land-holdings,
made him financially independent for life. Their married
life was apparently a happy one, and gave issue to nine
children.

Calhoun's public career may be very conveniently divided into two parts, with the turning point somewhere
between 1825 and 1827.[6] During the early part, certainly,
he was something of a nationalist. In the Twelfth Congress he, Henry Clay, and James Monroe were among the
"war hawks" who urged war with Great Britain. It was
war in the name of defense of our maritime rights, but
also war to remove the obstacles Britain put in the way of
Western expansion and the burdens imposed upon Southern export enterprise. They succeeded finally, in conjunction, of course, with the administration, in overriding the
opposition of John Randolph of Roanoke and of the New
Englanders, and in precipitating the country into the conflict. Calhoun worked prodigiously on measures to raise
troops and to provide funds. The obstructive tactics of the
representatives of New England could not dampen his
spirit. Even after peace was made, it was undoubtedly his
preoccupation with the problems arising out of the war
and with the task of building up the military strength of
the country that gave a nationalistic bent to his views. He,
and McDuffie and Hayne among his fellow Carolinians,
sought improved military establishments; encouragement,
through a protective tariff, of domestic industry with a
view to American self-sufficiency, especially in materials
for clothing and defense; and a judicious sytem of internal improvements, a good system of roads and canals
being necessary to unite the country, by the bonds of commerce, and to provide means of military communication
and movement in case of war. In his mercantilist inclinations, Calhoun went so far as to renounce expressly the

doctrine of *laissez faire,* declaring in 1816 that protection to manufacturers "must not depend on the abstract principle that industry, left to pursue its own course, will find in its own interest all the encouragement that is necessary. I lay the claims of the manufacturers entirely out of view, . . . but on general principles . . . a certain encouragement should be extended, at least to our woolen and cotton manufacturers."[7] He realized that what was necessary for the common good might often be seemingly opposed to the interests of particular sections, but believed that such burdens must be borne as the condition of national greatness.[8] As for constitutional limitations, "he was no advocate for refined arguments on the Constitution. This instrument was not intended as a thesis for the logician to exercise his ingenuity on. It ought to be construed with plain, good sense. . . ."[9]

In 1817 Calhoun entered Monroe's Cabinet as head of the War Department. He applied himself industriously to setting its jumbled affairs in order, clearing up old debts, effecting some economies, and proving himself an efficient executive. He showed ability also in tackling the task of administrative reorganization by introducing the "bureau" type of working unit and putting into effect a set of uniform regulations of work, which he had caused to be drafted. He claimed credit for inaugurating in the department systematic collection of medical data for use in scientific study. His views of public policy presumably remained unchanged. Certainly his departmental report on roads and canals, his diligent work in supervising the federal survey, and his suggestions in his last annual report as to the most desirable federal works showed a sustained interest is internal improvements.[10] Moreover, in a letter written in July of 1824 to Robert S. Garnett, he reasserted his adherence to a somewhat flexible rule of constitutional construction.[11] As late as May, 1825, he upheld his past course upon the tariff and other questions, at a public dinner given in his honor at Abbeville; he was then Vice-President, having been elected the preceding year.[12]

But Calhoun was not in these matter wholly representative of South Carolina or of the Southern States. Opposition to protection was articulate there from the very beginning of government under the Constitution; and in 1816, when Calhoun and his friends in Congress favored the tariff bill, they were not supported by the majority of Southern Congressmen.[13] The work of Judge William Smith and of Thomas Cooper in South Carolina began to bear fruit in the protests by local meetings and resolutions of the State legislature. The lead of South Carolina in 1820 was followed within a few years by other legislatures of the Southern States in a dozen or more resolutions against the tariff and internal improvmements.[14]

It was at about the same time that the agitation over the Missouri question disturbed the peace of Congress and gave unmistakable evidence of the growth of sectional hostility. The attempt to limit the extension of slavery undoubtedly aroused the resentment and apprehensions of many Southerners who instinctively joined hands in defense of their "peculiar domestic institution." Unfortunately the compromise did not settle the problem. In succeeding years many State legislatures continued to attack slavery in joint resolutions and petitions to Congress; and in various guises the question continued to recur in the debates of Congress itself. This sectional antagonism probably had some influence on the growing sectional alignment on the tariff,[15] although as yet the two issues were not generally joined or looked upon as two phases of a single contest for power between the sections. Calhoun apparently depreciated the seriousness of the danger to slavery at the time.[16]

In South Carolina opposition to protection had united

all parts of the State by 1827; and Calhoun, although somewhat reluctant for fear of damaging his political fences, showed his stand by defeating the tariff bill of that year with his casting vote as presiding officer in the Senate. The "tariff of abominations," adopted in 1828, aroused great excitement;[17] and the reply was the "South Carolina Exposition" of the same year. This had been written by Calhoun, but his authorship was kept secret. The document denounced the economic exploitation of the South involved in the "American System," making a strong case against the tariff in terms of *laissez faire* economics. The "consolidation" resulting from the usurpation of reserved power by Congress was deplored; and State interposition was put forward as the corrective for the evil. It was here that Calhoun first attempted philosophical treatment of his idea of the concurrent majority.[18] Once the way had been clearly pointed out, the nullification party, led by Hamilton, Harper, McDuffie, Turnbull, Rhett, and others, determined to put the State "on its sovereignty"; these "radicals" canvassed the electorate vigorously in successive elections, and, when Congress failed to provide relief in the tariff of 1832, secured the adoption of the Ordinance of Nullification by constitutional assembly.[19] The effect of this measure was to enlist the full authority of the State in preventing, through various ingenious devices, the collection of customs duties within the State. President Jackson countered with a proclamation in which he insisted that these revenues must be collected, that the State had no right to prevent their collection, and that if necessary the armed might of the federal government would enforce the revenue laws. Warlike gestures were made on both sides.[20]

Fortunately for all concerned, South Carolina postponed putting the ordinance into effect until Clay, in consultation with Calhoun (who had resigned as Vice-President to take Hayne's place in the Senate) and others, was able to put through one of his compromise measures, by the terms of which the duties were to be cut rather seriously, although gradually over a period of years. Calhoun supported the compromise,[21] but strenuously opposed the Force Bill that was carried through at the same time. This latter bill authorized the President to deal with nullification of federal law to the extent of employing military force. Calhoun engaged Webster in debate on many of the pertinent issues; and, by quoting Webster's own words, gave the great orator the forensic lacing of his life. He showed on Webster's own authority that the Constitution was a compact; he contended that any party to a compact has the right to judge of violations thereof, and, moreover, that the parties, either jointly or singly, have the authority to prevent such violations by an agent (the federal government) whose sole source of power is the same compact. Then he proceeded to elaborate the case in an argument, in legalistic and historical terms, for State sovereignty, which was the foundation stone for nullification.[22] One auditor of the debate, old John Randolph, exclaimed afterward that he "saw . . . [Webster] dying an hour ago."[23] Despite Calhoun's best efforts, the bill was passed. Nevertheless, he prevailed upon his home State to accept the compromise. The constituent assembly repealed the ordinance nullifying the tariff law, but at the same time adopted another nullifying the Force Bill.

Calhoun had by his course in the nullification controversy completely destroyed whatever ragged ties remained between him and President Jackson. Mrs. Calhoun's snubbing Mrs. Eaton, the wife of the Secretary of War, because of her questionable past had already affronted the old war-dog, for he and his wife had suffered in the past similar snobbery. Jackson's rage on discovering that Calhoun had, while in Monroe's cabinet, advised some discipline of his conduct in invading Florida with his troops on his own initiative, strained their relations beyond repair. Nullification, to Jackson, was simply another sin on the villain's head. Naturally Calhoun and his followers went with the opposition. However, as Calhoun himself deliberately declared, they were not converted to any of the principles of the Whigs; they joined them only in opposition to executive usurpations of power. "King Andy" was their common foe.

On Jackson's passing from the national scene, Calhoun and his following found it more congenial to swing back into the Democratic fold. Calhoun was especially sympathetic with Van Buren's efforts to deal with the currency problem after the financial panic of 1837; and he aided the administration tremendously in establishing the independent treasury system. Cries of desertion and inconsistency arose from the Whig camp. But Calhoun had always opposed (and in this at least he had been in agreement with Jackson) the enlistment of the credit and the support of the government in the service of business interests of the community. He had supported the establishment of the Second Bank of the United States as the only remedy available for the sad financial plight of the government after the War of 1812. Even then he had looked upon it as an evil to be tolerated only as long as necessary; and he had written his own safeguards into the bill which established the bank, after aiding the defeat of successive bills that he regarded as schemes to exploit the public credit. After the independent treasury was set up, he doggedly opposed all efforts to charter another United States Bank. So it was with the other pet policies of the Whigs. The tariff on imports was held generally low; the one success of the Whigs in raising it was rectified following the very next election, Calhoun aiding with his denunciations of the violation of the Compromise of 1833.[24] To forestall their best efforts, he cannily engaged himself in the detection of their various plans for depleting the treasury, whether by extravagant expenditures or division of the proceeds from the sale of public lands among the States, so as to necessitate raising the tariff duties higher. His activities in these matters won him admiration and gratitude throughout the Democratic party. His plans for winning the Presidency, which had, of course, been side-tracked earlier by the nullification episode, might yet have assumed serious proportions—had not his intransigent stand on abolition rendered impossible support from the Northern wing of the party.

Theodore Dwight Weld, the Tappan brothers, and William Lloyd Garrison had begun their work in the early 30's; and although discountenanced by many people in the North, it had assumed the proportions of a movement destined to endure and grow.[25] Even during the nullification controversy, Calhoun had felt that hostility to slavery was forcing a cleavage between the North and South on other important issues of public policy.[26] The efforts of the abolitionists to sow the seeds of discord in the South by sending incendiary matter through the mail and flooding Congress with hundreds and thousands of petitions were two especially insidious methods of propaganda that aroused Calhoun's fears. He did not want such use of the mails prohibited by the federal government, for that procedure would logically involve admission of that government's power to judge what matter was not incendiary and to enforce its delivery through the mails. Rather, he felt, the federal authorities should cooperate in the enforcement of laws of the several States on the subject. In this way each set of authorities would be acting clearly within its proper sphere, the federal officials in performing their duty of carrying the mails, the State officials in enforcing State laws for the protection of domestic institutions. This procedure had already been used in the case of quarantine laws and laws for the exclusion of free Negroes from certain States.[27] Congress, however, did nothing. With regard to the petitions to Congress, Calhoun was more successful in getting his way. He repeatedly hammered home the dangers of reception as the beginning of a process of gradual encroachment by which reception would lead successively to reference to committee, discussion of the merits of the petition, and assumption of power to deal with the subject. He finally persuaded the Senate to adopt the practice, if not the rule, of automatically laying these petitions on the table.[28]

Calhoun was further worried by the "underground railroads" that had developed in the North. He charged many Northern States with having nullified, not an unconstitutional law of Congress, but a part of the Constitution itself, by their "personal liberty" laws which rendered so very difficult the recovery of runaway slaves. That the abolitionists themselves were still small in numbers did not reassure him in the least, for he believed that the competition of the older parties for the support of the abolitionists, in the old game of politics, rendered them constitutionally incapable of dealing effectively with the problems abolitionism was creating. He lost all faith in the efficacy of political party action. Opposition in the North to the annexation of Texas only confirmed his views. He wrote his son-in-law, Thomas G. Clemson, that "the course of the northern wing of the party has been very bad on the abolition question," and that "if the annexation of Texas is to be defeated by the same spirit . . ., it is difficult to say what may be the consequences."[29] For his own part, he entered Tyler's cabinet as Secretary of State in order to complete the negotiation of the treaty of annexation which had been initiated by Upshur and in order to deal with the Oregon controversy.

The vigor with which he sought annexation of Texas (and certainly some of the credit of its final achievement belongs to him) and the compromising spirit in which he approached the Oregon boundary dispute were, of course, contrasted; and the difference was attributed to the desire of a Southern imperialist, eager for expansion only into territory where slavery would probably extend. Such partisan ignoring of the patent differences in the two situations cannot pass for the judgment of history. The validity of American territorial claim was certainly more palpable in Texas (given annexation) than it ever could have been to 54°40' as the northern boundary of Oregon; war was less inevitable on annexation of Texas than on seizure of British territory in the Northwest; and, besides, annexation of Texas would have expanded American territory in the South only as far West as it had already been pushed in the North. Calhoun himself did not believe that annexation of Texas would bring on war with Mexico if the boundary settlement were dealt with by the Americans in the proper spirit of conciliation. He consistently opposed the war, and laid the responsibility for its initiation on the President. Ordering American troops to proceed to the extreme limits of American claims for boundary, he held, was deliberately intended to provoke war. He washed his hands of it.[30]

The introduction of the Wilmot Proviso to exclude slavery from all territory acquired in the War with Mexico represented to Calhoun but the latest step of a party in the North whose persistent intention was to destroy the balance of the sections in the federal government and thereby deprive the South of any means of protection within its framework. The attempt to admit California as a free State, before it had even acquired territorial status, was a similar move. He believed that any action to divide the region into free and slave, or to prohibit the introduction of slaves into any portion of it, was entirely beyond the competence of Congress. The Missouri compromise was really unconstitutional,[31] and so would be any similar measure. The federal government as the agent of the sovereign States held the territory in trust for the common and equal benefit of all of them; and consequently it could not prevent a citizen of any one State from migrating into any part of the territory or carrying with him property, the legal status of which was recognized by his home State. The Missouri compromise was beyond the power of Congress, and yet the South had accepted it as a sort of extra-legal settlement of a problem. Now, however, as the North plainly showed no disposition to keep its part of the bargain, the South must assert its full constitutional right. Certainly a new State, when proceeding properly under Congressional authority to draft its constitution, had the power to settle the status of slavery within its bounds regardless of its geographical location; but Congress should not sanction the precipitate action of a handful of conspirators who demanded admission into the Union for California. There the anti-slavery men proceeded irregularly in thus striving to avoid organization as a territory first, and California remained wholly without power to determine for itself the status of slavery until authorization by Congress for voting on a proposed State constitution.

Calhoun had striven desperately over the course of years to find an adequate check for the attacks on slavery and the threats to the sectional interests of the South. He had sought to secure recognition of State sovereignty and of government by a concurrent majority through nullification; and late in life he proposed another scheme for government by concurrent majority—the establishment, by constitutional amendment, of a dual executive, each of the two members to represent the two great sections of the country and to possess an effective veto on laws of Congress.[32] He sought to suppress hostile agitation; and, although he believed that the constitutional recognition of slavery should have been sufficient to command Northern toleration of the institution, he took "higher ground" and vigorously defended it as a "positive good." He wrote to Hammond:

I have ever had but one opinion on the subject. Our fate as a people is bound up in the question. If we yield, we will be extirpated; but, if we successfully resist, we will be the greatest and most flourishing people of modern time. It is the best substratum of population in the world; and one on which great and flourishing commonwealths may be most easily and safely reared.[33]

He did not believe the labor system of the North actually afforded the laborers any more liberty than did the slave system of the South, or that the former was as humane as the latter. He appealed to the North to observe constitutional guarantees; and he warned the North, as many others had done, of Southern desperation. Naturally he sought expansion of Southern polity, and he was grieved that the North did not tolerate such efforts with as good grace as the South had shown toward expansion in the Northwest. He further sought to bind the West more closely to the South by economic bonds, the project of a railroad extending from South Carolina through Georgia to the Western States having long been a favorite with him. To the same end, at the Memphis convention in 1845, he made out something of a case to reconcile federal improvement of the navigation of the Mississippi with State rights doctrine.[34] The West must not be lost if the balance of the sections was to be maintained.

He was struggling "against the census returns," however. The industrial revolution in the North created economic power and resources superior to those of either South or West. Eastern manufacturing, stimulated by monopoly of the home market during the War of 1812 and encouraged by protective tariffs, made great new fortunes for Yankee thrift and initiative; the cotton, wool, and iron industries especially thrived. Commercial enterprise prospered; banks increased in size and numbers, and by 1830 more than four-fifths of the total number in the country were located in the North (or East). By 1860 the annual incomes earned in manufacturing, commerce, shipping, and banking practically equalled the capital investment. With a total assessed wealth of about four billion dollars, the North as a whole received an annual income of nearly one billion. By comparison the economic growth of the South was lethargic; the annual income of the section by 1860 was approximately only one-third that of the North. Southern agrarian economy became highly specialized in its dependence upon the few great staple crops of cotton, tobacco, and sugar. Prosperity, especially in cotton culture, ordinarily led only to the purchase of more Negro slaves and the expansion of acreage; and attempts either at industrial enterprise, under the inspiration of William Gregg, or at agricultural diversification generally failed. Thus the South came to rely upon the North, not only for a market, but for shipping, manufactures, supplies, and capital. The West, also largely agricultural, remained the poorest of the sections economically, even though it was the fastest growing in population. It was likewise dependent upon the North for essential credit, goods, and services.[35]

The South and West shared a basic antagonism toward the North (or East), arising out of this economic dependence. They distrusted Eastern banks, and their interests were opposed to tariff protectionism. But the conflict of interest between South and North proved more persistent and pernicious, breaking out in intermittent struggles over tariff protection and other public policies. The West was less dependent upon foreign markets than the South, and therefore bore less of the burden of the protectve tariff policy. Moreover, the North remained a larger market than the South for Western grain produce and was the chief source of funds for Western economic development. Despite the efforts of Calhoun and other Southern leaders to attract traffic from the West to the South, railroads and canals between North and West bore an ever increasing share of the intersectional trade. Further, Western economy was more akin to Northern in the employment of a system of free labor and in the enjoyment of some success in industrial and commercial enterprise during the last few decades of the middle period. These were the economic foundations for political alliance between North and West.[36]

These economic bonds alone, however, would not have produced a nationally successful political alliance that excluded the South. There were elements of economic antagonism between North and West; and certain economic ties bound the South to each of the other sections. In the rival bargaining for compromises between divergent sectional-economic interests, Southern politicians succeeded for some time in winning the support of Westerners and even of some Northerners. There were other factors in the situation, however. Western settlers who came from the North far outnumbered those who came from the South; and the latter were prevented from importing Southern plantation economy and a slave regime by geographic and climatic as well as political obstacles. Furthermore, an increasing number of Westerners were immigrants from Europe who had an antipathy to slavery. Germans and Scandinavians wanted no competition from slaveholding farmers, and many of the Germans held democratic ideals antagonistic to property in human beings. The Irish in all parts of the North despised the Negro and feared him as a competitor.[37] The abolition movement came gradually to capitalize this widespread latent hostility to slavery. Anti-slavery sentiment became a weapon increasingly employed in party warfare by reformer and political opportunist alike. The danger arose, as Calhoun had early discerned, that the emotional impact of abolitionism might forge existing economic bonds into a more durable political combination between North and West—one from which the South would necessarily be excluded. The South was faced by sectional isolation and permanent control of the federal government by a hostile majority.

Calhoun had long feared, and became at length convinced, that the slave States would have to take their fate in their own hands. He turned more and more toward reliance upon a united and determined South. He sought the calling of a political convention of the slaveholding States, pulling wires through political associates, local committees, and newspapers. He prepared an address, which he presented to the Southern members of Congress for their approval, and urged that they offer it to the people of the Southern States as an appeal for united action. The address repeated his earlier warning that "the day that the balance between the two sections of the country . . . is destroyed is a day that will not be far removed from political revolution, anarchy, civil war, and widespread disaster."[38] If united Southern resistance were not successful, he prophesied abolition, enfranchisement of the Negroes by a vengeful party bent on intrenching its domination of the South, political degradation, and social chaos.[39] In his last speech in the halls of Congress he voiced his firm convicton that "as things now stand

the Southern States cannot remain in the Union."[40] To
him, Clay's Omnibus Bill with its compromises could not
alter the situation. Only drastic reform, which was not
likely to be instituted, could keep the South in the Union;
and this would have to include restoration of the federal
character of the Union government, repeal of all laws by
which the "money power" had achieved a privileged position regardless of constitutional limitations, curtailment
of the powers of the President within strict constitutional
limits, election of the executive strictly in accordance with
constitutional provisions, establishment of a dual executive, and the repeal of the twenty-fifth section of the
Judiciary Act of 1789 (so that appeal could not lie from
State to Federal courts).[41] Only in such a reformed system
would the South be secure.

Calhoun died on March 31, 1850. He did not live to
see the remarkable accuracy with which his predictions
were fulfilled. He did leave behind him two works which
gave philosophical justification to his schemes of government by concurrent majority, attacked fiercely the old
philosophy of natural rights which had furnished the basis
for egalitarian doctrines, defended slavery, and presented
clearly his views on sovereignty and on the juristic nature
of the Union. He had begun work on these about 1843,
but the pressure of public business allowed him only spor-
adic intervals to devote to them. The first and shorter of
the two, the *Disquisition on Government,* was put in fairly
complete form before his death. It dealt entirely with the
theoretical aspects of the problems involved. The second,
the *Discourse on the Constitution and Government of the
United States,* which dealt specifically with the nature of
the Union and its federal government, was left somewhat
unfinished. The legislature of South Carolina had the two
published in a single volume, and the book became the bible

of the State rights school. It is from these works and from his speeches, reports, addresses, and letters that the political theory of Calhoun is to be derived.

B. INTERPRETATIONS

Various misconstructions of different phases of Calhoun's career have been made both by his contemporaries and by writers of later times. He has been accused of political opportunism in a "panting" pursuit of the Presidency.[42] His bitter disappointment at his failure in this quest caused him, it has been asserted, to seek disruption of the Union, for "he had rather be first man in the Slave States than the second man in the Union."[43] It was charged that he suffered something of a psychological fixation on the subject of slavery which rendered him incapable of rational treatment of the problems of politics. At various times, and especially in connection with the nullification episode, he was berated for desertion of his political allies and for inconsistency of views. It was often complained that he was too "metaphysical" in his reasoning and not, therefore, entirely to be trusted by "practical" men dealing with practical problems of government. This complaint may be dismissed as the wail of discomfited opponents who found it difficult to match his logical arguments and too great a task to dig up his premises and attempt to confute them. Certainly he wanted to be President, but his desire became no overruling passion. He did not want to unite the South in order to dominate it and use it to thrust himself into the chief magistracy. Time and again he took steps in the interest of his State and section which he knew would injure his availability as a candidate. Specifically, for example, he knew that Pennsylvania, where he

had some popularity, would not support him with nullification "on his head"; but this did not deter him from
performing his duty as he saw it .

It must be admitted that the nullification episode
marked a definite change in his views. He himself later admitted it. As to why he changed, it should be safe to say
that during his service in the House of Representatives
he had never contemplated the extent to which tariff protection might be pushed, the rates of 1816 having been
much lower than those of 1824 and 1828. His earlier
advocacy of moderate protection in however positive
terms did not logically preclude opposition to a much
higher tariff. Just after the experience of the war with
Great Britain his thoughts were centered upon the problem of building up the physical and industrial resources
of the country in order to insure an adequate national defense; his thinking was undoubtedly influenced by his preoccupation with the contingency of war, the Holy Alliance
in Europe probably causing no little disquiet to his mind.
Later a different aspect of protection was brought sharply
to his attention by the activities of the "radicals" in his
own State; and certainly he could not fail to sympathize
with the interests of his own section as he saw them. It was
one of the virtues of statesmanship to take into account
changed circumstances and shape one's course accordingly.
Only quack statesmanship prizes consistency above all
else; and in a rapidly changing world it is only the peculiarly rigid mind whose views change not at all. One of the
patent changes in the world about him was the growth in
the North of hostility to slavery.

Von Holst's interpretation of Calhoun in terms of a
fixation on slavery is an interesting one. "Calhoun," he
wrote, "is ... the representative of an idea. ... From about
1830 to the day of his death, Calhoun may be called the

very impersonation of the slavery question." Elsewhere Von Holst characterized him as "entirely a slave of slavery"; "one aim dominated his course"; "the slavery question drove him into the path."[44] This view, however, is much too simple. As a description of the rich complexity of the actual man in relation to his times, it is plainly inadequate. Although Calhoun devoted much of his time to a defense of the institution against various aggressions, he also spent himself in concern for problems of general government. He busied himself with the currency and banking problems; he sought to guard against wastes of public funds and against exploitation of the public lands in speculation; he studied problems of foreign policy that had no relation to slavery and he was an interested observer of political events in Europe. He deplored the rise in this country of the "spoils system," the corruption of the parties, and their domination by machine organizations.

Calhoun should be viewed rather as an unusually able and high-minded politician, one having ambitions but also virtues. He wanted high office, but was not willing to sacrifice his principles to secure it. He changed his views a few times, but he always had excellent reasons for doing so. He was the representative of a social order, a way of life, rather than merely of an idea. Slavery was one of the characteristics of life on the Southern plantation, and naturally it had to be defended. But that was not all. It was an order of agricultural capitalism; it had its own peculiar economic problems, its own customs and manners, pleasures and joys. Its claims were written into the laws of the States and into the federal Constitution; and it had its own set of values. It was as defender of this world of his that Calhoun defended slavery, fought the protective tariff, and guided generally his conduct in public affairs. He was certainly attached to the Union, but his love of his State and of the South was stronger. He was torn between two loyalties, had to place one above the other, but strove mightily to reconcile them.

It had pleased Providence . . . (he said) to cast his lot in the slaveholding States. There were his hopes, and all that was near and dear to him. His first duty was to them, and he held every other, even his obligations to this Government and the Union, as sacred as he regarded them, subordinate to their safety. He knew he would be assailed, both here and elsewhere, for this avowal; but he had long been accustomed to such assaults. They had no terror for him. . .[45]

C. EDUCATION, READING, AND CONTACTS

Calhoun possessed a mind of extraordinary keenness and toughness. His insight into complex social phenomena and the movement of the forces of history was beyond the ken of average men; and later events bore out a number of prophecies that he made with remarkable accuracy.[46] Close observation, hard and deliberate thinking, and bold pursuit of ideas to their logical conclusions characterized his treatment of the problems that interested him. His judgment of the "juncture" of affairs was usually sound, and he had a deal of facility in setting forth his views in debate. It has been said of him, probably with some exaggeration, that he always came to the halls of Congress the best informed man on any subject to which he directed his attention. On the other hand, it was often complained that he was too "metaphysical." His mental habit of following ideas into their logical interrelations annoyed some of his contemporaries and made him a formidable opponent.

Calhoun had developed his intellectual capacity to a considerable extent by solitary reading and contemplation. His institutional education was somewhat delayed. At the

age of thirteen, Calhoun was sent, for a short time, to the
academy of Reverend Moses Waddel, a Presbyterian
clergyman who was his brother-in-law. But the academy
closed, and young John came home. Up to the age of
nineteen, Calhoun wrote, his formal training had covered
little more than reading, writing, and arithmetic. Then,
on his brother's urging him to take up one of the professions, he deliberately made plans to spend seven years
in educating himself for the law (which was, of course,
the accepted training for politics also). He returned for
two years to Waddel's academy, which had re-opened, and
diligently applied himself to his Latin grammar and other
studies preparatory for college. He entered Yale in 1802
and graduated in 1804 with some distinction as a student.
Then, for approximately eighteen months he attended
Tapping Reeve's law school in Litchfield, where, although
he disliked the work, he applied himself conscientiously.
He participated here in the activities of a debating society.
His formal preparation for the law he completed by reading in the law offices of DeSaussure in Charleston and of
George Bowie in Abbeville.

    During this time he had not confined his reading to the
prescribed courses. He related an early experience of
having undertaken at the age of thirteen to read "the
whole of the small stock of historical works" contained in
Waddel's circulating library. Waddel was away from
home for the most of fourteen weeks, and the boy read
constantly. He went through Rollin's *Ancient History*,
two books by Robertson on *Charles V* and *South America*,
Cook's *Voyages*, Brown's *Essays*, Voltaire's *Charles XII*,
and Locke's *Essay on the Human Understanding*. His intense reading so impaired his health that his mother
ordered him to come home.[47] He retained throughout his
life a fondness for books of history and travel; and he
read practically no fiction. Certainly he read books on gov-

ernment and economics, including ancient and modern authors—among others Plato and Aristotle,[48] Demosthenes' speeches and Cicero's orations, Polybius, Machiavelli, Burlamaqui, and the Abbé Lammenais. He was a close observer of the interesting developments in Europe during his lifetime, and followed the news in the journals and in letters from relatives and friends. Among Englishmen, he had read Sidney, Locke, and Filmer, was acquainted with the works of Paley and Palgrave, and read much of Edmund Burke.[49] Aristotle and Burke were without doubt his favorite authors. Certainly he was influenced to some extent in his theorizing on politics by them, for now and then definite similarities appear. Finally, of, course, he was well-versed in the literature of American history, law, government, and economics, most frequent references having been made by him to Jefferson and Madison. He referred at times also to St. George Tucker,[50] Marshall, Henry Baldwin, and Henry Vethake. Naturally he read most of the current political writings of a controversial character; and it is believed that the works of John Taylor of Caroline[51] and of Thomas Cooper were influential in shaping his ideas.

The development of Calhoun's mind was undoubtedly influenced in part by the personalities with whom he lived or came into contact; and the impress made upon him by those commanding his respect during his youth was probably stronger than that of later acquaintances. His father, a man of singular independence and sharpness of mind, participated now and then in local politics ,and directed the attention of his son to public questions. He had opposed the ratification of the Federal Constitution by South Carolina; and Calhoun remembered his father's having "maintained that government to be best which allowed the largest amount of individual liberty compatible with social order and tranquility."[52] President Timothy Dwight of

Yale, staunch old Federalist, admired Calhoun's ability as a student, and often engaged him in debate as to the legitimate source of political power, Calhoun maintaining popular sovereignty, Dwight inclining to more aristocratic doctrine. Despite their disagreement on this subject, Dwight once expressed the opinion that the young man was of presidential caliber. Still another teacher may have sharpened Calhoun intellectually, the rigorously logical cast of Calhoun's mind being attributed in part to the influence of old Judge Gould of the Litchfield law school. Whatever contribution to his mental growth came from his intimates and political fellows of later years proved rather intangible; his association with John Quincy Adams, Daniel Webster and other prominent figures apparently changed him very little.[53] After his entrance into the national arena, politicians in South Carolina were generally more influenced by Calhoun than he was by them. However, his young and fiery political captain, James H. Hammond, who later came to advocate the death penalty for abolitionists, may well have shaped Calhoun's course to some extent on the fateful question of Negro slavery.[54]

This, in brief, was the background of one of the outstanding intellectuals of his time. With the exception of John Taylor, who may appropriately be considered a predecessor rather than a contemporary, he is the only one in the American stream of thought of the period properly to be deemed a political philosopher. Unlike most of his contemporaries, Calhoun attempted some systematic scrutiny of politics and achieved something in the way of original contribution to thought on government. He owed an intellectual debt, of course, to various of his American predecessors, especially to those of the State rights school, including Jefferson, Madison, and Taylor; but in certain respects he went beyond them and in significant ways broke with them entirely, as will appear later in this work. These fore-runners in the State rights school will be examined in the next chapter.

NOTES

1. Calhoun wrote years later of his having prepared "an English oration" for commencement at Yale on "the qualifications necessary to constitute a perfect statesman." [John C. Calhoun], *Life of John C. Calhoun* (New York, 1843), p. 6. His whole education was designed to prepare him for politics. See his remarks on his qualities as a statesman. *Ibid.*, pp. 52-53.
2. Or the reverse, as in the case of Clay's attempt to unite the West and the North with his "American System."
3. More accurately, his argument was for State sovereignty rather than simply for State rights, but the latter is customarily used to designate the school to which he belonged.
4. This apparently is the generally accepted date, although Meigs, his careful biographer, fixes it on March 17, a day earlier. William Meigs, *Life of Calhoun*, 2 vols. (New York, 1917), Vol. I, p. 48; U. B. Phillips, "John Caldwell Calhoun," *Dictionary of American Biography*, Vol. III, p. 411.
5. Calhoun, *Correspondence* (Washington, 1900), pp. 99-100.
6. Calhoun himself made such a division. [Calhoun], *Life of John C. Calhoun*, p. 70.
7. *Annals of Congress*, 14th Congress, Ist. Session, 1816, p. 837.
8. *Annals of Congress*, 14th Congress, 2nd. Session 1816-1817, p. 854.
9. *Ibid.*, p. 855.
10. Calhoun, *Works*, 6 vols. (Charleston and New York, 1851-1867), Vol. V, pp. 40-54, 137-147.
11. *Correspondence*, pp. 219-223. With regard to strict

construction, he wrote: "I feel confident that such . . .
rule must lead into perpetual difficulty and contradiction, which must finally bring into discredit those who
act on it, and thereby weaken their authority when it
may be most required. Believing that no general and
artificial rule can be devised which will not act mischie-
vously in application, I am forced to the result that any
doubtful portion of the Constitution must be construed
by itself in reference to the true meaning and intent of
the framers of the instrument; and consequently that
the construction must, in each part, be more or less
rigid, as may be necessary to effect the intention." *Idem.*

12. Meigs, *Life of Calhoun,* Vol. I, pp. 350-351.

13. Meigs, *Life of Calhoun,* Vol. I, pp. 188-189.

14. See Herman V. Ames, *State Documents on Federal
Relations* (Philadelphia, 1900-1906), pp. 133-157; J.
T. Carpenter, *The South as a Conscious Minority*
(New York, 1930), p. 56.

15. The Ohio legislature in January, 1824, proposed
gradual emancipation and colonization, and within a
year and a half the proposal was endorsed by eight
other Northern States. Ames, *State Documents,* pp.
203-4.

16. Meigs, *Life of Calhoun,* Vol. I, pp. 320-343.

17. *Niles' Register* reported that nothing would seem to
satisfy the "wild politicians of that country," and that
the newspaper articles were of a violent cast. *Niles'
Register* 34:300.

18. *Works,* Vol. VI, pp. 1-59.

19. Ames, *State Documents,* pp. 169-173.

20. The better accounts of the whole nullification episode
are to be found in D. F. Houston, *Nullification in South
Carolina* (New York, 1908) and C. S. Boucher, *Nullification Controversy in South Carolina* (Chicago,
1916). There is also Frederick Bancroft, *Calhoun and
the South Carolina Nullification Movement* (Baltimore, 1928). For briefer treatment see John W.
Burgess, *The Middle Period* (New York, 1897), Ch.
X; Edward Channing, *History of the United States,* 6
vols. (New York, 1921), Vol. V, Ch. XIII.

21. Benton, Senator from Missouri, related the story

that Jackson contemplated causing Calhoun to be tried for high treason. There was also talk of hanging. Thomas Hart Benton, *Thirty Years' View*, 2 vols. (New York, 1845-1856), Vol. I, pp. 342-344.

22. *Works*, Vol. I, pp. 262-309.

23. Walter L. Miller, "Calhoun as a Lawyer and a Statesman," *Green Bag* 11 : 277.

24. Charles A. and Mary R. Beard, *The Rise of American Civilization*, 1 vol. ed. (New York, 1930), Book I, pp. 678-679. For his course on the banking issue see the following speeches: *Works*, Vol. II, pp. 309-343, 344-376, 534-569, 569-586; Vol. III, pp. 60-92, 244-279, 279-330.

25. See Gilbert H. Barnes, *The Anti-Slavery Impulse* (New York and London, 1933), for correction of the view that Garrison was the chief leader of the abolition movement; he was rather the most notorious of the fanatical fringe.

26. See his letter to Virgil Maxcy, of September, 1830, quoted by Meigs, *Life of Calhoun*, Vol. I, pp. 418-419. In part it ran: "I consider the tariff but as the occasion rather than the real cause of the present unhappy state of things. The truth can no longer be disguised that the peculiar domestic institution of the Southern states, and the consequent direction which that and her soil and climate have given to her industry, has placed them in regard to taxation and appropriations in opposite relations to the majority of the Union; against the danger of which, if there be no protective power in the reserved rights of the states, they must in the end be forced to rebel, or submit to have their permanent interest sacrificed, their domestic institutions subverted by colonization and other schemes, and themselves and children reduced to wretchedness. Thus situated, the denial of the right of the state to interfere in the last resort more alarms the thinking than all other causes. . . ." p. 418.

27. *Works*, Vol. II, pp. 509-533.

28. *Works*, Vol. II, pp. 465-490, 625-633; Burgess, *The Middle Period*, pp. 252-270.

29. *Correspondence*, pp. 633-634.

30. Benton placed full responsibility for the war on Cal-houn. *Thirty Years' View*, Vol. II, pp. 639-649.
31. The United States Supreme Court joined him in this view several years later. See *Dred Scott v. Sanford*, 19 Howard 393 (1856). For an excellent exposition of the arguments of Calhoun, Rhett, and Jefferson Davis on the question of slavery in the territories, see A. C. McLaughlin, *Constitutional History of the United States* (New York, 1935), pp. 516-520, 126-527.
32. *Works*, Vol. I, pp. 391-392.
33. *Correspondence*, p. 369.
34. See his *Correspondence*, pp. 346-7, 353-6, 362-3, 365-7, 411-12, 412-16, 430-31, 494, 698; *Works*, Vol. V, pp. 246-311.
35. William E. Dodd, *Expansion and Conflict* (Cambridge, 1915), pp. 28, 40-42, 184-207; U. B. Phillips, *Life and Labor in the Old South* (Boston, 1929), pp. 148, 185-186; A. C. Cole, *The Irrepressible Conflict* (New York, 1934), pp. 58 ff.; R. B. Russel, *Economic Aspects of Southern Sectionalism* (Urbana, 1924), pp. 67 ff., 225-230; J. G. Van Deusen, *Economic Bases of Disunion in South Carolina* (New York, 1928), pp. 262-303, 328-330, and *passim;* L. C. Gray, *History of Agriculture in the Southern United States to* 1860, 2 vols. (Washington, 1933), Vol. II, pp. 933-936, 1043; *Statistical Abstract of the United States,* 1907 (Washington, 1908), pp. 19-20, 30-31.
36. Cole, *The Irrepressible Conflict*, pp. 14-15, 24, 103 ff.; Van Deusen, *Economic Bases of Disunion in South Carolina*, pp. 148 ff., 220-254; Beard, *The Rise of American Civilization*, Bk. I, pp. 636-640; Bk. II, p. 6.
37. Cole, *The Irrepressible Conflict*, pp. 98-100, 122-145, 263-264, 266, 267; A. M. Schlesinger, *New Viewpoints in American History* (New York, 1928), pp. 11-13.
38. *Works*, Vol. IV, pp. 343-344.
39. *Works*. Vol. VI, pp. 285-313.
40. *Works*, Vol. IV, p. 576.
41. *Works*, Vol. I, pp. 383-396.
42. William E. Dodd, *Statesmen of the Old South* (New

York, 1911). Dodd puts this view plainly in several passages. See especially pp. 110-111, 133-134. D. F. Houston in his monograph, *Nullification in South Carolina,* inclines to this view also.

43. John W. Draper, *History of the American Civil War,* 3 vols. (New York, 1867-1870), Vol. I, pp. 380-384. In like fashion, Parton averred that Calhoun probably caused the Civil War, James Parton, *Famous Americans in Recent Times* (Boston, 1869), pp. 113-171.

44. H. Von Holst, *John C. Calhoun* (Boston and New York, 1899), p. 7; H. Von Holst, *The Constitutional and Political History of the United States,* 8 vols. (Chicago, 1876-1892), Vol. I, pp. 462-463; Vol. II, p. 705.

45. *Works,* Vol. III, p. 178.

46. He predicted the opening up of Japan to foreign trade. *Works,* Vol. IV, p. 244. He foresaw that the emancipated Negroes would remain in a status of subordination to the white community in the South. *Works,* Vol. V, pp. 204-205. He forecast abolition, Negro suffrage, "carpet-bag" days in the South. *Works,* Vol. VI, pp. 285-313.

47. *Life of John C. Calhoun,* p. 5.

48. He advised A. D. Wallace, a young man contemplating entering politics, to read the elementary treatises on government, "including Aristotle's, which I regard as among the best," *Correspondence,* p. 469.

49. He once said that Burke was "the wisest of modern statesmen, . . . (one) who had the keenest and deepest glance into futurity." *Works,* Vol. III, p. 591. References to and quotations from these writers are to be found scattered throughout his speeches and writings. See *Works,* Vol. II, pp. 64, 140, 274-275; Vol. III, pp. 164, 479, 481-482, 591; Vol. IV, pp. 507-512; Vol. VI, p. 230; his *Life,* pp. 5-6; his *Correspondence,* pp. 468-469. See also Meigs, *Life of Calhoun,* pp. 99 and *passim.*

50. Especially the appendix to his edition of Blackstone's *Commentaries. Works,* Vol. II, pp. 286-289.

51. In 1823 Calhoun referred to Taylor in a letter to S. Gouveneur. "I was surprised to find how accurate his

information is as to passing events," he wrote. *New York Public Library Bulletin* (1899), Vol. III, p. 325.
52. [Calhoun], *Life of John C. Calhoun*, p. 6.
53. Over the course of years Calhoun and John Quincy Adams changed from cordial friends to rather intractable opponents. To Calhoun, Adams became that "mischievous, bad old man." *Correspondence*, p. 513. To Adams, Calhoun changed from a fair, candid, intelligent, and patriotic statesman of "enlarged philosophical views" to the "high-priest of Moloch—the embodied spirit of slavery," his speeches being "glaring, unblushing, daredevil inconsistencies." John Quincy Adams, *Diary*, Nevins ed. New York, 1929), pp. 191, 265, 544.
54. See Hunt, *John C. Calhoun* (Philadelphia, 1908), Ch. XV. Theodore D. Jervey's *Robert Y. Hayne and his Times* (New York, 1909) is one of the best works extant for the story of the relationship between the prominent politicians of that period in South Carolina. See also Elizabeth Merritt, *James Henry Hammond, 1807-1864* (Baltimore, 1923).

Part II

Background of
State Rights Doctrine

2
Background of State Rights Doctrine

A. INTRODUCTION

CALHOUN'S ADHERENCE TO the cause of State rights in the fight of South Carolina against the protective tariff of 1828 marked definitively a new departure in politics for him. In the course of years he became the outstanding champion of the cause; and he developed a very ingenious, and in some respects unanswerable, political theory in its support. Prior to this, however, State rights had already become a tradition in the politics of the country. It was an article of faith in the political creed of one of the great political parties, and the exposition of its meaning and various consequences had enlisted the efforts of several eminent defenders. To the whole State rights school, the problem was to reconcile sufficient strength in the Union, for protection against foreign aggression and for satisfactory adjustment of relations among the several States, with the complete freedom of each in its internal affairs. State sovereignty secured the latter for Calhoun, while his theory of the concurrent majority was intended to show how the requisite reconciliation with the former was to be secured. His exposition of the legitimacy, justice, and practicality of his solution of the problem called forth his best efforts. In the process he assumed a more particularistic position than many of his predecessors in the State rights school (who had relied to some extent on the theory

of divided sovereignty), and he discarded their dangerous frame of reference—the doctrines of the social compact and natural rights. The natural liberty and equality
of men were not readily compatible with the institution of
human slavery. Before discussing in detail the theory of
Calhoun, some attention must be given to this background
of State rights doctrine.

The history of particularist sentiment in this country
reaches well back into colonial times; and, of course, it
proved a handicap in the prosecution of the war for independence and an obstacle to the establishment of an efficient common government. Official assertion of the rights
of the States under the Constitution may be said to have
found expression first in the resolutions of several of the
State conventions on ratifying the Constitution itself. The
New York convention declared the right of the people to
"reassume" the powers of government whenever necssary
to their happiness, and reserved every power not "clearly
delegated" to the federal government for the State or its
people. Several of the ratifying resolutions set forth the
rule of strict construction, that of New Hampshire, for
example, offering a clarifying amendment declaring that
"all powers not expressly and particularly delegated"
were "reserved to the several states."[1] It was to satisfy
the fears of some of the States, of course, that the reservation was added to the Constitution. The attempts of the
Federalists, especially those under the leadership of Alexander Hamilton, to strengthen the powers of the federal
government by various measures, including funding, assumption, protection of manufactures, and the establishment of the Bank of the United States, called forth opposition in the name of State rights. The Alien and Sedition acts evoked the famous protest in the Virginia and
Kentucky Resolutions.[2]

Later, when the Republican (anti-Federalist) party,

professed guardian of the rights of the States, came into power in the federal administration, it strained a constitutional point in order to purchase Louisiana and provoked Federalists into sober proposals of secession from the Union by the Northern States.[3] During the War of 1812, a war precipitated by the Republican party, disaffected New England Federalists met in the Hartford Convention, and adopted resolutions recommending resistance by the States to certain war measures of Congress.[4] After the war, particularist opposition to the Bank, internal improvements, and the protective tariff was carried on in Congress by members from all parts of the country, sectional cleavage not becoming apparent until the third decade of the century. Holmes and Webster of New England joined John Randolph, William B. Giles, and Nathaniel Macon in opposition to centralization. The Supreme Court experienced difficulties arising from the jealousy with which the States guarded their rights; its exercise of appellate jurisdiction over the State courts evoked, perhaps, the most bitterly hostile criticism. When the centralizing tendencies of Marshall's work in a remarkable series of decisions was appreciated, he became the subject of scathing attacks on the part of Spencer Roane, who had the backing and approval of Jefferson.[5]

It is not intended here to go into all of these events in detail.[6] Rather it must suffice to examine the ideas of the more representative leaders and thinkers who contributed to the State rights body of doctrine. More especially, it is intended to confine consideration to the Southern men who were in the agricultural tradition, and thus more properly to be deemed predecessors of Calhoun. And it is interesting to note that the most prominent of these were Virginians. To the ideas of Jefferson, Madison, Taylor, Tucker, and Roane, little remained to be added until the time of Calhoun and nullification.

B.   NATURAL RIGHTS PHILOSOPHY: LIMITED GOVERNMENT

Thomas Jefferson was the most prominent political leader of the early State rights school. He was the organizer and head of the political party that took origin chiefly in opposition to the centralizing and "consolidating" program of Hamilton and the Federalists. One of the most significant expressions of this opposition to centralization was his authorship of the famous Kentucky Resolutions, a protest of the State legislature against the Alien and Sedition laws and a warning against federal usurpation of State rights. However, the logical starting point of his political ideas he put in the familiar but happily phrased passage of the Declaration of Independence in which he appealed to the "inalienable rights" of men.[7] For the happiness and prosperity of mankind, all men were equally endowed by God with individual rights to life, liberty, and property. Government established by the deliberate agreement and individual consent of men for the protection of individuals in the enjoyment of their natural rights could not justly go beyond its allotted sphere. Serious abrogation of these natural rights by the government was just cause for popular revolution. There was little originality in the Declaration. Jefferson simply gave expression in a few words to a political creed that was already widely held throughout the colonies, and that had been expounded fully by James Otis, Samuel Adams, John Dickinson, Thomas Paine, and others.[8] Jefferson's appeal to "the Laws of Nature and Nature's God" in justification of revolution by an oppressed people was certainly a valid one in the then prevailing "climate of opinion." Later, the philosophy of the Declaration was copied into the various State constitutions, and has persisted in them down to the present time, "perfunctorily safeguarding the liberties of mankind." Conventional acceptance of this great tradition seems to defy changes in the climate of opinion.

Jefferson's belief in the equality of all men in the possession of certain natural rights accounts for his dislike of slavery and his interest in gradual emancipation and colonization. But his abstract concepts of the natural liberty and equality of men did not betray his common sense into doctrinaire demands for immediate abolition. He wrote to a friend: "We have the wolf by the ears, and we can neither hold him nor safely let him go."[9] Even in the politics of his time he was not an equalitarian democrat, for certainly he was profoundly distrustful of the proletariat of the cities. Moreover, he was not at all averse to high property qualifications on the suffrage. Nevertheless, he was really representative of the agricultural elements in the community, which comprised a large majority of the population; in this sense, he was more democratic than the leading politicians of the Federalist party.[10]

According to Jefferson, the limitation of government to its proper sphere was of the very essence of republican government, and this limitation comprised as an important element the division of the country (United States) into States, the "true barriers of our liberty." These smaller units were closer to the people and consequently more safely trusted than the larger political organization of the Union. He thought that the general government might well "be reduced to foreign concerns only" and the States relied upon for competent administration of domestic affairs." It was not surprising, then, that when he became excited over the alarming assumptions by the federal government of powers not expressly delegated to it, he appealed to "nullification" by the States as the rightful remedy. The Constitution was a compact to which each of the States acceded as "an integral party, its co-states forming, as to itself, the other party. . . ."; and "as in all other cases of compact among powers having no common judge, each party has an equal right to judge for itself, as well of infractions as of the mode and measure of redress."[12] He did not go further into an exposition of the nature or procedure of this remedy, but certainly here was the forerunner of Calhoun's theory of nullification.

Jefferson defended State rights, then, not to protect the rights of the minority from the majority, or the reverse, but to maintain a system of limited government, government that would not violate the established sphere of individual liberty. It has been asserted that Jefferson really was not devoted to the doctrine of State rights, but adopted the doctrine only in so far as it was politically useful in promoting the interests of the agricultural community. Thus Beard characterizes the Louisiana purchase as a violation of the reserved rights of the States for the sake of increasing the strength of the agricultural States.[13] It need not be denied that Jefferson's actions did not always suit his words. Nor, on the other hand, is it any great point that Jefferson was not devoted to State rights for their own sake; all government, to him, was but a means to an end. The agricultural interest was in great part the interest of the country, and he thought that the agricultural interest was best served by State rights. When a situation arose that made the contrary appear true, he certainly manifested scrupulous regard for his professions of political faith.[14] There was no doubt of his attachment to agriculture as a way of life. He had great admiration for the character of the people devoted to its pursuit, and he meant as a patriot to serve its interests.[15]

John Taylor of Caroline,[16] "the philosopher of Jeffersonian democracy," was said seldom to have differed from Jefferson on any important point.[17] Both apotheosized agrarian life and supported the cause of State rights; both maintained doctrines of democracy and individualism.

Certainly Taylor used his pen vigorously in attacking their common political foes; and, although usually discussing current issues, he went beyond them in the course of his writings and developed a fairly complete political theory. He was not entirely clear on all points, however; his unusual use of words and the diffuseness of his treatment made him somewhat difficult to understand.[18]

Taylor, like Jefferson, approached the problem of government from the point of view of the inalienable natural rights of individuals and of the social compact theory. Upon the basis of a rather indefinite conception of the state of nature, he maintained that the individual possessed certain rights prior to and above all political association. Among these were the rights to life, liberty, and property, the natural right of self-government deriving from the conception of the moral liberty of the individual, and the natural right to property deriving from the right of the individual to the fruit of his labor. These rights bore the sanction of the law of nature which imposed universal moral sanction.[19] Because all men possessed these rights equally, it was only through their consent given by means of a social compact that powers of government were legitimately to be established. "The sovereignty of the people arises and representation flows out of each man's right to govern himself. With this individual right political structures are built. Individuals, in forming a society, may arrange their rights in such forms as they please . . ."[20] Although Taylor did not explain the nature of the social compact clearly, he emphasized the continuing superiority of the natural rights of the individual over the sovereignty of the society created by it. Thus one's natural right to property must always be protected. "The freedom of property from the indefinite despotism of sovereignty is the best security . . . against the unjust laws by which social liberty is so often injured . . . The wise and just principle even denies to the sovereignty of the people a right to the private property of individuals. . . ."[21] Upon the largest possible amount of freedom for the individual to pursue property and happiness depended progress in the arts and sciences—the advance of civilization. Past history showed this.

Upon the basis of his theory of the social compact, then, Taylor accepted popular sovereignty,[22] that principle of the American revolution which asserted responsibility of government to the people. And he was a political democrat not only in maintaining the equality of men in political rights but in believing that by and large men were equal in talents and virtues. Aristocracy had no legitimate basis upon which to rest, for it was a general law of nature that talent was not hereditary.[23] The wide distribution of wealth was also favorable to democracy in this country. "Talents and virtue are now so widely distributed as to have rendered a monopoly of either, equivalent to that of antiquity, impracticable; and if an aristocracy ought to have existed, while it possessed such a monopoly, it ought not also to exist, because this monopoly is irretrievably lost. The distribution of wealth produced by commerce and alienation, is equal to that of knowledge and virtue . . ."[24]

Thus it appears that, although Taylor used the term "sovereignty," and appeared to conceive it as legitimately residing only in the people, he did not contemplate the legal omnipotence of the politically organized people.[25] From his point of view it was always highly desirable to restrict the sphere of government to the police functions. It was to the end of securing limited government and of holding it within its proper bounds that the great American principle of division was adopted. "Power is divided by our policy that the people may maintain their sovereignty. . . . Our principle of division is used to reduce power

to that degree of temperature which may make it a blessing and not a curse, its nature resembling fire, which, uncontrolled consumes, in moderation, warms."[26] Power was
first divided between the people and the government, "re-
serving to the people the control of the dividend allotted
to the government." This "dividend" was then parcelled
out between the federal and State governments; and these
parts in turn split up among various legislative, executive,
and judicial bodies. By thus dividing the powers of government and placing them in separate hands, the people
would be able to enforce responsibility (through elections) and prevent that "coalescence of political power"
which was always "fatal to civil liberty." Representation,
division, and responsibility—the earmarks of a republican
government as distinguished from monarchy, aristocracy,
and democracy—rendered most difficult the concentration
of the powers of government into the hands of one group
and thereby minimized the temptation to seek such concentration for purposes of political plunder. So it was
that "our policy divides power and unites the nation in
one interest."[27]

Hence any attempt, save by the people themselves, to
change the division of power made by the people was a
hostile move pregnant with danger to civil liberty and
private rights. Any attempt of an interested group, impelled by man's natural lust for power,[28] to extend the
action of the central government beyond its alloted sphere
into the domain of the State governments, or *vice versa*,
was to be resisted by the intelligent and patriotic. Experience had proved that there was grave danger of the former. Although in his earlier writings Taylor had been inclined to doubt the efficacy of the check and balance principle as a means of securing the end of limited government,
by 1822 he had become sufficiently alarmed at the progress of "consolidation" to advocate a mutual State-feder-

al veto on constitutional questions. Each government was competent to judge of the extent of its own powers, and neither authorized to enforce its judgment on the other.[29] Definitive alteration of the federal division of powers was to be secured only upon concurrence of three-fourths of the States. Thus protection of the rights of the States was part and parcel of maintaining a whole system designed to the end of securing limited government and individual liberty.

Taylor despaired of any help from political parties. He deplored the facilities they afforded to selfish minorities, interested in "paper, patronage, and protection," for pushing their policies at the expense of the majority who constituted the agricultural interest; and he condemned the psychological trickery of parties in fostering blind party loyalty and so beclouding the real issues. He recognized the sectional aspects of the politics of the time, sometimes viewing the cleavage as between North and South, and at other times as between inland and maritime regions. Taylor thoroughly deprecated the attempts to seize upon slavery as a mark of distinction to set off the South from the other sections, and, by arousing hostility to the institution, to form a political alliance of the other sections for the purpose of securing a "monopoly of the offices of the government and of the partialities of Congress." Such a "geographical balance of power" would "beget new usurpations of internal powers over persons and property, and these will beget a dissolution of the Union." Sectional oppression and exploitation could but result in civil war or revolution. Just as every individual possessed an inherent moral right of self-defense, so each of the States had a right to self-preservation. Although Taylor inclined to deplore slavery in the abstract, he felt that it was a subject to be dealt with only by the States, as had already been determined by the federal compact. He felt sure that the Southern States would not submit to compulsory emancipation and he was not one to wish them to risk the social catastrophe that had befallen the white people of Santo Domingo upon emancipation of the blacks.[30]

James Madison, the "father of the Constitution," was another of those essentially in the tradition of John Locke. Private rights of life, liberty, and property must be conserved to promote the public welfare; and it was in the protection and security it afforded these rights of individuals that government found its justification, although Madison seldom referred to these as natural rights. Security for these rights involved the principle of limited government, and the realization of this principle required checks and balances in the governmental structure. The whole complicated mechanism of the federal system was designed by the "Founding Fathers" to check oppression by majorities in the State legislatures. To Madison, the central government was to be competent to afford such protection, but was itself largely to be inactive, passive, incapable of great harm.[31]

Although Madison had taken a leading part in the movement for a stronger government for the Union, had even advocated a "national" government for a time, he found his place in opposition to the great fiscal measures of Hamilton in the first Congress. And thereafter through a long public life and in retirement his sentiments were those of a strict constructionist and champion of the rights of the States. Earlier he had thought there was little danger of the invasion of the sphere of State authority, for the large expanse of territory over which the federal government was to be established would include such a number and variety of parties and interests as to render extremely improbable any combination of them bent on exploiting the others. Moreover, as he contended when championing ratification, since the State governments were closer to the people and since their patronage and sphere of authority would remain much larger than those of the federal government, there was little danger of the latter's encroaching upon the rights of the States.[32] The history of all confederations showed the contrary tendency.

However, the fears of the particularists had led him to consider the possibility of a "clear, palpable, and dangerous" usurpation of power by the federal government. He wrote in the *Federalist*:

In the last resort a remedy must be obtained from the people, who can, by the election of more faithful representatives, annul the acts of the usurpers. The truth is that this ultimate redress may be more confided in against unconstitutional acts of the federal than of the state legislatures, for this plain reason, that as every such act of the former will be an invasion of the rights of the latter, these will be ever ready to mark the innovation, to sound the alarm to the people, and to exert their local influence in effecting a change of federal representatives.[33]

Here in 1788 he suggested the remedy which was invoked in 1798-1799 against a federal statute clearly subversive of the Constitutional guarantee of freedom of speech. As he explained late in life, it was his view that the Virginia and Kentucky Resolutions were simply an appeal to the "co-states" to "throw the rascals out." If they sounded warning of more drastic action, it was only to protest that such usurpations and oppressions might provoke revolution.[34]

Madison could not accept nullification, because he did not believe the States alone were sovereign. In the movement for ratification of the Constitution he had put forward the idea of divided sovereignty, and he held to it to the end of his days. Sovereignty, to him, meant the possession of legislative power and "the physical means of

executing it," and certainly the federal government possessed such power and means quite as legitimately as the
States. Within its sphere of delegated powers the general
government was sovereign; to the several States remained
a "residuary and inviolable sovereignty over all other subjects."[35] In fact, it was this division of sovereignty that
made possible this new compound form of government of
ours. As he described it, it was federal in its origin and in
the extent of its powers; national in the use of its powers;
and partly federal and partly national in the source of its
powers and in the authoritative mode of amendment.[36]
Certainly Madison saw clearly a definite set of relations
between the general government, the local units, and the
people, which he believed had been established by the
Constitution. Although he was devoted to the maintenance
of the rights of the States, he gave no support to the idea
of State sovereignty. He recognized that the interests of
the North and South were antithetical in some respects,[37]
and yet firmly believed that there was sufficient common
ground to make union mutually advantageous. A governmental system that provided such union effectively without
bringing those interests into conflict would be "something
new under the sun," and was best to be viewed in terms
of divided sovereignty. This concept of divided sovereignty, or "sovereignty of the spheres" as Taylor labeled it,
was accepted by the Supreme Court and found expression
in numbers of its decisions for many years.[38]

St. George Tucker, Virginia lawyer and judge was also
one of the more prominent of the early State rights school.
In the appendix to his edition of *Blackstone's Commentaries*,[39] Tucker set forth the familiar theory of natural
rights and social compact, citing frequently Locke, Rousseau, Paine, Vattel, and Pufendorf. From the state of
nature where the "laws of nature and of moral obligation"
prevailed and where all men were equal in liberty and

rights, men withdrew upon instituting a political society by common consent. Tucker appeared at times to believe that the consent of each was necessary, but in other passages the requisite consent seemed only that of a majority.[40] Nor did he make the nature of his concept of the social compact entirely clear; his attempt to join the ideas of Rousseau and Locke made for some confusion. In one place, he wrote: "Government . . . may be regarded as coeval with civil society itself, since the agreement or contract by which each individual . . . agreed with all the rest that they should unite into one society . . . would probably be immediately followed by the decree . . . made by the whole people of the form or plan of power, which is what we now understand by the Constitution of the state . . ."[41] And yet elsewhere he designated the federal constitution as a social compact.[42]

By means of a number of compacts the people of the various American States had set up a number of State governments and a federal government, all possessing a limited authority derivative from the people. That "supreme, irresistible, absolute, uncontrollable authority, which is denominated sovereignty" resided only in the people of the several states.[43] From this it would apparently follow that sovereignty was indivisible, but his use of the term was somewhat loose. He wrote in places of portions of sovereignty. And, when he declared that each State retained an "entire liberty of exercising, as it thinks proper, all those parts of its sovereignty, which are not mentioned in the Constitution . . . as parts that ought to be exercised in common,"[44] he showed that his thinking was not entirely free of Madison's idea of divided sovereignty. Despite some confusion in his ideas, however, it is clear that he was a strict constructionist and more. The ordinary procedure to prevent the usurpation of power by the federal government was for the State legislatures to appeal for election of new representatives or to resort to amendment of the federal Constitution. However, the Union was but a confederacy that could be dissolved by mutual consent, and secession was consequently within the rights of the States. The dissolution of the Union under the old Articles of Confederation constituted a precedent that was still valid.[45]

William Rawle in his elementary treatise on the Constitution[46] proved very similar in his views to Tucker, but he was much more assertive of the right of secession. He viewed the Constitution as a compact; and he shared the confusion with regard to sovereignty. He clearly held to an idea of divided sovereignty early in his treatment. Later he declared that the people of each State possessed the authority to determine whether to continue membership in the Union, deriving such authority from the right people have in all cases to determine how they will be governed. Secession could be effected by amendment of the State constitution; and such action would not destroy the Union as to the rest of the States. However, failure to elect Senators was not to be deemed secession.[47]

C. HISTORICAL AND LEGALISTIC ARGUMENTS

The first generation under the Constitution witnessed the beginnings of the development of the case for State rights in historical and legalistic terms. At various junctures the nature of the Union was brought under scrutiny and conclusions reached in this regard without reference to the social compact theory or the rights of man. Argument proceeded in the light of the intentions of the "Founding Fathers," or of what was to be inferred as to their intentions from what they did. Arguments were derived from the logical, legal, or customary meanings of the words in the Constitution. The past history of the States was raked over to find support for the particularist position. Comparing or identifying the Constitution with an international treaty or a business deed of trust furnished bases for argument. Such argument did not, of course, occur in isolation, but was linked up with others in terms of general principles of government or of the tenets of political economy. Generally they were used in debates in speech or writing which had for their immediate focus the exercise by Congress or the President of a disputed power or the assumption by the Supreme Court of jurisdiction questioned by the adherents of the State rights school.

John Taylor attacked the assumption he detected in Marshall's language in the Bank decision that there was a single people of the United States. "The people" were the several peoples of the individual States. The members of the Federal Convention had been selected as representatives of the States; they had voted as units representing the States; and they had submitted their work to be ratified by representatives of the people of each State separately, the Constitution binding no State that did not so ratify. Further, internal evidence was to be derived from the Constitution in that Senators were to be chosen by the States and to represent them equally and that the regulation of suffrage for the House of Representatives was left to the States. The President was elected indirectly by the States. Moreover, only the States voting by a three-fourths majority could ratify amendments to the Constitution[48] Common consent was necessary to constitute a people, and there was no historical evidence that such consent had ever been given to form a people of all the inhabitants of the United States. Such a proposition would have been rejected in 1787-1789.[49] He even turned his attention to the logical implications of the meanings of words. "States" was plural, and "Union" could only be attributed to a plurality. If there had been a single, collective people, there would have been only one State and no union of States.[50] He could but agree with Tucker's earlier assertion that "The Union is . . . an association of states, or a Confederacy."[51] Tucker had reached his conclusion also in part from a consideration of the agency of the States in the operation of the federal government. Thomas Cooper contended that although the nationalists in the Federal Convention led by Hamilton, Morris, and even Madison, had attempted to establish a "consolidated" government, they had been defeated by the guardians of State rights. The latter had succeeded in making the federal government a creature of the States, a government of limited, specifically enumerated powers.[52]

The reservation of powers to the States in the Tenth Amendment was no idle phraseology; and to give it effect the implied powers of the federal government should be restricted to those "indispensably necessary." Only such were "proper." Otherwise the reserved powers of the States would be subject to unlimited invasion through construction. To Taylor, Marshall's decision in *McCulloch v. Maryland* opened up a vista of unlimited amendment of the Constitution by interpretation. Marshall's argument amounted to saying that the States could be deprived of their reserved right to tax property by the federal government's creating a corporation and declaring it exempt from State taxation. Although the Federal Convention had rejected a proposal to give Congress the power to create banks,[53] the Supreme Court implied such power from the fiscal powers of Congress. Thus the "necessary and proper" became the "convenient" or "remotely related." Moreover, Taylor pointed out the assertion of federal supremacy in every case of conflict between delegated and reserved powers was inconsistent with Marshall's own avowal that the federal and State governments were each sovereign in their respective spheres.[54] In similar vein did he and Cooper attack the perversion of the power to levy import duties into a power of protection. The burdening of the industry of one part of the country in order to subsidize that of another was a manifest violation of the provision of the Constitution for uniformity of taxation and for impartiality in regulation of commerce among the several States. Cooper also attacked the constitutionality of internal improvements by the federal government.[55]

Perhaps Marshall's most able opponent on constitutional questions involving the rights of the States was Spencer Roane, a Virginia judge whose appointment as Chief Justice of the United States by Jefferson was thwarted by Adams' last-minute offer to John Marshall.[56] On the Bank case he met Marshall's every argument with another just as logical and just as clearly based on the letter and spirit of the Constitution and yet leading to an antithetical conclusion.[57] In an opinion rendered a, few years earlier, in refusing, as a judge of the highest court of Virginia, to execute the decree of the Supreme Court in *Martin v. Hunter's Lessee,* Roane established himself as a leading particularist. He claimed there was no power in the Supreme Court of the United States to extend its jurisdiction over the highest court of a State. The "supreme law of the land" clause only bound the State judges to apply the Constitution and laws "in pursuance thereof" in cases arising before them, but there was no warrant in it for implying review of their judgments by the Supreme Court. "All cases arising" under the federal Constitution and laws were covered by the judicial power of the United States; but, as the Constitution did not look upon the State courts as part of the federal judicial organization, a case which was instituted in the State rather than the federal courts did not arise under the Constitution. The States were not to be robbed of this sphere of authority by mere construction.[58] Thereafter Roane resorted to the press to attack Marshall's decisions, especially that in *Cohens v. Virginia* in which Marshall expressly denied State sovereignty. Roane flung in his face Marshall's own speech in the Virginia ratifying convention of 1788, in which the latter had declared that the sovereignty of Virginia must be maintained.[59]

The development of the historical and legalistic case for State rights was to receive great stimulus from Calhoun and his contemporaries, but its culmination was only reached after the Civil War in the monumental work of Alexander H. Stephens. This glimpse of its early growth must suffice here.

D. LAISSEZ FAIRE ECONOMICS

Part of the case for State rights, as urged by its early exponents, was in terms of *laissez faire* economics. They probably derived the latter to some extent from the Physiocrats (who, it should be noted, shared their fondness for agriculture) and in part from the classical economists of England. The latter definitely influenced the writings of Thomas Cooper on the subject. Jefferson, Madison, and Tucker all believed that government should leave the individual free to pursue his own private economic interests largely unhampered by governmental regulation, for the simple reason that the individual knew his work better than the government could know it. Such free private enterprise would yield a greater volume of output, and society would profit thereby. Madison was of the opinion that "if industry and labor are left to take their own course, they will generally be directed to those objects which are most productive, and this in a more certain and direct manner than the wisdom of the most enlightened Legislature could point out."[60] Jefferson opined that "agriculture, manufactures, commerce, and navigation, the four pillars of our prosperity, are the most thriving when left free to individual enterprise."[61] And again: "Were we directed from Washington when to sow, and when to reap, we should soon want bread."[62] Thomas Cooper demanded to know: "Is a county-court lawyer from Pittsburgh competent to direct the commercial capitals and dealings of the merchants of New York, Boston, or Philadelphia?" Certainly not, was his answer. Legislators, ignorant of necessary details and devoid of experience and skill in the management of capital, could only mismanage and inflict loss upon the aggregate national capital.[63]

Of course, the argument of these State rights exponents for economic liberalism were just as applicable to the State governments as to the federal government in most respects. However, there was the difference that the State governments were closer to domestic affairs and thus presumably better qualified to judge of them. Moreover, in general it was only the federal government that presumed to regulate seriously the large business concerns of the community, possibly because it alone had constitutional competence to regulate commerce among the States and with foreign countries. It also controlled the currency of the country. Whatever the conditioning circumstances may have been, classical political economy proved a weapon in the service of the State rights school. Demonstration that a *laissez faire* policy was superior to an alliance of business and government in securing social goods and a denial of the constitutional competence of the government to do what business interests desired worked to the same conclusion: non-interference in the economic world. That the rights of property and contract were to be maintained was an assumption unquestioned by them. The right to private property was a natural right.

It was chiefly, of course, the protective tariff policy that drew the fire of the economic liberals; John Taylor and Thomas Cooper were the most prominent and able of the early particularists in this field. Taylor had long protested against what he deemed attempts to rear in America an artificial aristocracy of paper and patronage, a minority fattened by the special privileges involved in the use of the government credit through the Bank of the United States. But the tariff was, if possible, even more indefensible; and he devoted practically all of his book, *Tyranny Unmasked*, to showing that it was crass economic exploitation, detrimental to the weal of the people for the benefit of a few. The "favorable balance of trade" argument was fallacious in that it assumed that money, or specie, was a kind of wealth more desirable than food, clothing, and other merchandise. In reality, money of itself had little utility, and only as a means of exchange did it serve its purpose. It could always be obtained from other countries in exchange for goods. He also pointed out the great difficulty, if not impossibility, of determining when the balance of trade was "favorable." The "home market" argument, that the growth of manufacturing in America would develop a greater demand for agricultural products, was misleading, because the cost of that development would be paid by all consumers at home in the higher prices paid for manfactured products. Moreover, laboring men who were forced into factories to work would undoubtedly be exploited, damaged in morals, and reduced to pauperism, as experience with the factory system in England had shown. Finally, the restriction involved would deprive the government of a source of revenue, invite re-taliation by foreign countries, and destroy our commerce abroad.[64]

The advantage of protection to the country was chimerical, proceeding on the false assumption that the wealth of the country was something other than the wealth of all the individuals living in the country. People as individuals would be much better off in the pursuit of agriculture, for there was an abundance of available land in America. This land was a natural resource whose culti-vation should not be neglected, an advantage not enjoyed by all peoples, a gift of nature, the utilization of which offered the greatest possible economic return. The true interest of this country was agriculture. To give a few manufacturers special privileges by law, and thereby to transfer to them property that belonged to the great farm-ing population, was tryranny.[65] "A political economy which takes away individual savings by exclusive privileges might have been exemplified could Nero have killed his mother by the hands of mercenaries before he was born," he expostulated.[66]

Thomas Cooper, President of the College of South Carolina, and probably the first teacher of political econ-omy in America,[67] set forth in several books his classical economic doctrine,[68] but his pamphlet, *On the Alteration of the Tariff,* marshalled his main arguments in close array and achieved great popularity and influence. Many of his points were like those of Taylor, but they were more di-rectly put and not dulled by endless repetition and digres-sion. Economic loss to society was incurred by the employ-ment of capital in pursuits that could only show profits with the aid of artificial restriction of market. The pro-tective tariff really meant subsidizing the inefficiency and carelessness, the lack of judgment, skill, and experience, on the part of American manufacturers. Removal of the discipline of competition not only enabled the manufacturers to charge higher prices, but to foist on the consumers inferior products. There was a direct contrariety of interest between those avaricious seekers after special privilege and the community. "Their object is monopoly; to make the farmer sell at the manufacturer's price, and buy at the manufacturer's price. It is for the interest of the community that there should be competition among them; it is their object to exclude it."[69]

It was for the interest of society to take advantage of natural resources; and geographical specialization, even international specialization, was the natural result. He thought it neither desirable nor possible that America should be economically independent of other countries. Certainly the new "home market" could not approach absorbing our agricultural exports. International trade was for the good of mankind, for the resulting mutual dependence begat exchange of good feeling and of moral, intellectual, and cultural advantages. In a word, free trade promoted the cause of peace and civilization.[70] Matthew Carey, economist of the protectionists, acknowledged the great effectiveness of Cooper's onslaught.[71]

In summary, it may be said that the predecessors of Calhoun in the State rights tradition resorted to general principles of government, legalistic and historical arguments, and *laissez-faire* economics to support their cause. Some of them maintained State sovereignty; others held to the idea of divided sovereignty, while a number of them confusedly tried to hold both concepts at the same time. A few of them, with an instinct for caution, generally avoided the term "sovereignty." Certainly it was a word bandied about without precise definition, applied variously to law-making power, to any power of government, and to the power of the people to hold government responsible or to alter or abolish it. Some of their difficulty with the idea of sovereignty was doubtless due to the prevalence of the philosophy of the natural rights of individuals. These rights, plus the social compact, were used to establish principles of limited government and popular sovereignty. But in some cases even popular sovereignty was deemed inferior to certain natural rights of individuals which were never surrendered through any social or political compact. Locke rather than Rousseau was the intellectual godfather of American theorists. Defence of State rights fell naturally in line with the principle of limited government, serving as a check to enforce observance of its limits on the part of the federal government. Because the "Founding Fathers" avoided the term "sovereignty" and did not locate it, the field was clear for disputes as to constitutional construction. And disputes followed with constant appeal to the logic of legal analogy and historical evidence. Defenders of State rights also availed themselves of classical political economy, because it reinforced the prevailing natural rights philosophy in the conclusion that government (including the federal government) should confine itself to protection against foreign aggression and maintenance of peace and order at home.

This was the heritage of State rights doctrine which Calhoun received on his turning to the defense of the planter aristocracy of the South. That he wrought important changes in the doctrine did not mean a complete break with the tradition. There was the same respect for private rights, especially property rights; and there remained the same regard for limited government. Moreover, Calhoun and his allies were the true successors of the early school in carrying on the representation of a purely agricultural regime. State rights proved their common political weapon.

NOTES

1. Jonathan Elliot (ed.), *Debates in the Several State Conventions on the Adoption of the Federal Constitution,* 5 vols., 2nd ed. (Philadelphia, 1888), Vol. I, pp. 327 ,322, 325, 326; Vol. II, pp. 177, 545. The resolutions of Rhode Island and Virginia also asserted the right of the State to "reassume" the powers of government. *Ibid.,* Vol. I, pp. 327, 334.
2. *Resolutions of Virginia and Kentucky . . . and Debates in the House of Delegates of Virginia in December,* 1798, *on the Same* (Richmond, 1832).
3. H. C. Lodge, *Life and Letters of George Cabot* (Boston, 1878), pp. 338-341, 435-438; Octavius Pickering, *The Life of Timothy Pickering,* 4 vols. (Boston, 1873), Vol. IV, pp. 53-54.
4. E. P. Powell, *Nullification and Secession in the United Sates* (New York, 1897), pp. 200-233. The resolutions ran in part: "Therefore Resolved, that it be and hereby is recommended to the Legislators of the several States represented in this Convention, to adopt all such measures as may be necessary effectually to protect the citizens of said States from the operation and effects of all acts which have been or may be passed by the Congress of the United States, which shall contain provisions, subjecting the militia or other citizens to forcible drafts, conscriptions, or impressments, not authorized by the Constitution of the United States." Ames, *State Documents,* pp. 83-84.
5. Edward S. Corwin, *John Marshall and the Constitution* (New Haven, 1919), Ch. VII; Ames, *State Documents,* pp. 7-15; William E. Dodd, "Chief Justice Marshall and Virginia, 1813-1821," *American Historical Review* 12 : 776-787.
6. See the essay, "The State Rights Fetish," by A. M. Schlessinger in his book, *New Viewpoints in American History* (New York, 1922), Ch. X; John J. Lalor, ed., "Nullification," *Cyclopedia of Political Science, Political Economy, and of the Political History of the United States,* 3 vols. (Chicago, 1883), Vol. II, pp. 1050-

1055; Powell, *Nullification and Secession in the United States.*

7. The passage: "We hold these truths to be self-evident, that all men are created equal, that they are endowed by their creator with certain inalienable rights, that among these are life, liberty and the pursuit of happiness—that to secure these rights governments are instituted among men, deriving their just powers from the consent of the governed—that whenever any form of government becomes destructive of these ends, it is the right of the people to alter or abolish it, and to institute new government, laying its foundation on such principles, and organizing its powers in such form, as to them shall seem most likely to effect their safety and happiness." See Thomas Jefferson, *Writings*, 10 vols. Ford ed., (New York, 1892-1899), Vol. II, pp. 43-45.

8. See B. F. Wright, *American Interpretations of Natural Law* (Cambridge, 1931), Ch. IV.

9. Letter to John Holmes, quoted by Calhoun. *Works*, Vol. IV, pp. 492-493.

10. Charles A. Beard, *Economic Origins of Jeffersonian Democracy* (New York, 1915), pp. 429-437, 450-461.

11. Jefferson, *Writings*, Vol. IX, p. 308; Vol. I, p. 113; Vol. VII, pp. 451-452; Vol. III,p. 4.

12. Jefferson, *Writings*, Vol. VII, pp. 289-301.

13. Charles A. and Mary R. Beard, *The Rise of American Civilization*, 1 vol. ed. (New York, 1930), Bk. I, pp. 422-423.

14. See his proposal for a constitutional amendment to sanction the Louisiana purchase. Ford's edition of *The Federalist* (New York, 1898), p. 686.

15. His classic statement in his *Notes on Virginia* ran in part: "Those who labour in the earth are the chosen people of God, if ever he had a chosen people, whose breasts he has made his peculiar deposit for substantial and genuine virtue. It is the focus in which he keeps alive that sacred fire, which otherwise might escape from the face of the earth. Corruption of morals in the mass of the cultivators is a phenomenon of which no age nor nation has furnished an example. It is the mark

set on those, who not looking up to heaven, to their own
soil and industry, as does the husbandman, for their subsistence, depend for it on the casualties and caprice of
customers. Dependence begets subservience and venal-
ity, and suffocates the germ of virtue. . . . While we have
land to labour then, let us never wish to see our citizens
occupied at a work-bench, or twirling a distaff. . . ."
Notes on the State of Virginia (London, 1787) pp.
274-275. John Taylor echoed his sentiment, saying:
"At the awful day of judgment, the discrimination of
the good from the wicked is not made by the criterion
of sects or of dogmas, but by one which constitutes the
daily employment and great end of agriculture. The
judge upon this occasion has by anticipation pronounced
that to feed the hungry, clothe the naked, and give
drink to the thirsty are the passports to future happiness; and the divine intelligence which selected an agricultural state as a paradise for its first favorites, has
here again prescribed the agricultural virtues as the
means for admission of their posterity into heaven."
John Taylor, *Arator* (Petersburg, 1818), pp. 188-189.
16. Taylor was a Virginian, a soldier, legislator, and a
planter, one who obviously preferred life in the last
capacity. He served in the army during the American
revolution, took part in politics as a Republican, and
sat in both the State and federal legislatures. See H. H.
Simms, *Life of John Taylor* (Richmond, 1832). His
fame must rest chiefly on his writings, the more important of them including the *Arator*, a book of agricultural essays; and his four more comprehensive works
on government and politics, *Inquiry into the Principles
and Policy of the Government of the United States*
(Fredericksburg, 1814), *Construction Construed and
Constitutions Vindicated* (Richmond, 1820), *Tyranny
Unmasked* (Washington, 1822), and *New Views of
the Constitution of the United States* (Washington,
1823).
17. Simms, *Life of John Taylor*, pp. 144, 179-180.
18. In his *Inquiry,* perhaps his most important single
book, Taylor used John Adams' *Defense of the Constitutions of Government of the United States* (1787-

-1788), as an intellectual punching bag. It must be said in all fairness that Adams' ideas were not always correctly represented by Taylor.

19. *Inquiry*, pp. 2, 76, 161; *Construction Construed*, pp. 32, 78. Taylor sometimes used the concept of natural law as meaning the dictates of God and "right reason"; at other times he meant rather scientific law (invariant relation between two or more variables) ; still again he derided the use of the term as irrational. See *Inquiry*, pp. 11-12, 123, 402.

20. *Inquiry*, p. 412.

21. *Construction Construed*, p. 67.

22. For the sake of peace also, Taylor thought that political sovereignty should be located where the preponderance of physcial force resided. *Inquiry*, pp. 448-449.

23. *Inquiry*, pp. 27-29, 403.

24. *Ibid.*, p. 29.

25. *Construction Construed*, p. 25.

26. *Inquiry*, p. 400.

27. *Inquiry*, pp. 409, 80-81, 422, 428.

28. *Construction Construed*, p. 298.

29. *Tyranny Unmasked*, pp. 256-284.

30. *Tyranny Unmasked*, pp. 291, 299, 316; *Construction Construed*, pp. 291-314.

31. Madison's Journal in the *Formation of the Union Document*, 69th Congress, 1st. session, House Doc. 398 (Washington, 1927), pp. 397, 412, 418, 450.

32. *The Federalist*, Ford ed. (New York, 1898), pp. 62-63, 348, 315-316; *Formation of Union Document*, pp. 250-252.

33. *The Federalist*, pp. 300-301.

34. Madison, *Writings*, 9 vols. (New York, 1900-1910), Vol. VI, pp. 326-332; Vol. IX, pp. 573-607.

35. *Ibid.*, Vol. IX, p. 569; *The Federalist*, p. 251. Although not developed explicitly as a theory of divided sovereignty, something of a forerunner of Madison's concept was the argument of American revolutionists that, as between the American colonies and Great Britain, custom and therefore the imperial constitution sanctioned a division of governmental power—a division not subject to change at the discretion of the mother

country. See A. C. McLaughlin, *Constitutional History of the United States* (New York, 1935), pp. 43 ff.

36. *The Federalist*, p. 252.

37. *Formation of Union Document*, pp. 310-311, 369, 381.

38. See *Chisholm v. Georgia*, I *Law Ed.* 447 (1792); *Ware v. Hylton*, 1 Law. Ed. 582 (1796); *McColloch v. Maryland*, 4 *Law Ed.* 602 (1819); *Worcester v. Georgia*, 8 *Law. Ed.* 512 (1832); *Collector v. Day*, 20 *Law. Ed.* 125, 126 (1871); *Tennessee v. Davis*, 25 *Law Ed.* 650 (1879); *Flint v. Stone Tracy Co.*, 55 *Law Ed.* 413-414 (1910); *United States v. Lanza*, 67 *Law. Ed.* 314, 317 (1922).

39. Tucker, "View of the Laws of Virginia as a Member of the Federal Union," appendix to *Blackstone's Commentaries*, 5 vols. (Philadelphia, 1803).

40. *Ibid.*, Vol. I, pp. 8-11.

41. *Ibid.*, Vol. I, p. 10.

42. *Ibid.*, Vol. I, pp. 20-21, 144, 150.

43. Tucker, "View of the Laws of Virginia . . .", Vol. I, pp. 5-6, 8-9.

44. *Ibid.*, Vol. I, p. 171.

45. *Ibid.*, Vol. I, pp. 151-153.

46. William Rawle, *A View of the Constitution of the United States of America* (Philadelphia, 1825.)

47. *Ibid.*, pp. 25-27, 288, 289, 295-299.

48. Simms, *Life of John Taylor*, pp. 183-184.

49. *Construction Construed*, pp. 46-47.

50. *Construction Construed*, pp. 39-50. He also made use of the words, "Congress" and "federal." *New Views of the Constitution*, pp. 5-9.

51. Tucker, *Blackstone's Commentaries*, pp. 141-142.

52. Dumas Malone, *Public Life of Thomas Cooper* (New Haven, 1926, p. 296. Taylor also argued this. *New Views of the Constitution*, p. 265.

53. *New Views of the Constitution*, pp. 29-30, 275. In the Convention the proposal to give Congress the power to grant charters of incorporation was repected, because among other things such power would enable Congress to establish a bank. See *Formation of the Union Document*, pp. 563, 564, 724-725.

54. Simms, *Life of John Taylor*, pp. 189-190. *Construction Construed*, pp. 125-128.
55. Cooper, *Two Tracts: On the Proposed Alteration of the Tariff*, etc. (Charleston, 1823), pp. 4-5; Malone, *Public Life of Thomas Cooper*, pp. 296-298.
56. Dodd, "Chief Justice Marshall and Virginia", *American Historical Review* 12: 776.
57. John P. *Branch Historical Papers*, Vol. II, 51-76.
58. Edward S. Corwin, *John Marshall and the Constitution*, pp. 176-177.
59. Dodd, "Chief Justice Marshall and Virginia," *American Historical Review* 12 :783.
60. Madison, *Writings*, Vol. V., p. 342.
61. Jefferson, *Writings,* Vol. VIII, p. 123.
62. *Ibid.*, Vol. I, p. 113.
63. *Two tracts: On the Proposed Alteration of the Tariff*, etc., p. 6.
64. Taylor, *Inquiry*, Chs. IV-V and *passim; Tyranny Unmasked*, pp. 72-80 and *passim*, 138-141, 195-198, 240-242, 168-172, 177-194.
65. *Tyranny Umasked*, p. 41.
66. *Ibid.* p. 28.
67. Malone, *The Public Life of Thomas Cooper*, pp. 302-306.
68. Especially his *Lectures on the Elements of Political Economy* (Columbia, 1826), and *Manual of Political Economy* (Washington, 1833).
69. *Two Tracts: On the Proposed Alteration of the Tariff*, etc., p. 11.
70. *Ibid.*, pp. 6, 11-13, and *passim*.
71. Malone, *Public Life of Thomas Cooper*, pp. 291-292.

Part III

Society and Government

3
Society and Government

A. HUMAN NATURE

CALHOUN BEGAN THE exposition of his political theory in his *Disquisition on Government* with an express assumption as to the nature of man. The universal presence of government wherever men lived led him to conclude that government must be rooted in "the law of our nature." He felt that some explanation of human nature was necessary, therefore, to an understanding of government, just as some hypothesis by way of explanation was prerequisite to man's thinking about the solar system. Experience taught that man was a social being, for man everywhere in all history was found only in society. Living in society, he had sufficient social sense to sympathize with his fellows, but he was also a selfish being. Calhoun believed that although man was "so formed as to feel what affects others, as well as what affects himself, he is at the same time so constituted that his direct or individual affections are stronger than his sympathetic or social feelings . . ."[1] Calhoun rarely used the word "selfish," preferring terms that were more coldly scientific in carrying no derogatory implications. Judge William Harper, his fellow nullifier, was more blunt. "Man loves himself better than his neighbor," he declared, this constituting the "selfish principle" in man.[2] In a word, Calhoun compounded his assumption as to human nature by adding something of the "economic man" of the classical economists to Aristotle's "political animal."

These aspects of human nature that Calhoun believed most significant had long received recognition in political and social thought, though probably not in exactly the same juxtaposition which he gave them. In fact, his conception was an ingenious combination of two somewhat contradictory dogmas. The idea of the inherently social character of man was derived from the great Greeks of antiquity, Plato and Aristotle, and had come down through the centuries as part of the widely accepted Aristotelian tradition. Calhoun did not attempt any analysis of the concept into the necessary interdependence of men for the satisfaction of organic and spiritual needs, as did Plato and Aristotle, but simply relied upon empirical generalization. The *a priori* rationalism of some of the contract writers, among the more modern predecessors of Calhoun, led them to dissent from the idea of the essentially social nature of man. Probably Hobbes put the most striking emphasis upon the purely egoistic character of man, picturing him as a creature of appetites and aversions who was the natural enemy of every other man.[3] The Greek philosophers had not ignored this side of human nature, and yet had not thought that it altered man's character as a "political" being. But in the late eighteenth and early nineteenth centuries English political economists, possibly influenced by Hobbes' doctrine and certainly following the lead of David Hume and Adam Smith, were creating the fashion of stressing individual self-interest as the only human motive of importance in economic activity. The hedonistic psychology of the Utilitarians predominated. Calhoun, however, could ignore neither of the two conceptions of human nature, and sought to use both in combination, justifying himself by appeal to experience.

Calhoun thought this view of human nature valid for various reasons. In the first place, he juggled the two factors of the algebraic equation to which he had reduced man, and found the logical consequences untenable—even absurd. Man was not to be conceived as having an equal balance of selfish and social feelings, nor a preponderance of the latter over the former. This rejection of the alternatives was substantiated by the few exceptions to the rule. He recognized the altruistic relationship between mother and baby; and believed that certain peculiar individuals, through the influence of education and habit, acquired notably unselfish characters. But the deep impression such instances made was proof of their unusual nature, proof that they were exceptions to the general rule.[4] Moreover, he found support of his view in observation of the conduct of the people about him, especially in public life. Time and again in his letters and speeches Calhoun commented upon the influence of self-interest upon the actions of men. "I have seen enough public men," he wrote, "to come to the conclusion that there are few indeed whose attachment to self in not stronger than their patriotism and their friendship. The principal difference is only in . . . degree. . . ."[5] Even moral and religious sentiment rested ultimately upon interest. This character of man was not to be changed by any increase of knowledge or intelligence, or by any influence of education or environment.[6]

This self-interest took on generally an economic stamp. The "most powerful passions of the human heart" were the love of gain and the love of power. And in politics the masses were prone to be motivated more by desire for economic gain than by considerations of justice, peace, and harmony. Calhoun deviated from the concept of the "economic man" of the political economists, however, to the extent that he saw one might err in the calculation of one's interest. Self-interest was not always intelligently pursued. Thus manufacturers in the United States mistakenly sought protection, he wrote to Abbott Lawrence, for free trade would be more beneficial to them in the long run.[7]

Calhoun thought this predominence of selfishness a characteristic of all animated existence. It was, perhaps, to be derived from the law of self-preservation, from the desire to live, or the will to exist. And God, the creator of all things, was therefore the source of this particular character of man. "He, in his infinite wisdom and goodness, has allotted to every class of animated beings its condition and appropriate functions, and has endowed each with feelings, instincts, capacities, and faculties best adapted to its allotted condition."[8] Existence in this world required a selfish nature, and God had accordingly supplied it.

Several writers have seized upon Calhoun's attributing the nature of man to divine ordination as proof of his reliance upon a theory of natural law.[9] Since he made this formula for human nature the basis of his political theory, it was even asserted that he fell in line with the natural law tradition in America.[10] This, it would seem, makes too much of Calhoun's appeal to God as an ultimate cause. Naturally as a good Presbyterian he looked upon the Christian God as the prime mover of everything in this world. But it must not be overlooked that his linking up of this postulate as to human nature with a divine sanction was not at all essential to his theory. His view of the nature of man was a generalization which he felt could be validly drawn from universal experience. It may well be viewed as an empirical judgment drawn from long years of observation and reflection upon the conduct of men and from his study of history. In this sense only did he believe it "the law of our nature" " . . . without which government would not, and with which it must necessarily exist."[11] If such generalizations as to the fruits of experience are to be designated natural law, they must be carefully distinguished from other senses in which the term is used. John Taylor, as we have noted, used the term in the same sense that Calhoun did, but he also used it in quite a different sense in which it carried the connotation of a natural, or pre-political, order.[12] Calhoun did not use the concept in the latter sense, and he did not fall within the American stream of natural law theory. He made no appeals to it as to the dictates of "right reason" or justice.

Today, of course, his assumption might be criticized as reducing the human equation to too few factors. Modern psychology indicates that man's motives form a complex of many factors, some of them of a very elusive nature. On the other hand, the behaviorists might argue that, if man is either gregarious or selfish, he becomes so by learning and is not so constituted by nature. It should be noted, however, that Calhoun made no pretensions to a complete analysis of human nature; his conception was simply an abstract representation of certain qualities which he considered significant in political relationships. He recognized it as a fundamental assumption, and it was one that he shared in part at least with many others of his time.[13] He thought there was valid support for it. He wrote that in politics " . . . we must take men as they are, and do the best we can with them, constituted as they are."[14] He started, then, with this assumption as to human nature to build up his political theory; and he recognized the abstract nature of his results and desired to see to what modifications they were subject in practice.[15] It was the pursuit of self interest by individuals and groups that complicated and made so very difficult the problems of government and politics. It was probably the most important of the imponderables.

B. THE LOGICAL ORIGIN OF GOVERNMENT

The selfish character of our nature would logically lead to conflict between individuals. Calhoun discerned a "tendency to a universal state of conflict between individual and individual, accompanied by the connected passions of suspicion, jealousy, anger and revenge,—followed by insolence, fraud, and cruelty . . ."[16] He contemplated a sort of Hobbesian war of each against all, with the resulting social chaos. However, Calhoun was not positing a state of nature fashioned after Hobbes. He was simply asserting that without government men would live in anarchy, which he felt must be an unpleasant condition, man being constituted as he was. It was out of the evils of anarchy that arose the imperious necessity for government, if the human race were to be preserved and perpetuated. Thus, wherever men lived, and they always lived in society, there was government. The social and political state was the only natural one for man.[17] Calhoun was, in fact, attempting a reconciliation between what he deemed valid elements of two distinct traditions. With Aristotle he believed government was an activity normal and natural to man, requiring not even rationally any contract for its institution. Its universality among men attested to its satisfaction of fundamental human needs. In singling out the source of the necessity of government, Calhoun turned to the lower nature of man, an explanation of long standing going back to the early fathers of the Roman Catholic Church and given more immediate currency by various contract theorists. John Taylor, among the Americans, for example rejected Godwin's doctrine of the essential goodness of men, and based his social compact theory on the idea that the need for government arose out of the evil moral qualities of men.[18] But Calhoun, unlike many adherents of the social compact theory, did not conceive that government in restraining the lower nature of man exhausted its legitimate sphere, for man was also a social being. Government, arising of absolute logical necessity for one reason, might well be used by men for other reasons.

Calhoun's followers reiterated his view variously. The tendency of each to sacrifice the interests of others to his own, according to them, required a controlling power in the community to curb it. "Without it, the strong would arrogate to themselves all advantages at the expense of the weak," asserted Judge Harper, who acknowledged his indebtedness to Calhoun. The resulting anarchy would be not so much the absence of government as the government of the worst, or "kakistocracy"; it would be a "horrid hell."[19] Thomas Cooper declared that "To prevent the mischiefs arising from the selfish exercise of power by individual over individual, men increased their power for particular purposes by union."[20] This was no reference to any specific act of union, for men always lived in communities and always possessed government. As George Fitzhugh agreed, some kind and amount of government was an absolute necessity to men, who really wanted good government, not liberty.[21] These writers, like Calhoun, were visualizing men without government and finding in such a state a reason for government.

Here and elsewhere throughout his political theory, Calhoun contemplated a community of people possessing political organization and independence of every other similar community. The concept of the state was there; but Calhoun nowhere made it explicit. He placed supreme power, designated as sovereignty, in the body of the people of such a community. His implicit concept of the state will be considered in the chapter on sovereignty.[22] It should be noted here, however, that on occasion Calhoun apparently founded popular sovereignty on a basis not entirely consistent with the course of his theory or with his treatment of the logical origin of government. Naturally he accepted popular sovereignty, the right of a people to self-government, as the great principle established by the American Revolution. And early in his political career he was inclined to accept the traditional derivation of self-government from natural rights. He once declared in Congress: "We have a government of a new order, perfectly distinct from all others which have preceded it—a government founded on the rights of man; resting not on authority, not on prejudice, not on superstition, but reason."[23] And he went on to assert his faith in the ultimate triumph of its principles throughout the civilized world. Here plainly, he was using the vernacular of his predecessors with all the paraphernalia of the natural rights of man, the social compact, and so on. This was in 1816 long before he began the formulation of his systematic theory. That he found some difficulty in divorcing himself from the old ideology is shown in his statement as late as 1831 that in a state of nature no man had a right to govern another without his consent.[24] However, he did tear himself away from the old philosophy of natural rights of men. When he came to the mature formulation of his ideas, he found another source for popular sovereignty in the pragmatic efforts of men to mitigate the abuses of governmental authority. Government itself was rooted in the nature of man.

C. ATTACK ON THE SOCIAL CONTRACT THEORY

Calhoun set forth his attack on the philosophy of the Declaration of Independence at its fullest, perhaps, in his speech on the Oregon Bill in June, 1848. As an advocate of Southern interests, he was opposing the growth of the sentiment for the exclusion of slavery from the territories of the United States. He denied the constitutional right of either Congress or the territorial government (of Oregon, in this case) to exclude slavery, and maintained that the "squatter" sovereignty argument of Cass and Douglas had no legal foundation. The unfortunate hostility to slavery, from which the movement for exclusion derived sustenance, rested at bottom upon the old anarchical theory of the natural liberty and equality of all men. With courage and stoic determination, Calhoun rejected this traditional theory. He subjected the proposition that all men are created free and equal to careful analysis, beginning with a rather scholastic attack on the choice of words. In the first place, according to the Bible, only two were "created"; all other people were born into the world. Then, men were not born; only infants were. And certainly all would acknowledge that infants were not born free, what with their subjection to parents, guardians, or older people generally.

While infants they are incapable of freedom, being destitute alike of the capacity of thinking and acting, without which there can be no freedom. Besides, they are necessarily born subject to their parents, and remain so among all people, savage and civilized, until the development of their intellect and physical capacity enables them to take care of themselves. They grow to all the freedom of which the condition in which they were born permits, by growing to be men. Nor is it less false that they were born "equal." They are not so in any sense in which it can be regarded; and thus . . . there is not a word of truth in the whole proposition as expressed and generally understood.[25]

If one considered how different even the same person was at different periods of life, one would realize how impossible in fact was the assumption of equality. In like vein, Cooper argued that no human being ever had been

or would be born free, or live free from the control of his
fellow men. Moreover, "no set of men, from six hundreds
to six millions, were ever born equal in size, in strength,
in health, in natural intellect and capacity for improvement. And if they were, the variety of circumstances to
which they are exposed from birth will produce inequali-
ties from the very first month of existence. Where is the
use of basing political theory on a false fact?"[26]

Calhoun did not believe that the postulate of natural
liberty and equality was necessary to the vindication of the
American Revolution; an appeal for defense of chartered
rights and of the traditional rights of Englishmen would
have sufficed. American colonials had borrowed the ideas
from English writers on government, such as Sidney and
Locke; and these writers had qualified "free and equal"
by adding "in the state of nature." He believed that they
had contemplated man in such a state only "for the purpose of reasoning"; i. e., that their state of nature was a
purely hypothetical one. In this fashion it was possible
to conceive man as living alone and isolated, or in society,
or in political society—i. e., in a community having government. One might reason as to the rights or duties of
man in any of these states without being concerned for the
moment whether he could exist therein. In the first of
these, certainly he would be free and equal in the sense that
each would be exempt from control by others from whom
he lived apart. "But it is equally clear that man cannot
exist in such a state; that he is by nature social, and that
society is necessary, not only to the proper development
of all his faculties, moral and intellectual, but to the very
existence of his race."[27] To reason upon an hypothesis that
was never to prove true, was to reach conclusions of no
practical value. Bledsoe and Dabney, Virginians who followed Calhoun in many respects, furthered the criticism
by pointing out the subjective variation in social contract

theories, those of Hobbes and Locke differing greatly.[28]
The social and political was the only natural state for man.
Thus Calhoun, who was always an interested observer of
European political affairs, wrote his daughter that there
was little prospect for success in the French Revolution of
1848, for the French lacked the proper elements for a free
popular government and labored under a total misconception of the principles underlying such a government.

Indeed, her conception of liberty is false throughout. Her
standard of liberty is ideal; belongs to that kind of liberty
which man has been supposed to possess in what has been
falsely called a state of nature,—a state supposed to have
preceded the social and political, and in which, of course,
he must have lived apart, as an isolated individual, without society, without government. In such a state, if it were
possible for him to exist in it, he would have, indeed, two
of the elements of the French political creed, liberty and
equality; but no fraternity. That can only exist in the social
and political; and the attempt to unite the other two, as
they would exist in a supposed state of nature, in man, as
he must exist in the former, must and ever will fail. The
union is impossible, and the attempt to unite them is
absurd. . . .[29]

Since the state of nature was such a poor one, and
since man was nowhere to be found living in it, it was
rational to conclude that it never existed. It followed that
the origin of government was not to be found in any social
compact—either as an historical fact or as a hypothetical
convention on which to base the ethical justification of
government. Government found its justification in making
possible existence of man in society. Although Calhoun
felt that the social compact was predicated upon the
worthless concept of a state of nature, and also that it was
superfluous in explanation of the origin of government, he
made frequent use of the term "compact" in treating of

the nature of confederate and federal government. But, of course, compact in this connection was a "political compact," something quite distinct from the social compact. It was rather to be identified with a solemn treaty between independent governments, or compared to a contract between individuals (with certain differences). Compacts there certainly were between governments, but none between individuals to establish government. Nor was a constitution a social compact,[30] but rather an organic act of a people already organized to give a certain form to its organization.

Despite all of this attack on the natural liberty and equality of men, the state of nature, and the social contract theory, one of Calhoun's critics of later times found what he believed an implicit contradiction between this attack and Calhoun's basic assumption as to human nature.

Here we see the continuance of the old concepts of natural law doctrine. That was to be expected, because the whole political theory in America was dominated by this theory, a theory of a pre-political state, in which the evil propensities of human nature find free play, and would soon lead to the destruction of the race if a controlling power, that is, the power of the state, did not intervene. . . . A stateless condition was unbearable and stood in contradiction with the social tendencies of man; therefore political authority (*eine Staatsgewalt*) must take its place. Political authority is something necessary, natural; in the nature of man we find the proximate cause for the foundation of the state; but man has received this natural character from God. . . . Thus we find in God the ultimate cause of political association.[31]

Although much of Calhoun's thought is there, this statement leaves a totally erroneous impression, for Calhoun's men without government were wholly hypothetical. He made a clean break with the concept of a state of nature. Moreover, he certainly was not of those in America who used the natural law doctrine as a basis for a claim to natural rights. Rights of individuals were only those sanctioned by the community. And again, as has been noted, the fact that Calhoun dubbed "natural" his formula for human nature, as he observed it to work in his time and in past history, or even that he declared it determined by God, did not put him in the stream of American natural law theory. Calhoun's chief appeal in this regard was to the fruits of experience—to the verdict of history. That one might question his reading of history is no adequate denial of his empiricism; that his use of the empirical approach may have been influenced by subjective factors does not actually impeach Calhoun's rejection of natural law as a valid criterion for human reasoning. Elliott, however, gave his misconception of Calhoun away when he inserted a footnote quoting the Declaration of Independence to prove his point that, according to Calhoun, it lay within the free will of men to establish through compact or agreement their own form of government.[32] As we shall see later,[33] Calhoun felt that shaping the organization of a government through the adoption or alteration of a constitution was not a process merely of rational deliberation and agreement of men, but one dependent on a variety of circumstances quite beyond control of the rational decision of the moment.

In his attack on the state of nature and on the natural liberty and equality of men, Calhoun was definitely making a break with his predecessors. Jefferson, Madison, and Taylor had all been adherents of the contract theory in the Lockeian tradition; and they had all appealed to the natural rights of man. Calhoun had some difficulty in erasing all traces of similar doctrine from his thinking, but, it is submitted, he succeeded. Many of his contemporaries who followed him in his defense of State rights were not so successful. They adopted much of his theory, but now and again lapsed into the old vernacular. Robert Turnbull preached nullification to his fellow Carolinians in 1832, and found himself still appealing to the natural rights of man.[34] Governor Troup of Georgia rejected nullification but asserted the right of secession. He declared: "Here . . . is a contract involving rights and obligations on the face of it; it purports to be perpetual and irrevocable, but is it so in fact? Can it be so between independent communities, who are bound by the laws of God and nature to protect and defend themselves; to take care of their own happiness and interests—are those communities to be bound from generation to generation without the possibility of finding absolution?"[35] Here are some of the jargon of natural rights, but it should be noted that the emphasis was shifting from the rights of the individual to those of the community. Many years later Jefferson Davis, in justifying secession, appealed in words almost identical with those of the Declaration of Independence, to the inalienable right of a people to change its government.[36]

To Calhoun, as to Edmund Burke somewhat earlier, these doctrines of the natural rights of men to liberty and equality were destructive of social order and safety. These "French principles" were really anarchical at bottom; they made the proper construction of government most difficult and were causing Europe much trouble. Among his followers, Fitzhugh and Dabney confirmed his judgment that these doctrines really constituted a denial of all human authority; and Hammond cited the horrors of the French Revolution as their logical corollary.[37] To Calhoun, these false ideas threatened to thwart all of the efforts of European peoples to reform their social and political condition. Likewise, American abolitionism, originating in these ideas, was proving a formidable menace to Southern institutions. Finally, the progress of equalitarian ideas and practices among the lower classes throughout the country seemed to him to be rushing the country into "some new and untried condition."[38] Time alone would reveal the outcome.

However, he believed he detected in the natural rights body of doctrine principles just as inimical to the interests of the industrial capitalism of the North as to the slave owners of the South. The ideal of equality, carried out to its logical conclusion, constituted an attack on all property rights. Explain it away as one might, by pointing out that equality of rights naturally leads to inequality of possessions, etc.,[39] the germ of "agrarianism" was there. Calhoun wrote to Duff Green that if and when these subversive doctrines should be logically applied, " . . . the first victims would be the wealthy and talented of the North. We of the South are by far the most safe. The intelligence of the North must see this, but whether in time to save themselves and the institutions of the country, God only knows. But whenever their eyes may open, they will be astonished to find that the doctrines which they denounce as treason are the only means of their political salvation, while those, which they so fondly hugged to their bosom, were working their certain destruction."[40] His estimate of the immediacy of the danger was somewhat askew, but he was followed by writers of a different cast in his belief that the logical conclusion of the democratic ideal was socialism.

In denying either historical or logical validity to the social contract theory, Calhoun was pioneering in American thought. He was moved in part by the desire to maintain consistency with a more Aristotelian view of political relationships than that prevalent in America of his day. He initiated for the new world the work already begun in the old by Hume and Bentham in the preceding century, and carried on in the nineteenth by the English utilitarians, of destroying the vogue of contract theory in political thought. Calhoun's convictions on this subject revealed no direct evidence of debt to Hume or Bentham, but, in addition to the influence of Aristotle, they were shaped without doubt by the lack of any sense of historical continuity in the contract theory. On this latter point, Calhoun could but share Burke's feeling of distrust. Moreover, in the form prevalent in America, contract doctrine was inseparably bound up in the dangerous dogma of the natural liberty and equality of all men. Underlying his complete rejection of *naturrecht* contract theory was Calhoun's clear appreciation of its real or potential incompatibility with human slavery. If every man had a natural right to liberty, and government were instituted by compact only to protect man in the enjoyment of his natural rights, then government was not justified in protecting the institution of slavery. Such application of the doctrine was plainly an attack on the labor system of the South, and it was proving annoying, and even alarming, in the hands of abolitionists of the Garrison breed. Rational men must be convinced of the error of abolitionism, in part at least by the destruction of its intellectual foundation.

D.   PURPOSES OF GOVERNMENT

To Calhoun, the ends to be secured by political organization, as has probably been indicated already, included in the first place, the preservation and perpetuation of the race, i. e., of the people included within the jurisdiction of the government.[41] The community must be preserved through the protection of its individual members from violence, injustice, or anarchy within, and from danger of attack from without. "If it fail in either, it would fail in the primary end of government, and would not deserve the name."[42] Even those who appealed to the natural rights of individuals for severe restriction of the activities of government conceded this much. The second great purpose of government was the perfection of the society through fostering or aiding the development of individuals in their spiritual, moral, and intellectual capacities. The "main spring" to such development was the "desire of individuals to better their condition," Calhoun using for his own purposes this pet motive to which Adam Smith had appealed in his arguments for *laissez-faire.* To insure its efficient performance, the proper amount of liberty and security in the possession of the fruits of one's exertions must be provided by the government.

Calhoun nowhere considered in any detail the justification of the institution of private property, although he felt the force of the attack on one kind of property— slaves. He met this attack by criticizing its basic ideas of the natural liberty and equality of all men. Positively, he sought justification for slavery as it existed in the concrete circumstances in the South of his time. But of property in general he had little more to say than that its secure possession was a necessary inducement to the efforts of individuals to improve their lot. In other words, it was a necessary condition of the advance of civilization. Its sanctity was generally accepted by his contemporaries, and he probably saw little reason for doubting or substantiating unquestioned truth. Americans generally followed Locke in the view that protection of private property was one of the main functions of government; and some of the framers of the Constitution, notably Gouverneur Morris of Pennsylvania, John Rutledge of South Carolina, and Rufus King of Massachusetts, had practically held that this was the sole important function of government, primitive freedom having been surrendered only so that property might be protected. Without recourse to *natur-*

recht theory, Judge Harper and William G. Simms, representatives of the State rights school, declared also the fundamental importance of property, Simms arguing that only by the accumulation of property could men escape their destiny to labor. However, Thomas Dew clearly went beyond Calhoun's position in asserting the right of property to exemption from political authority. In this regard, Dew's position was nearer that of Chancellor James Kent, the classic expounder of the doctrine of vested rights of property in America.[43]

To Calhoun and to the general current of American thought, the maintenance of the right of property meant also the maintenance of inequality of property; for as individuals differed in native ability, health, and strength, so would some achieve more success in the acquisition of worldly goods.[44] This was natural and proper in the interest of the material welfare of the community.

The preservation and perfection of men in society, then, were the ends of government. These were general ends as old as Aristotle, who had observed that government, originating in the necessities of the life of men, continued in existence to promote the good life. Calhoun and Aristotle may have contemplated different public policies as conducive to the development of the higher qualities of men, but their broad flexible criteria of the legitimate sphere of governmental function were essentially the same. Calhoun thus claimed for American thought the heritage of the modern western world from ancient Greece. His rejection of any attempt at doctrinaire limitation and fixation of governmental function through a narrow and rigid conception of the purpose of government followed consistently his denial of the validity of natural law and natural right doctrine. Although Calhoun inclined to favor *laissez-faire* public policy as best suited to the agricultural civilization in which he lived, he did not generalize his opinion into a theory of the purpose of government. And in this he departed from the individualistic American tradition that government was a necessary evil, the legitimate sphere of which was completely consumed in the preservation of the life, liberty, and property of the citizen. To Calhoun, the preservation and perfection of men constituted at once the justification for existence of government and a flexible general guide for distinguishing between the proper spheres of liberty and authority.

NOTES

1. *Works,* Vol. I, pp. 2-3; Vol. VI, p. 53. Alexander H. Stephens, óne of the most prominent of the later leaders in the State rights school, was also impressed with the selfish propensities of human nature and with the absolute necessity of political association. See his "Letter to J. Henly Smith, September 16, 1860," *American Historical Association Annual Report,* 1911, Vol. II, pp. 498-499; *Constitutional View of the War between the States,* 2 vols. (Philadelphia, 1868-1870), Vol. I, p. 7. George Fitzhugh, his follower in the defense of slavery, offered no real modification of Calhoun's view on asserting that: "Man is by nature the most social and gregarious and, therefore, the least selfish of all animals." Fitzhugh, *Cannibals All!* (Richmond, 1857), pp. 55, 341. R. L. Dabney, another of the champions of slavery believed that man was destined for social existence by will of God. Dabney, *Defence of Virginia* (New York, 1867), pp. 251-252.
2. *Speech before the Charleston State Right and Free Trade Association, April 1, 1832, explaining and enforcing the Remedy of Nullification,* pamphlet (Charleston, 1832), pp. 9-10.
3. Thomas Hobbes, *Leviathan,* Everyman ed. (London and New York, 1914), pp. 63-66.

4. *Works,* Vol. I, pp. 3, 5-6.
5. *Correspondence,* p. 692. Cf. Alexander H. Stephens, "Letter to J. Henly Smith, January 22, 1860," *American Historical Association Annual Report,* 1911, Vol. II, pp. 457-458.
6. *Works,* Vol. I, p. 74; Vol. II, p. 24.
7. *Works,* Vol. VI, pp. 79, 85, 202; Calhoun, *Correspondence,* pp. 654-655.
8. *Works,* Vol. I, pp. 6-7. R. L. Dabney, in his postbellum apology for Virginia, derived the social nature of man from the same source. *Defence of Virginia* (New York, 1867), pp. 251-2.
9. See Edward G. Elliott, "Die Staatslehre John C. Calhouns," *Staats—und volker-rechtliche Abhandlungen,* Vol. IV, No. 2 (1903), pp. 21-25 and *passim;* Benjamin F. Wright, Jr., *American Interpretations of Natural Law* (Cambridge, 1931), pp. 272-273.
10. Elliott, "Die Staatslehre John C. Calhouns," p. 21.
11. *Works,* Vol. I, pp. 1-2.
12. See *supra,* Ch. II.
13. Thomas Cooper, for example, in his *Lectures on Political Economy* (Columbia, 1826), shared the classical economists' concept of the "economic man." pp. 9, 56-57, 189-190.
14. *Correspondence,* p. 693.
15. *Ibid.,* p. 752.
16. *Works,* Vol. I, p. 4.
17. *Ibid.,* Vol. I, pp. 4, 57-58; Vol. VI, p. 53. A. H. Stephens accepted Calhoun's view as axiomatic. See *Constitutional View of War between the States,* Vol. I, p. 7. Myres misrepresents Calhoun as having contended that "government was not created by voluntary consent . . ., but originated in force and was continued by force." S. D. Myres, Jr, "Politics in the South," *Arnold Foundation Studies in Public Affairs,* Vol. III, No. 1, pp. 14-15.
18. Taylor, *Inquiry,* pp. 76, 166-167, 161, 436.
19. William Harper, *Speech . . . explaining and enforcing . . . Nullification,* pp. 9-10; "Memoir on Slavery," *Pro-Slavery Argument* (Philadelphia, 1853), p. 78.
20. Cooper, *Manual of Political Economy* (Washington,

1833), p. 105. Bledsoe and Dabney offered a different explanation of government as natural and inevitable for men, one smacking somewhat of natural law. God imposed upon all men the duty of caring for his fellows, and government arose necessarily as the most useful instrument for the discharge of this moral obligation. A. T. Bledsoe, *Essay on Liberty and Slavery* (Philadelphia, 1856), pp. 27-28, 33-34; R. L. Dabney, *Defence of Virginia*, pp. 251-252.

21. Fitzhugh, *Sociology for the South* (Richmond, 1854), pp. 31, 353.
22. See *infra*, Ch. VI.
23. *Works*, Vol. II, p. 152.
24. *Works*, Vol. VI, p. 138.
25. *Works*, Vol. IV, pp. 507-508.
26. *Manual of Political Economy, pp.* 104-105. Thomas Dew in his defense of slavery did not attempt directly to refute the ideas of natural liberty and equality; he dismissed them as abstractions too remote from actual circumstances to furnish a basis for legislation. He declared: "No set of legislators ever have, or ever can legislate upon purely abstract principles, entirely independent of circumstances, without ruin to the body politic which should have the misfortune to be under the guidance of such quackery. Well and philosophically has Burke remarked that circumstances give in reality to every political principle its distinguishing color and discriminating effect." "Review of the Debate in the Virginia Legislature, 1831-32," reprint from the *Political Register,* October 16, 1833, p. 789. William Gilmore Simms expressed the attitude of the Calhounian school in declaring that all men are equal "each in his place" in accountability to God and in the protection of the laws. This was the sum total validity of the doctrine of the equality of men. Simms," Morals of Slavery," *Pro-Slavery Argument*, pp. 252-253. Jefferson Davis and practically all Southern secessionists repudiated the ideal of equality as applied to the black and white races. See Davis' *Globe,* 36th Congress, 2nd session, p. 487. See also Ch. VIII *infra*.
27. Calhoun, *Works,* Vol. IV, p. 509.

28. Bledsoe, *On Liberty and Slavery*, pp. 30-33; Dabney, *Defence of Virginia*, p. 253.
29. Calhoun, *Correspondence*, p. 758.
30. In this regard Calhoun differed from several of his predecessors, St. George Tucker notably inclining to identify constitutions with social compacts. See his *Blackstone's Commentaries*, (Philadelphia, 1803), Appendix to Vol. I, pt. i, pp. 4, 20-21, 144-145.
31. Edward G. Elliott, "Die Staatslehre John C. Calhouns," pp. 21-22.
32. Elliott, "Die Staatslehre John C. Calhouns," p. 22.
33. See *infra.*, Ch. V.
34. Turnbull, *Oration delivered before the State Rights and Free Trade Party . . . on the Fourth of July*, 1832, pamphlet (Charleston, 1832), pp. 4-5.
35. Troup, *Letter to a Gentleman in Georgia on the Rights of the States*, etc., pamphlet (Milledgeville, 1834), pp. 8-9.
36. Davis, *The Rise and Fall of the Confederate Government*, 2 vols. (New York, 1881), Vol. I, pp. 153, 184. And yet Davis strictly adjured the doctrine of the natural rights of individuals as historically unsound and subjectively variable. See *Ibid.*, Vol. I, pp. 570-571. Judge Harper, as closely as he had followed Calhoun in purely political theory, nevertheless wrote in terms of natural right and natural law in treating of slavery. "It is the order of nature and God that the being of superior faculties and knowledge . . . should control and dispose of those who are inferior. It is as much in the order of nature that men should enslave each other . . ." Harper, "Memoirs on Slavery," p. 14.
37. Fitzhugh, *Cannibals All*, pp. 80-81; Dabney, *Defence of Virginia*, pp. 241-242; J. H. Hammond, "Letters on Slavery," *Pro-Slavery Argument* (Philadelphia, 1853), pp. 149-150. Fitzhugh believed that he had found the origin of anarchical natural-rights political doctrine in the Reformation which gave birth to the idea of private judgment. Transferred from religious to political application, "the right of private judgment . . . leads to the right to act on that judgment, to the supreme sovereignty of the individual, and the abne-

gation of all government." Fitzhugh, *op. cit.*, 80-81.

38. Works, Vol. IV, p. 512; *Correspondence*, pp. 367, 758.

39. As Cooper did in the fashion of the political economists, *Manual of Political Economy*, pp. 104-106.

40. *Correspondence*, pp. 344-345.

41. *Works*, Vol. I, pp. 4, 51-52, 58.

42. *Ibid.*, Vol. I, p. 52.

43. See Max Farrand, ed., *Records of the Federal Convention of 1787*, 3 vols. (New Haven, 1911), Vol. I, pp. 533-534, 541-542; Harper, "Memoir on Slavery," p. 11; Simms, "Morals of Slavery," pp. 259-261;Dew, "Review of the Debate in the Virginia Legislature, 1831-32," p. 799; James Kent, *Commentaries on American Law*, 4 vols., 13th ed. (Boston, 1884), Vol. II, pp. 319-320.

44. This was, of course, a conclusion of long acceptance. See Kent, *Commentaries on American Law*, Vol. II, pp. 328-329. Alexander Hamilton in the Federal Convention had felt that inequality of property would exist as long as liberty, and was, in fact, the result of liberty. See Farrand, *Records of the Federal Convention of 1787*, Vol. I, p. 424. Tucker and Cooper of the State rights school also expressed the same general view. Tucker wrote: "But some men have more strength than others; some more health; some more industry; and some more skill and ingenuity than others; and according to these and other circumstances the products of their labour must be various, and their property must become unequal. The rights of property are sacred, and must be protected; otherwise there could be no exertion of either ingenuity or industry, and consequently nothing but extreme poverty, misery, and brutal ignorance." Tucker, *Blackstone's Commentaries*, Vol. I, p. 28 of appendix. Cooper asserted such inequality arose from the laws of nature. *Manual of Political Economy*, pp. 105-106. Generally speaking, Americans of this period considered property only as the product of one's labor when justifying it.

4

Liberty Versus Authority: The
Great Problem of Goverment

A. THE CRITERION

CERTAINLY IN HIS great concern for preserving a large
sphere of individual liberty entirely free of governmental
control (given the protection of established institutions)
and of freedom of the community to manage its own affairs, Calhoun was the true heir of his Virginian fore-runners. In fact, most Southerners of the middle period were
pronouncedly attached to the cause of liberty—a striking
and, to some, incongruous fact, about which Edmund
Burke observed that it was because freedom was to the
Southerners not only an enjoyment but a mark of rank
and privilege.[1] Thomas R. Dew, Virginia defender of
slavery, added, perhaps somewhat wishfully, that this attachment was also because of the perfect spirit of equality
prevalent among the whites, a spirit made possible in the
South as in Greece of old by the institution of slavery.[2]
And obviously also other reasons included the *laissez-faire*
inclinations of agricultural capitalism and the reliance
upon the States for protection of their minority interests
against interference by the central government. Of course,
Calhoun's attachment, unlike that of his predecessors and
even some of his political allies, was not in terms of the
natural right of the individual. Having achieved a new
philosophical orientation, he had no need of the traditional

American frame of reference to support his regard for the Southern ideal of liberty. Turnbull and Rhett among his fellow Carolinians strayed from their master on occasion and did not show his scrupulous care in avoiding a doctrine not easily reconcilable with slavery.[3] Jefferson Davis and others of the State rights school experienced similar difficulty.

To Calhoun it was not a matter of natural right, but one of the conditions of human progress that the individual should be allowed a large field of action free of community control. Here, as we have seen, he relied upon the desire of the individual to improve his lot as a motive which society should capitalize by offering the individual liberty to seek this improvement in his own way and security in the fruits of his efforts. Individuals pursuing their own interests in their own way made for both individual and social progress. The "highest wisdom of the State" was "a wise and masterly inactivity."[4] However, inasmuch as security in possession of the fruits of one's efforts was essential to progress, government must have sufficient authority to afford such security. Moreover, as preservation of society was primary and perfection secondary, authority must be competent to insure the former even when at times such action meant the serious limitation or abandonment of the latter objective. In his own words, "by assigning to each (liberty and authority) its appropriate sphere, all conflicts between them cease . . ." But such assignment must vary according to circumstances, some of which are "physical—such as open and exposed frontiers . . . Others are moral—such as the different degrees of intelligence, patriotism, and virtue among the mass of the community, and their experience and proficiency in the art of self-government . . ."[5] A community must be prepared for a large share of liberty. In a word, the genius of a people as well as strategical factors must be taken into account in drawing the line in a given community between liberty and authority.[6]

Prudent judgment of the quantum of authority most efficient to securing the ends of order and progress, in the light of the conditioning circumstances, was the only guide in drawing the line between the rights of the individual and those of the community. It followed that abstract concepts of the natural rights of man would be of little service in this regard. The rights of individuals were those sanctioned by the community.[7] When the individual claims a right which the community does not sanction, his only recourse is through persuading the community to his point of view. It was for this reason that certain rights, as those of freedom of speech, of press, and of assembly, were to be safeguarded to the individual by the community with particular tenderness. Experience had shown these to be "great moral agents" for effecting changes that reason revealed as necessary. For the rest the individual must depend upon the power of truth to win its way into the human heart.[8] His almost Miltonian fervor for the preservation of liberty of expression through speech and print placed Calhoun surely within the pale of political liberalism, his argument appealing to the resulting wisdom of the community for just government. This justification may have been but his view of the "truth" which Milton had wanted to secure earlier; certainly it conformed to prevalent American ideals, however philosophically supported.

Naturally, according to Calhoun, all individuals would not agree in their judgment of the quantum of authority necessary, or of the way in which the accepted authority should be used, to achieve the designated ends, which in themselves were so general as to be acceptable to almost everyone. The sense of the community alone was determining. Of course, now and then the judgment of the community might not be accurate; and people might be accorded more or less liberty than they deserve. Calhoun granted that some people might not enjoy all the liberty of which they were capable.[9] However, he thought it un-questionably true that no people could long possess more liberty than that to which they were fairly entitled. If such a people did not have the requisite virtues, or if other circumstances were unpropitious, their liberty would probably degenerate into license; and the resulting anarch-ical conditions would soon be displaced by despotism. True liberty was always dependent upon the virtues of the people.[10]

It follows . . . that it is a great and dangerous error to suppose that all people are equally entitled to liberty. It is a reward to be earned, not a blessing to be gratuitously lavished on all alike—a reward reserved for the intelli-gent, the patriotic, the virtuous and the deserving—and not a boon to be bestowed on a people too ignorant, de-graded, and vicious, to be capable of either appreciating or of enjoying it. . . . This dispensation seems to be the result of some fixed law; and every effort to disturb or defeat it, by attempting to elevate a people in the scale of liberty above the point to which they are entitled to rise, must ever prove abortive, and end in disappointment. The progress of a people rising from a lower to a higher point in the scale of liberty is necessarily slow. . . .[11]

When the character of a people gave little promise of capacity for freedom, it was sheer stupidity to experiment with granting liberty in the name of the natural right of the individual. Calhoun had a strongly conservative sense of social continuity. The great common liberty, the right of the community to self-government, was not to be sacri-ficed for some "vague, indefinite, erroneous, and most dan-gerous conception of private individual liberty."[12] That the sense of the community, then, might dictate unequal enjoyment of liberty as between different orders in the same community, he readily granted. There should be equality before the law, but not complete uniformity of legal rights and duties. In fact, the latter was not only unessential to liberty, but would destroy both liberty and happiness. Here Calhoun remained conveniently vague about the meaning of "equality before the law"; and at the same time he attempted to muster the old argument for justifying inequality in the possession of property to the defense of inequality in the enjoyment of liberty. Inequality, not merely in actual freedom, but in legal status was justified, he felt, by the inequality of different individuals and groups of individuals in their abilities and virtues. Thus Calhoun and his school availed themselves of the Greek idea of "proportional equality," with an eye, no doubt, to conforming their theory to the social stratification of Southern society. To Dabney, true equality required a varied distribution of social privilege and legal right among the members of a community to fit the distribution of ability and virtue. As William Gilmore Simms, Calhoun's fellow Carolinian, put it, all men enjoyed the equal protection of the laws "each in his place."[13] According to Calhoun, equality of the less able in legal freedom would hold back the superior in their pursuit of their own welfare, and thus destroy the latter's liberty and retard progress. "It is, indeed, this inequality of condition between the front and rear ranks in the march of progress which gives so strong an impulse to the former to maintain their position, and to the latter to press forward in their files. This gives to progress its greatest impulse."[14] Emulation of their superiors by a group of people bound by the law to a servile status would not seem today much of a stimulus to achievement; the handicap in the race was too large. But such was his argument.

However little value may be attributed to Calhoun's argument for inequality in the enjoyment of liberty under

the law (since there can be no scientific certainty as to who
are the superior), it must be granted that as regards the
nature and amount of liberty to be accorded individuals
by the law his rejection of *a priori* right marked an advance over his predecessors. His position again revealed
the influence of the Greek point of view, in which rights
of individuals as against the community found no place.
Under Calhoun's influence, this came to be the view of the
State rights school generally. In Europe before the time
of Calhoun, Hobbes and Rousseau had both arrived at essentially the same position, but their philosophical premises were those of the natural law school. Probably Bodin
belonged more truly to the Aristotelian tradition in this
regard. Calhoun, however, owed his inspiration directly
to Greek sources. In practical application, Calhoun's high
regard for the sociological conditions in a community
would indicate an indistinct line of division between liberty
and authority at times, or no line at all—rather a con-
tinuum of gradual shading. At any rate, his criterion put
into use would mean a process of constant adjustment to
fit changing conditions, adjustment with an eye single to
the welfare of the community. His criterion, then, for
drawing the line between liberty and authority was not a
very precise one; it would offer no end of trouble in use;
but it was, and remains, perhaps, as exact a one as could
be accepted, even today.

B. ABUSE OF AUTHORITY

Probably the greatest problem of government, to Calhoun, was the abuse of authority—abuse in various forms
which inevitably meant the subversion of whatever liberty
was sanctioned by the better sense of the community. He
began his contemplation of the problem in the twenties,

impelled by the desire to comprehend the opposition of South Carolina to federal protection of manufactures by tariff laws in terms of the underlying fundamental principles. As time passed, he found other applications of the same principles. Abuse was certain. "If there be a political proposition universally true—one which springs directly from the nature of man, and is independent of circumstances—it is that irresponsible power is inconsistent with liberty, and must corrupt those who exercise it."[15] Human individuals must wield the authority of government, and invariably these individuals, being subject to the "law of our nature" and thereby being more or less self-seeking, are prone to use their power to their own ends often irrespective of the common good. Men have long striven to eliminate or to mitigate such abuses by checks incorporated into the structure of the governmental mechanism. Men should work to mould the constitution or "organism" of their government so that the possibility of abuse would be reduced to a minimum. A government provided with appropriate checks was constitutional government. "Such an organism, then, as will furnish the means by which resistance may be systematically and peaceably made, on the part of the ruled, to oppression and abuse of power on the part of rulers, is the first and indispensable step forming a constitutional government."[16] This must be the work of men, for although men are impelled by their very nature to live in the political and social state, the proper checks on the abuse of power do not arise of themselves. When the movement of social forces (or the "juncture" of affairs) gives men the opportunity, if they are sufficiently enlightened, they will seize upon it in order to provide the constitutional checks necessary to safeguard that liberty which is the condition of our advancement in civilization.

The first step in this task is the establishment of representative government. Calhoun called it the "primary and indispensable principle" of the suffrage, the election, that is, of the governing by the governed. This involves the rejection of monarchy or any other form of irresponsible government, for people had learned by experience that they suffer if they blindly revere certain great families.[17] The people must choose their own rulers and hold them responsible. This will "make those elected the true and faithful representatives of those who elected them instead of irresponsible rulers as they would be without it; and thus, by converting it into an agency and the rulers into agents, to divest government of all claims to sovereignty, and to retain it unimpaired to the community. . . ."[18] The point was (and it was made by John Stuart Mill somewhat later in his defense of representative government) that representative government gives those whose interests are at stake a surer and more effective part in the government; and the probability is, therefore, that those interests will be less likely to suffer from the activity of the government. The elected rulers will have a selfish interest in the misuse of their powers just as is the case with hereditary rulers; but, the electorate, if it intelligently pursues its own selfish ends, will check such misuse by throwing out of office the guilty parties. Such were the latent advantages of this "modern improvement in government" when compared with "ancient usage" that Calhoun believed it was destined to spread throughout the civilized world.[19]

Calhoun accepted representative democracy as part of a glorious American tradition, as the principle of government for which the United States was the leading champion. William Harper, Jefferson Davis, Alexander H. Stephens, and others prominent in the State rights school reaffirmed this acceptance.[20] The American Revolution had been fought to uphold the right of a people to self-government, an idea which involved not merely independence but also popular sovereignty. The old American tradition followed John Locke in positing the responsibility of the governing to the governed as derived from the natural rights, liberty, and equality of individuals. Thomas Jefferson and John Taylor had added little in this regard to the argument of the Englishmen. Calhoun, however, put his support upon different ground—simply the utilitarian argument that democracy would enable at least a majority of the people to protect its interests against abuse by the government. As compared with monarchy or aristocracy, democracy provided greater restriction upon the universal tendency of governors to prostitute their authority for selfish ends.

Calhoun was aware that the power of the voter to protect his interest was subject to a number of limitations. In the first place, not all voters were equally enlightened and intelligent in the exercise of the suffrage, but this he felt did not impeach the validity of the general principle. He was intimately acquainted with many of the pitfalls which lay in the path of the voters' enforcing the responsibility of their elected agents to themselves. Political parties grew up of necessity in connection with representative governments, for in no other way could the preferences of the voters be made articulate—in no other way could choice be effected. But according to Calhoun's realistic view, these parties on developing elaborate organizations tended to become ends in themselves, and the individuals most potent in the control of their activities were prone to use them to their own ends. True representation of the will of their adherents tended to be lost from view. Thus Calhoun argued against election by general ticket for fear of the power it would throw into the hands of the party organization. As political patriarch in South Carolina in 1846, he was opposing popular election of presidential electors, because it would tend to upset the balance established in the State legislature between the lower country and the up-country.

In the first place, . . . it is impossible for the great body of voters to be guided by their individual knowledge in selecting the candidates, either from personal acquaintance or reputation, which is indispensable to that exercise of judgment in making a selection necessary to constitute an election. And in the next, the scattering of the votes would be so great that the result as to who would have the plurality of votes would be mere accident and no indication of the voice of the State. . . .

The first conseauence would be that a few prominent and influential individuals would enter into a secret concert to control the election, which need not be very extensive when the scattering would be so great. The next would be for others to enter into like concert to defeat them; and finally there would grow out of this state of things two parties with all the usual machinery of caucus, conventions, cliques, and managers to control the election. . . .

Instead of giving the election directly to the people, as its supporters assume, it would divest them of it, and place it under the control of intermediate and irresponsible cliques and political managers as certainly as it is adopted. This ever has and must be its result, and by laws as uniform and certain in the moral world as gravitation is in the physical.[21]

Here was criticism of the operation of the party system much in the fashion of later arguments against the long ballot. The game of politics as it came to be played after the advent of Jacksonian Democrats on the national scene was surely adequate to give the close observer some insight into the tendency toward the development of machine politics and boss rule through party machinery. Calhoun believed this development made a travesty of popular government. It was a commonplace in the contemporary political warfare to point out the divergence and even opposition of interest between party and country. But it was particularly disturbing to Calhoun that there should arise what appeared to him a party with no principles at all, a party whose sole interest was in the patronage which accrued to control of government office. What was more alarming was that this party, by taking a middle position between the two parties of principle—that is, by straddling or beclouding the real issues—was achieving great success in winning the "spoils" of office and attracting to its service large numbers of loyal workers who bowed abjectly to the leaders of the party in order to gain the desired end. "Never did a free people exhibit so degraded a spectacle—give such evidence of loose attachment to principle, or greater subserviency to power."[22] His comments on the political degeneracy of his times run throughout his letters. Believing, as did Stephens after him, that "in all free governments the laws . . . cannot be much above the tone of public opinion," Calhoun must have contemplated a sorry spectacle indeed.[23]

Moreover, the competition between parties was becoming so keen that they were losing all sense of values in the wild scramble after votes. No group of people was spurned, and in order to win support the party would make almost any sort of promise, regardless of consistency with other promises, or it would attempt to reconcile the most obvious contradictions. Politicians made "strange bedfellows" even in those days. Thus it was possible for any opportunistic group, by playing off one party against another, to obtain an influence far greater than that to which its real strength entitled it. Naturally Calhoun feared the success of such strategy when used by the abolitionists of the North. When party members concerned themselves only with the results of the next election, the game of

politics was becoming vicious.[24] It did not allow the better
sense of the community to assert itself.

The spoils system which supplied the life blood of the
degenerate variety of the political game was, of course,
anathema to Calhoun. His anxiety was not so much because of the injury to the public service involved in the
periodical overturn of employees, but rather because of
the deleterious effects upon the party workers and the
voters. However, the former consideration was not entirely absent from his thoughts; and occasionally his utterances contained sentiments which would have done justice to a civil service reformer of a much later day. During the attacks in Congress on President Jackson's use of
patronage, he declared: "I, for my part, must say that
according to my conception the true principle is to render
those who are charged with mere ministerial offices secure
in their places, so long as they continue to discharge their
duty with ability and integrity."[25] Merit rather than
partisanship should be the principle of public personnel
administration. Public office was a public trust which
should be bestowed upon able and conscientious men instead of those who are zealous and slavish in the service
of party. If "to the victor belongs the spoils" were to become the rule of general application, it would directly and
inevitably convert "the entire body of those in office into
corrupt and supple instruments of power, . . . raise up a
host of hungry, greedy, and subservient partisans, ready
for every service however base and corrupt."[26] The resulting extension of the power of patronage and of the
spirit of "subserviency and man-worship" would sap the
strength of patriotism, subvert liberty, and establish despotism. A free people would have sold its birthright for a
mess of pottage. However exaggerated one may consider
his characterization of the spoils system, it should be
noted that Calhoun himself never availed himself of sev-

eral opportunities for sharing the spoils of office. In this regard, his record was above reproach.

Thus Calhoun in order to restore some sanity to the electoral process was willing to grant permanence of tenure to ministerial public officers despite his fears of the growth of bureaucracy. Healthy representative government required that real issues play some part in elections. Bureaucracy he feared, of course, just as he did the recognition of any special privilege on the part of the government. All such special privilege constituted a latent menace to the liberty of the community at large. During all the latter part of his public career he considered the special privilege granted the manufacturers in tariff protection an encroachment on the liberty of the rest of the community as well as a deprivation of their property. So also he joined Andrew Jackson in opposition to the rise of a "separate monied interest" which would fatten on the use of government credit and special privilege in the exercise of the power of the government to control the currency. He believed a close alliance between the political and money powers one "more dangerous than Church and State."[27] Moreover, he discerned a tendency for one sort of special privilege to beget another. The more government regulates the labor and wealth of a country, the larger grows the executive department in size, activity, and power; it tends to become an irresponsible and despotic power—a bureaucracy.[28] He was at one with old John Taylor in his deprecation of special privilege, the latter representing it as minority exploitation of the majority. And he used the very stuff of Jefferson's ideas when he advocated curtailing the administrative activities and expenditures of the government.[29]

Calhoun's distrust of the capacity of the electorate was again demonstrated in his little animadversion on the power of the press. He admitted that the free press as an or-

gan for influencing public opinion was "a new and important political element" which might become of great
service in informing and educating the voters. The individual voters themselves might benefit thereby; but no
increase of knowledge and intelligence, no influence of education, would alter the inherent impulse to pursue selfish
ends. Public opinion was not the opinion of the whole
community. "On the contrary . . . public opinion is usually
nothing more than the opinion or voice of the strongest
interest, or combination of interests; and not infrequently
of a small, but energetic and active portion of the whole.
Public opinion in relation to government and its policy is
as much divided and diversified as are the interests of the
community. . . ."[30] The press was but the organ of these
various interests and was used by them as a means of controlling public opinion and of so moulding it as to promote
their peculiar interests and to aid in carrying on party
warfare. The press was as incompetent as the suffrage itself to counteract the tendency to oppression and abuse of
power. In brief, his position was that so long as representative government existed, party struggles for office and
patronage would continue with all of the attendant evils;
and the press, although ideally a source of enlightenment,
was inevitably drawn into the struggle, diverted from its
ideal path and enlisted in the service of special interests.
So his hard-headed realism made Calhoun skeptical of the
enthusiasms of the moment.

Calhoun's distrust of an unadulterated general suffrage was further revealed in his concern that leadership
in politics should be assumed by men of talent and property. Those men who possessed the means and capacity for
education and leisure were those most capable of being enlightened and patriotic. Independence of means furnished
a surer foundation than anything else for that integrity
of character requisite for statesmanship, a quality seem-

ingly giving way to hypocrisy, cant, and political toadying. Having security, a man does not feel impelled to push his personal fortune; he is more likely to feel a sense of public responsibility and to give unselfish service. "I . . . deem it the duty of every man of education and leisure," he wrote to John Ewing Calhoun, "to bring himself forward in public business. It is thus dignity will be given to public affairs and the State usefully served."[31] Undoubtedly he sympathized with the arguments that had been made in various of the State constitutional conventions to the effect that possession of property was evidence *par excellence* of attachment to the community. Ownership of property, especially landed property, had long been considered to be a sure indication of a stake in and a faithful attachment to the permanent interest of the community, and therefore suitable qualification for the suffrage and for office-holding. Several members of the Federal Convention, including Pierce Butler and John Rutledge of South Carolina, had even argued that property was the only just measure of representation in the federal legislature.[32] Calhoun was a conservative in that he wanted to retain in public affairs a predominant influence for the "solid" elements of the community. He was himself a representative of the old order of aristocratic leadership. It was, perhaps, for this reason that he realized that the name "democrat" did not fit him so well as that of "republican."[33]

However, he was also devoted to "popular institutions"; and at times he showed no hostility toward an extension of the suffrage. He felt, for example, that the freehold suffrage in Rhode Island was too restricted, and he later wrote Dorr that he had no objection to lower qualifications.[34] However, he opposed "Dorrism," which he interpreted to mean a demand for universal suffrage as a matter of right regardless of legal sanction. He did not regard the suffrage, as did Taylor, as a substitute for one's natural right to govern oneself. It was consequently a matter of gratification to him to learn that England had successfully passed the crisis caused by the Chartist movement.[35] Curiously enough, however, Calhoun on occasion seemed to have more faith in the general electorate than he did in more select bodies. He advocated a change in the process of choosing the President so as to make the election a more direct expression of the popular will. Here, as in his opposition to presidential nomination by caucus or convention method, he was probably moved by the desire to weaken the influence of the party organizations.[36]

In decrying the evils of party politics, Calhoun joined several noteworthy predecessors who had made it a commonplace of American thought that party purposes and practices often ignored the common good. In his famous farewell address, George Washington had solemnly deprecated, much in the fashion of David Hume earlier, the injury to the general welfare inflicted by the strife and passion arising from the rivalry of parties.[37] Madison had recognized the same danger, but optimistically anticipated a balance of interests within the party system which would temper its excesses. John Taylor, however, experienced no such optimism, being particularly impressed by the psychological devices by which parties made irrational appeals to the public.[38] "Nations are always enslaved by the ingenuity of creating a blind confidence with party prejudices. A reigning party never censures itself, and the people have been tutored to vote under two senseless standards, gaudily painted over with the words 'Federalist' and 'Republican,' repeated and repeated, without having any meaning . . ."[39] Calhoun added further to the indictment by his criticism of the "spoils system" and of boss-controlled machines. In thus anticipating the gist of much later political criticism, Calhoun was concerned with showing the pit-falls confronting majority protection of its own interests even when the majority controlled the government.

In general, it may be said, Calhoun believed that responsibility of the governing to the governed could be enforced by the principle of election, i. e., by means of representative government—as far as the majority was concerned. However, he fully admitted many qualifications of this general proposition. Although the voter might be uninformed and stupid at times, although he might be misled by demagogues and a partisan press, although he might be duped into suffering special privileges for the benefit of energetic minority groups, although his control of his representative might be knocked awry at times through the machinations of party, in the long run his weapon with which he could turn out unfaithful representatives was an adequate one as long as he was one of the majority. A greater danger of abuse in representative government was that the majority would resort to unjust oppression and selfish exploitation of the minority. In fact, the tendency to such abuse of authority was ever present, for majorities were no more exempt than individuals, or hereditary rulers, or a bureaucracy, or parties, or functional groups, from the temptation to sacrifice the interests of others to one's own—an impulse springing from human nature.

In every politically organized community with representative institutions, there must be a majority and a minority; and the cause of liberty and justice required that the former should not trample underfoot the interests of the latter. If the community were a small and homogeneous one, there would probably be little temptation to such abuse and oppression. But even there Calhoun felt the patronage of the new government would suffice to divide the people into majority and minority, and create a diversity of interest.[40] Obviously, the larger the community was, the greater would be the variety and diversity of interests. "The more extensive and populous the country, the more diversified the condition and pursuits of its population, and the richer, more luxurious and dissimilar the people the more difficult it is to equalize the action of the government, . . ."[41] That is, the more difficult it became to insure that the laws imposed equal burdens and benefits upon the various interests. The situation was certain to be aggravated where there existed a diversity of economic interests spread over a wide area.[42]

That no one interest constituted a majority did not alter the problem. The less dissimilar interests would combine upon what they had in common until a majority party was formed, and then in a system of majority rule the minority would be at its mercy. Parties, he believed, were influenced by many different factors, including similarity of origin, language, institutions, political tradition, customs, interests, color, and contiguity of situation. Geographical contiguity was one of the strongest of these; because man tended to sympathize with the familiar, and because interests were generally more similar within a given region.[43] Thus it was that parties tended to become "sectional" or "local" in character and that majority oppression tended to become sectional exploitation. The close party organization and discipline that was necessary to hold together the various interests within the majority led to concentration of control in the hands of a few leaders who would then, for weal or woe, hold in their hands the fate of the country.[44] If the minority party or section had no constituted means of self-protection, it would certainly be ground under the heel. Government by unalloyed majority rule would inevitably lead to an appeal to arms, to revolution. And the right to revolution, as a moral right, he could not deny. "While I . . . openly avow myself a conservative," he said, "God forbid that I should ever deny the glorious right of rebellion and revolution. Should corruption and oppression become intolerable and not otherwise [to] be thrown off—if liberty must perish, or government be overthrown, I would not hesitate at the hazard of life to resort to revolution . . ."[45] It should be observed that he found, or expressed, no sanction for this in natural law or in the natural right of the individual. Revolution was action that had no legal validity whatever.

In his belief that unchecked majority rule would lead inevitably to oppression of the minority, Calhoun certainly was in agreement not only with predecessors in the State rights school, but with the framers of the Constitution. The Founding Fathers in many of the provisions inserted in the Constitution were motivated by the desire to limit majority rule. Protection of minority rights was an American tradition, one derived in part from that wise old Frenchman, Montesquieu. Consequently, Calhoun and his fellow Carolinians were not giving voice to something strange and new in asserting as axiomatic that a majority would oppress a minority. To Thomas Cooper, it was indubitable that " . . . as a general rule, the majority must decide against the minority . . ., unless there be a special contract which takes the particular case out of the general rule."[46] It was Judge Harper's belief that any government that admitted of such oppression was imperfect.[47] Further, it was declared by Rhett that failure to protect the minority was tyranny. "To destroy or silence a minority in a popular representative government," he said, "is to destroy liberty itself. The minority is the great check, the sole restraint on a majority."[48] Jefferson Davis affirmed that "the tyranny of an unbridled majority" was "the most odious . . . form of despotism."[49]

Further and more specifically, it was a conviction with Calhoun and many other Southerners that the general tendency to oppression was realized in the political situation of their times. The South as a minority section had been subject to exploitation and oppression through the operations of the federal government for a long time; to some, since the adoption of the first tariff bill by Congress. In 1789 William Grayson had feared that the Southern States would be "the milch cow out of whom the substance would be extracted."[50] And years later Congressman Archer, of Virginia, declared that "the gentlemen" appeared to assume that the South was some beast of burden, saddled, and themselves booted and spurred to ride.[51] Robert J. Turnbull in his famous series of essays on *The Crisis* (in 1827) preached that the "interest of the North and West are diametrically opposed to the interests of the South . . .," and that the people of the North were using the government to abolish the competition of European manufacturing, making the South "the Ass that is to bear all the burden and expense of the contest."[52] Robert Toombs and Alexander Stephens of Georgia; Thomas L. Clingman of North Carolina; C. C. Clay, Jr. and William L. Yancey of Alabama; and Jefferson Davis of Mississippi—all became convinced of sectional exploitation. In proof of this, they argued that there was in pensions, bounties, grants of land and expenditures for internal improvements on the one hand and in revenue collections on the other a disproportionate distribution of benefits and burdens between North and South, all in favor of the North.[53] In 1845 Yancey declared that, although the slave States since 1789 had paid sixty-three per cent of the common revenues, the free States had received in disbursements for internal improvements ten million dollars compared with three million for the slave States.[54] M. R. H. Garnett, a pamphleteer, found for the same period the disproportion in footing the bill even greater. The South had paid seven hundred million out of a total of nine hundred

million collected in import duties, while if the contributions had been in proportion to federal numbers the South
would have paid only two-fifths and the North three-fifths
of the total.[55] This was the unequal action of the federal
government which Calhoun deplored repeatedly; and that
it was effected by apparently impartial laws couched in
general terms rendered it none the less real. "I greatly
fear," he wrote in 1828, "that the weak part of our system will be found to consist in the fact that in a country
of such vast extent and diversity of interest, many of the
laws will be found to act very unequally, and that some
portions of the country may be enriched by legislation at
the expense of the others."[56]

All of this was substantiation of his general proposition that, regardless of considerations of justice, propriety,
and even legality, a majority was strongly impelled to oppress a minority. Reason, truth, and justice booted little
when they stood in the way of interest. Nor would mere
guarantees and limitations written into a paper constitution be any more efficacious, for a war of constructions
could but be concluded in favor of the majority. "No government based on the naked principle that the majority
ought to govern, however true the maxim in its proper
sense, and under proper restrictions, can preserve its liberty even for a single generation."[57] Men must strive to secure a constitutional organization of the government that
for its ordinary functioning would compel interests, or sections, to be just to one another. This would mean effective
checking of majority rule. He did not agree with Cooper
in the argument that the majority ought to rule because of
its superior force.[58] Nor did he agree with Rousseau that
the majority ought to govern because the minority was
simply mistaken as to what was its own real will. The
"simple numerical majority" possessed no inherent, or divine, right to govern—any more than did kings.[59] Hu-

man beings, subject to various limitations of circumstances, could shape their governments, alter or limit majority rule, and judge by experience what arrangement was superior—all with just as much (or more) show of right as some claimed for majority rule. Reason and experience demonstrated, he felt, that government by "concurrent majority" was the proper solution to the problem of how to make the majority just to the minority and at the same time to secure the fundamental ends of government.

In his insistence upon the justice of protecting the minority from oppression by the majority, Calhoun strove to emphasize the idea that simple majority rule was not an imperative of democratic doctrine, but simply a matter of convenience. On this point he was at one with Edmund Burke in opposition to mere doctrinaire dogma. He could not sympathize with Rousseau's metaphysical attempt to dissolve all real difference of interest between majority and minority and thus identify the will of the majority with the will of all; nor could he accept the argument of Locke that rule by simple majority arose from inherent necessity and an original social compact. Calhoun knew from experience that political bodies could and had acted by the rule of increased majority; action by simple majority was ordinarily used to expedite business only when no fundamental conflict of interest was anticipated. The danger was that uncritical democratic doctrine tended to foster the belief that the will of a bare majority could never be justly challenged. Burke contemplated virtually the same situation when he asserted the "infinite importance" of not suffering the "people" "to imagine that their will, any more than that of kings, is the standard of right and wrong."[60] As old John Taylor declared, majorities were not endowed by nature with political power; and, although Calhoun did not accept his social contract apparatus, Calhoun was in essential agreement with Taylor on insisting that human invention on deviating from simple majority rule did not necessarily do violence to justice or abrogate democratic principle.

NOTES

1. Thomas Dew, "Review of the Debate in the Virginia Legislature, 1831-'32," reprint from *Political Register,* Washington, Oct. 16, 1833, p. 822.
2. Dew wrote: "Another and more efficient cause . . . is the perfect spirit of equality so prevalent among the whites of all the slaveholding States. Jack Cade, the Irish reformer, wished all mankind to be brought to one common level. We believe slavery in the United States has accomplished this in regard to the whites, as nearly as can be expected or even desired in this world. The menial and low offices all being performed by the blacks, there is at once taken away the greatest cause of distinction and separation of the ranks of society. The man to the North will not shake hands familiarly with his servant, and converse and laugh and dine with him, no matter how honest and respectable he may be. But go to the South, and you will find that no white man feels such inferiority of rank as to be unworthy of association with those around him. Color alone is here the badge of distinction, and the true mark of aristocracy, and all who are white are equal in spite of variety of occupation." *Ibid.,* pp. 822-823.
3. See Laura A. White, *Robert Barnwell Rhett: Father of Secession* (New York and London, 1931), pp. 17, 24, 52-53. Turnbull's speech, cited *supra.,* Ch. III, note 34.
4. *Works,* Vol. VI, p. 143.
5. *Ibid.,* Vol. I, pp. 53-54.
6. *Ibid.,* Vol. IV, pp. 510-511.
7. Thus the rights of individuals, according to Calhoun, were always predicated upon social order and progress. Cf. the statements to the same effect of Harper, Bledsoe, and Fitzhugh: Harper, "Memoirs of Slavery,"

Pro-Slavery Argument (Philadelphia, 1853), p. 11; Bledsoe *Essay on Liberty and Slavery*, pp. 30, 39; Fitz-hugh, *Cannibals All*, pp. 115-116. Cf. Simms' definition of true liberty as the enjoyment of the place in society for which one is fit by one's abilities and efforts. Simms, "Morals of Slavery," *Pro-Slavery Argument*, p. 258. Jefferson Davis agreed essentially with Calhoun, quali-fying his acceptance of traditional American theory as stated in the Declaration of Independence by the as-sertion that the individual is entitled "to all the free-dom . . . consistent with the safety and rights of others and the weal of the community. . . ." *Rise and Fall of the Confederate Government*, 2 vols. (New York, 1881), Vol. I, p. 153. Thomas Cooper in general shared these views, but once gave expression to a dif-ferent view of the basis of rights, one unlike either Calhoun's or those of the social contract theorists. He wrote: "The natural foundation of right is power. There is no other. It is power that renders the human being the commander of the brute, the male of the fe-male, the man of the child, the strong of the weak, the wise of the ignorant. . . ." And so the community, of the individual. Such a statement of the view that might makes right was, indeed, a rare one for the time and place. See his *Manual of Political Economy*, pp. 104-106.

8. *Works*, Vol. VI, pp. 235-237, 335.

9. Thus Dabney and Bledsoe, Virginian advocates of the State rights school, followed his lead in recognizing that a state might deny a moral right to individuals, even though a well governed one would not do so. Dabney, *Defence of Virginia*, pp. 252-253; Bledsoe, *Essay on Liberty and Slavery*, p. 22.

10. *Works*, Vol. I, pp. 54-55. Alexander Stephens, some-thing of a disciple of Calhoun, shared this idea; but on the eve of the Civil War was inclined to very pessi-mistic views of the virtues of the American people. Per-haps they were not capable of free government. See his letters to J. Henly Smith in *The Correspondence of Robert Toombs, Alexander H. Stephens, and Howell Cobb* (Washington, 1913), pp. 457-458, 498-499. Cf.

the views of Simms and Fitzhugh to the same effect. Simms, "Morals of Slavery," p. 266; Fitzhugh, *Cannibals All,* pp. 115-116.

11. *Works,* Vol. I, pp. 55-56.

12. *Ibid.,* Vol. IV, p. 345.

13. Dabney, *Defense of Virginia,* pp. 255-256; Simms, "Morals of Slavery," pp. 252-253. Both Dabney and Bledsoe viewed the subject of liberty and authority from the basis of natural law (the will of God) which sanctioned no natural liberty of the individual apart from, or paramount to, government. In the use of the natural law criterion, they departed from Calhoun's leadership. See Dabney, *idem;* Bledsoe, *On Liberty and Slavery,* pp. 102-137.

14. *Works,* Vol. I, pp. 56-57. To anticipate in part Calhoun's defense of slavery, it may be noted that he was certain of the superiority of the white race. Its superiority was not relative merely to the black, but to all other races, history showing no instance of successful free government among the colored races. *Ibid.,* Vol. IV, p. 411. William Gilmore Simms agreed that the right of self-rule enjoyed by a people lacking capacity for it could only result in savagery and anarchy. Simms, "Morals of Slavery," p. 266.

15. *Works,* Vol. VI, p. 29.

16. *Ibid.,* Vol. I, p. 12.

17. *Correspondence,* p. 187.

18. *Works,* Vol. I, p. 14.

19. *Correspondence,* pp. 210-213.

20. Harper, *Speech before Charleston State Rights . . . Association, April* 1, 1832, p. 9; Davis, *Rise and Fall of the Confederate Government,* Vol. I, pp. 141, 153; Stephens, *Constitutional View of the War between the States,* Vol. I, pp. 39, 40; Vol. II, pp. 296-297. Cf. St. George Tucker, *Blackstone's Commentaries,* Vol I, Appendix, pp. 8-10, 14.

21. *Works,* Vol. VI, pp. 256-258; see also Vol. I, pp. 369-370.

22. *Works,* Vol. II, p. 401.

23. *Ibid.,* Vol. II, pp. 24, 46, 392-394, 399-421; Vol. V,

p. 162; *Correspondence*, pp. 307, 310, 317, 339, 358, 442-443, 462, 469, 567, 568-569, 700, 726, 733. Alexander H. Stephens attributed general political degeneracy in this country in 1860 to the lamentable lack of public virtue, courage, and patriotism among public figures. Letters to J. Henly Smith, *Annual Report of American Historical Association*, 1911, Vol. II, pp. 457-458, 498; A. H. Stephens, *Reviewers Reviewed* (New York, 1872), p. 56. Cf. Brownson's commentary on the political degeneracy of the time in Orestes A. Brownson, "Mr. Calhoun and the Baltimore Convention," *Works*, 20 vols, (Detroit, 1884), Vol. XV, pp. 473-483; W. E. Dodd, *Expansion and Conflict* (Cambridge, 1915), pp. 96-97; A. C. Cole, *The Irrepressible Conflict* (New York, 1934), pp. 28-30.
24. *Works*, Vol. II, pp. 399-401, 530-532.
25. *Works*, Vol. II, p. 446.
26. *Ibid.*, Vol. V, p. 152. See also Vol. I, pp. 17-22; Vol. II, p. 323.
27. *Works*, Vol. III, p. 91.
28. *Ibid.*, Vol. VI, pp. 200-201.
29. Economy in public expenditures was a constant theme throughout his speeches and writings. See *Works*, Vol. III, pp. 389-390; Calhoun, *Life of John C. Calhoun* (New York, 1843) pp. 24-26; *Works*, Vol. IV, pp. 140-157; *Correspondence*, pp. 200-201, 338.
30. *Works*, Vol. I, pp. 74-76.
31. *Correspondence*, p. 178.
32. See Farrand, *Records of the Federal Convention of 1787*, Vol. I, pp. 533-534, 541-542; C. E. Merriam, *American Political Theories* (New York, 1903), pp. 84-86.
33. *Correspondence*, pp. 399-400. For his comments on the participation of men of means in politics, see *Ibid.*, pp. 178-179, 179-180, 204-205, 394-395.
34. *Works*, Vol. VI, pp. 233-234; *Niles' Register* 72: 148.
35. *Correspondence*, pp. 644-645, 750, 754; *Works*, Vol. VI, pp. 224-230. To Taylor, election was "a resource for exercising a natural right." *Inquiry*, p. 413.

36. *Correspondence,* pp. 217, 230, 528, 552-555; *New York Public Library Bulletin,* Vol. III, pp. 328, 329.
37. J. D. Richardsom, ed., *Messages and Papers of the Presidents,* 10 vols. (Washington, 1899), Vol. I, pp. 218-219.
38. See Roy Irwin Kimmel, *The Political Ideas of John Taylor of Caroline* (M. A. Thesis, Yale University, 1931), p. 109 and *passim* .
39. *Tyranny Unmasked* (Washington, 1822), p. 291.
40. *Works,* Vol. I, pp. 17-22.
41. *Ibid.,* Vol. I, pp. 15-16
42. *Ibid.,* Vol. II, pp. 251-252.
43. *Ibid.,* Vol. I, pp. 232-233. With obvious concern over the development of sectionalism within the United States, Upshur agreed with Calhoun that in the absence of constitutional restraints differences of "interests, pursuits, and character" determined by geographical lines made for grave danger of majority oppression of the minority. Upshur, *Enquiry into the True Nature and Character of Our Federal Government* (Philadelphia 1863), p. 125. Reprint from Petersburg ed., 1840. James Hamilton, Jr., was also impressed with the danger of majority despotism over the minority (and with the sectional aspect of the alignment in the United States). See his *Speech on the Operation of the Tariff on the Interests of the South* (Charleston, 1828), p. 4.
44. *Works,* Vol. I, pp. 41-42.
45. *Ibid.,* Vol. II, p. 615.
46. *Consolidation. An Account of Parties in the United States from the Convention of 1787 to the Present Period,* second ed., (Columbia, 1839), p. 34.
47. *Speech before Charleston State Rights . . . Association,* April 1, 1832, pamphlet (Charleston, 1832), pp. 9-10.
48. White, *Robert Barnwell Rhett,* p.52.
49. Jefferson Davis, "Inaugural Address, Feb. 22, 1862," *Messages and Papers of the Confederacy,* 2 vols. (Nashville, 1905), Vol. I, p. 188.
50. J. T. Carpenter, *The South as a Conscious Minority* (New York, 1930), pp. 29-30.

51. *Speech on the Tariff Bill, delivered in House of Representatives,* April 1, 1820, pamphlet (Washington, 1820), pp. 2-3.
52. *The Crisis, or Essays on the Usurpations of the Federal Government,* pamphlet, (Charleston, 1827), pp. 9, 51.
53. Carpenter developed this case rather sketchily in his book already mentioned. See *op. cit.,* pp. 28-33. J. G. Van Deusen in his *Economic Bases of Disunion in South Carolina* (New York, 1928) gave more extensive attention to this argument and reached the conclusion that the facts did not entirely support it although the protective tariff policy undoubtedly reduced purchasing power in South Carolina. See pp. 30-34 and Ch. III. Alexander H. Stephens recognized that the Southern States had been in the minority in the Union from the beginning in 1789. See *Constitutional View of the War between the States,* Vol. II, p. 308.
54. John W. DuBose, *The Life and Times of William Lowndes Yancey* (Birmingham, 1892), p. 153.
55. *The Union, Past and Future: How it Works and How to Save It,* pamphlet, 4th ed. (Charleston, 1850), pp. 14-15.
56. *Correspondence,* pp. 266-267. See also *Ibid.,* pp. 249-250, 265, 317-318; *Works,* Vol. IV, pp. 22, 32, 179, 182-184. Jefferson Davis felt also that the fight to exclude slavery from the territories was made but for purposes of clinching the power of a sectional (Northern) majority bent on further exploitation of the South. Successful exclusion was exploitation. See his *Rise and Fall of the Confederate Government,* Vol. I, pp. 31-34, 47-49. To one E. B. Bryan the conflict of interest between the sections was so fundamental that they were "at war, inevitable, unavoidable war." Bryan, *The Rightful Remedy* (Charleston, 1850), pp. 110-152. Cf. W. H. Trescott, *Position and Course of the South* (Charleston, 1850); Langdon Cheves, *Speech ... before ... the Nashville Convention, on Friday, Nov.* 13, 1850 (Columbia, 1850); John Scott, *The Lost Principle* (Richmond, 1860), pp. 10-11.
57. *Works,* Vol. VI, p. 33; Vol. I, pp. 32-33. He wrote,

"But of what avail could the strict construction of the minor party be against the liberal interpretation of the major, when the one would have all the powers of the government to carry its construction? In a contest so unequal the result would not be doubtful. The party in favor of the restrictions would be overpowered. At first they might command some respect and do something to stay the march of encroachment; but they would in the progress of the contest be regarded as mere abstractions; and indeed, deservedly; should they indulge the folly of supposing that the party in possession of the ballot box and the physical force of the country could be successfully resisted by an appeal to reason, truth, justice, or the obligations imposed by the Constitution." p. 33.

58. See *supra.,* note 7 of this chapter.

59. *Works,* Vol. VI, pp. 229-230. A similar view, even though expressed in terms of the social compact theory, was offered by John Taylor. ". . . Majorities and their rights are creatures of social compact, and not endowed by nature with political power . . . However compounded, they are a social being, and no social duty can accrue to any majority, but to one established by social compact, because no other majority exists possessed of any political rights." *Inquiry into the Principles and Policy of the Government of the United States* (Fredericksburg, 1814), p. 415.

60. Burke, *Reflections on the French Revolution,* Everyman ed., (London and New York, 1910), pp. 90-91.

5

The Concurrent Majority

A. THE NATURE OF THE CONCURRENT MAJORITY

REPRESENTATIVE GOVERNMENT, according to Calhoun, in order to be truly representative, must provide adequate protection for every substantial minority. This was to be secured through the use of the "concurrent majority," the superior of two modes of taking the sense of the community. He explained: "One regards numbers only, and considers the whole community as a unit, having but one common interest throughout; and collects the sense of the greater number of the whole as that of the community. The other, on the contrary, regards interests as well as numbers, considering the community as made up of different and conflicting interests, as far as the action of the government is concerned; and takes the sense of each, through its majority or appropriate organ, and the united sense of all, as the sense of the entire community. The former of these I shall call the numerical or absolute majority; and the latter, the concurrent, or constitutional majority. I call it the constitutional majority, because it is an essential element in every constitutional government,— be its form what it may."[1] The ideally perfect "organism" of government would give true and full representation to every interest by so dividing and distributing the powers of government that each interest would have an effective part in making and executing the laws or a veto on their execution. Even though such perfection might be impossible of attainment, practically the same protection to the minority would be afforded by an organism that took the sense of "a few great and prominent interests only." In such case, it would require such a large proportion of the whole community to concur in the making of laws that the temptation to plunder the remaining few would be too weak as a motive for the abuse of power.[2]

It was, of course, in his contemplation of the nature of our federal Union and the constitutional amending power of three-fourths of the States that Calhoun struck upon the general idea. This increased majority requirement, if it could be made effective, would provide enforcement of the limitations of the Constitution upon the federal government and would protect thereby the interests of any substantial minority of States. His underlying motive was clearly the fashioning of an instrument by which the Southern States, long a minority of the States of the Union, might prevent federal legislation—on the tariff, bank, internal improvements, and possibly even on slavery —which they deemed antagonistic to their interests and disruptive of the economic bases of their social order. This increased majority of the amending power was a concurrent majority. Calhoun's insistence upon the superiority of the amending, "creating," or constitution-making power over the law-making power led him to further generalization as to the "concurrent" or "concurring" majority. He first used the term, it appears, in his letter of Aug. 28, 1832, to James Hamilton, Jr., containing a very long discussion in which he treated most of the questions raised by nullification.[3] Calhoun, Harper, Hamilton, McDuffie, Hayne, and others were trying to lead the people of South Carolina into vigorous opposition to federal tariff protection of manufactures. Calhoun wrote that the concurrent majority was one compounded of majorities in each of the social classes or geographical sections into which the community was divided. Class and territorial lines marked the most important differences of interest in any community. Differences and contrariety of interest were necessarily existent in all political communities; and it was in guarding against the unequal action of the laws, when applied to dissimilar and opposing interests, that the concurrent majority performed its essential task.[4]

Were there no opposition of interest, there would be no problem. But such opposition did exist in every community "however small or homogeneous." In all government, whether of a corporation or a community, conflict of point of view and interest must immediately spring up between management and stockholder, and between majority and minority. A majority of three out of five persons joined together to spend a sum of money would tend to ignore the interest of the other two; it would be to its selfish advantage to do so. The same was true of a majority of thirteen out of twenty-four States. The only just reconciliation of these opposing interests was to be effected by determining the will of each separately and giving it the force of law only when in agreement with that of the other.[5] This was the one solution of the problem of majority oppression and exploitation of the minority: "To organize society in reference to this conflict of interests which springs out of the action of government, and which can only be done by giving to each part the right of self-protection, which, in a word, instead of considering the community of twenty-four a single community, having a common interest, and to be governed by the single will of an entire majority, shall upon all questions tending to bring the parts into conflict, the thirteen against the eleven, take the will, not of the twenty-four as a unit, but of the thirteen and eleven separately,—the majority of each governing the parts, and where they concur governing the whole,—and where they disagree, arresting the action of the government."[6]

With his passion for logical precision and clarity, Calhound pondered incessantly upon the idea of the concurrent majority, viewing it from every aspect, until he had reduced it to "bare-bone" essentials. The nearer his argument approached mathematical demonstration, the more satisfied he was. The story is told of his having attempted to win the approval of one farmer Jones, at whose house he spent the night on a return trip from his gold mine in Georgia. Jones had given vent to his hostility to nullification. Calhoun, with some amusement and patient persuasion, sought to convince him that an association of seven equal partners, four shoemakers and three tanners, would give rise to economic exploitation of the minority if all decisions of the partnership were made by a simple majority. The opportunity for exploitation existed, and (human nature being what it was) it would probably be seized. However, that opportunity would be removed if the association could act only when a majority of the shoemakers and a majority of the tanners could agree. Surely seven rational men could act by concurrent majority.[7]

The ideal government was that of the whole community, the unanimous approval of all the constituent interest groups giving sanction to all its acts. This ideal Calhoun considered "too perfect to be reduced to practice in the present," but government by the concurrent majority provided a step in the right direction away from government by the absolute majority, which was but government by the strongest interests, "the most tyrannical and oppressive" that could be devised.[8] Government by increased majority vote, then, was the essence of the concurrent majority when it was so compounded as to reflect agreement of the most important interest groups in the com

munity. Simple majority rule, or the "numerical" majority, was to be tolerated as a matter of expediency only
within any group that was not divided in interest for any
important purpose. Where individuals were wholly united
in interest so that decisions of the group would affect all
equally, voting might still be done by a simple majority.

Identification of the social units that were to be considered interest groups, therefore, was of fundamental importance to government by the concurrent majority in any
community. In the past history of the world Calhoun
found that the important interest groups had been "artificial and separate" social classes; the nobility, commoners
or freemen, and serfs or slaves. In the America of his
time, however, there were happily no such artificial distinctions (slavery being overlooked for the moment).
Rather the important conflicts of interest arose out of sectional and economic differences. Here the important interest groups were "almost exclusively geographical, resulting mainly from difference of climate, soil, situation,
industry, and production. . . ."[9] "In a large community,
spreading over a country of great extent, and having a
great diversity of interests, with different kinds of labor,
capital, and production," he asserted a little later, "the
conflict and oppression will extend not only to a monopoly
of the appropriations on the part of the stronger interests,
but will end in unequal taxes, and a general conflict between the entire interests of conflicting sections, which, if
not arrested by the most powerful checks, will terminate
in the most oppressive tyranny that can be conceived, or
in the destruction of the community itself."[10] These were,
perhaps, more natural divisions of society, but needed no
less protection by the use of the principle of the concurrent
majority than where the distinct interests existed between
social classes. As a matter of fact, the dangers of conflict
and of unjust exploitation and oppression, and therefore

the necessity of protection, were greater in the case of such separate and dissimilar "geographical" interests. The multiplicity and diversity of these interests in our country explained the complexity of our federal system of government with its division of powers and the separation of powers and checks and balances within its various component parts. The principle of the concurrent majority found embodiment in many parts and relationships of the whole structure.[11]

In emphasizing the fundamental political importance of economic and geographic factors, Calhoun was following an old and respectable tradition, which enlisted in various ways the support of Aristotle, Bodin, Harrington, Montesquieu, and Madison. The ancient Greek philosopher held that political power follows wealth, and that democracy can work, therefore, only where wealth is fairly widely distributed among the citizens. James Harrington, in seventeenth-century England, set forth an essentially similar argument. Aristotle was certain that economic change was one of the chief causes of political revolution. James Madison, then influenced to some extent by English materialism of the late eighteenth century, was in essential agreement with Aristotle, Harrington, and Montesquieu in observing that the most important source of political conflict was the "various and unequal distribution of property": differences of economic interest moved men to form separate factions, or parties, which sought control of public policy for their own welfare.[12] Calhoun affirmed Madison's view, but had a much more intense impression of the danger of oppression of a minority by a combination of a majority of such factions. Both attached great importance to the geographical factor as determinant of differences of economic interest. Further, Calhoun may have shown some trace of the influence of the theory, developed by Bodin and Montesquieu, of the direct relation between physical environment on the one hand and human character and political capacity on the other. He believed that differences of climate and geography weakened the capacity of different people for sympathy and mutual appreciation. Different physical environments conditioned differently their mental patterns .

B.   APPLICATIONS OF THE PRINCIPLE.

Calhoun found numerous examples of the use of the principle of the concurrent majority throughout the history of western civilization. He felt convinced that there had not existed a single "free" state whose institutions were not based upon this principle; not one, in other words, which did not in some way or other depend upon the assent of its different political interests for the operation of its government.[13] He cited the instance of the ancient government of Sparta in which the plural executive was used to secure consultation of the diverse interests in the community in the ordinary operation of the government.[14] Possibly it was his admiration for the efficiency with which this device secured protection for the landed aristocracy in the Greek city-state that led him in the later years of his life to meditate its utilization in the federal government of the United States. He proposed vesting the powers of the federal executive in two officers, one from the North and one from the South; and he would have required the approval of each for the validity of all acts passed by Congress. This would certainly have given the two sections a concurrent voice in the actions of the government.[15]

To Calhoun, the most notable instance in antiquity of thorough application of the principle of the concurrent majority in the political institution of a country was that

of republican Rome. There, after the expulsion of the Tar-
quins, a fierce and bitter conflict of interest between the
hereditary order of patricians and the common people, or
plebeians, culminated in a strike of the army against further
military service as long as the unjust exploitation of the
lower ranks of society continued. Fortunately at this critical juncture moderate counsel prevailed among the nobility, and the affair was settled by concessions and compromise. The institution of the tribunate was established to
provide protection for the interests of the plebeians. The
incumbents of this office, elected by the plebeians, were
given a veto on the passage of all laws and a negative on
the entire action of the government, thereby giving the
two orders of the Roman body politic a concurrent voice
in the government (the patricians remaining predominant
in the traditional political organization). It was in this
change from a government of patricians only to one of
the whole Roman people that the solid foundation was
laid for "Roman liberty and greatness."[16] This provided
the unity of interest and stability of government at home
that enabled Roman patriots to extend the dominion of
their government and the influence of their laws over the
greater part of the then known world. Thus Calhoun
joined the old Greek historian, Polybius, in admiration for
Roman political genius. To Calhoun, the later degener-
ation of the government of Rome into rule by corrupt and
profligate factions and then into military despotism was
no impeachment of the value of government by concurrent
voice. Protection of the plebians against oppression by
the patricians had been fully secured; and later degeneracy
was to be attributed to other defects of their political system—notably in the control over their provinces.

The most extreme application of government by concurrent majority Calhoun found in the history of Poland.
For more than two centuries during the period of Poland's

greatest power and renown (when she twice saved Christ-
endom from invasion by the dread Turk), the election of
the king required the concurrence of every individual in
an assembly of one hundred and fifty to two hundred
thousand of the nobility and gentry. So also in all the proceedings of its Diet unanimous consent of the King, senate, bishops, and the deputies of the nobility and of the
gentry of the palatinates was requisite. Such extreme application of the principle would have been thought impracticable had it not actually existed, Calhoun wrote—
apparently ignoring the fact that he was merely describing
empty formulae that had no reality in actual practice. He
cited no instances in which a member of the gentry, for
example, defeated the election of a King or the passage of
a law.[17] He found what was probably a more genuine example of government by unanimous consent in the Iroquois Confederacy of the Six Nations of Indian tribes in
America. In the Iroquois Council, the highest governing
body, each of the seven representatives of each of the six
nations possessed a veto on all decisions. To the resulting
harmony in council and action Calhoun attributed their
great power and success in conquest.[18]

Although it represented a less successful experience in
comparison with that of the Roman government, Great
Britain too offered an example of the establishment in
actual political institutions of the concurrent voice of the
various interests of the realm. There, throughout a long
process of gradual change, marked by many gyrations of
political fortune, the conflict of interest between the monarch and the nobility drew onto the political scene the
plain people through rivalry for their support. Concessions
were made to them until finally they secured an effective
participation in the government as a third estate. There
was established, wrote Calhoun, a government by the concurrent and joint action of three estates, the king, the lords

temporal and spiritual, and the commons. The king represented the "tax-consuming interest," i. e., the military and bureaucracy. Calhoun looked upon the lords as the balance of the system, the conservative factor that interposed and preserved the equilibrium between the other two estates whose interests in the public finances were largely antagonistic. The three orders were so blended in the legislative department that the separate and concurring act of each was necessary to make law.[19]

Throughout all of this discussion Calhoun was careful to stress that constitutional government (which he identified with government by concurrent voice) was the product of circumstances, not merely of human contrivance or invention. Generally speaking, it arose at some critical juncture out of a struggle between conflicting interests when choice hovered between compromise and appeal to arms. Human effort might certainly prove of value in such a crisis by calming the opposed parties and bringing forth a conciliatory attitude, but without a fortunate combination of circumstances, it would prove unavailing.

Their construction has been the result not so much of wisdom and patriotism, as of favorable combination of circumstances. . . . It would seem that it has exceeded human sagacity deliberately to plan and construct constitutional governments with a full knowledge of the principles on which they were formed or to reduce them to practice without the pressure of some immediate and urgent necessity. Nor it is surprising that such should be the case, for it would seem almost impossible for any man, or body of men, to be so profoundly and thoroughly acquainted with the people of any community which has made any considerable progress in civilization and wealth, with all the diversified interests ever accompanying them, as to be able to organize constitutional governments suited to their condition. But even were this possible, it would be difficult to find any community sufficiently enlightened and patriotic to adopt such a government without the compulsion of some pressing necessity. A constitution, to succeed, must spring from the bosom of the community, and be adapted to the intelligence and character of the people, and all the multifarious relations, internal and external, which distinguish one people from another. If it do not, it will prove to be . . . but a cumbrous and useless machine. . . .[20]

Complexity of the structural arrangements and paucity of disinterested motives, then, made the establishment of constitutional government a difficult process. All forms of government by concurrent voice were of more complex structure than the absolute forms; and among the former the popular was the most complex and difficult of construction. This was true, in the first place, because in the absence of two or three orders, or classes, based upon artificial distinctions, the interests that became articulate were the "natural" ones, resulting from diversity of pursuits, conditions, situation, and character of the people. These latter were usually much more numerous, especially in a country of great extent, than the two or three contesting groups of aristocratic and monarchic forms; and consequently they required a more elaborate organization to give each interest a concurrent voice. Moreover, Calhoun found that in an aristocracy the people were rarely, in their attempts to secure protection of their interests, animated by any desire to abolish the nobility. Ordinarily their aspirations were tempered by their traditional reverence for great families; and thus they were predisposed to be satisfied with such participation in the government as would enable them to correct abuse and check oppression. Among the nobility also there were occasional statesmen with the rare sense and fine patriotism to counsel moderation and acceptance of the reasonable demands of the people. Where the situation was further complicated by the existence of an hereditary monarch, the people usually profited by the struggles between him and the nobility. Their support for the one or the other would be gained ultimately through gradual concessions of participation in the powers of government. An effective check upon the other parties would be established in the long run. In popular governments of the numerical majority, on the other hand, the attitude of the people was quite different. The coalescence of the various interests in the attempt to achieve a majority generally gave rise to a struggle between two parties for the whole power of government, the object of the minority being the expulsion of the majority from control, that of the majority to maintain their hold. The struggle became essentially like that of rival pretenders to the throne in an absolute monarchy.[21] The lack of the disposition to compromise made popular constitutional government a rare phenomenon. "Ours," Calhoun asserted, "may with truth be said to be the only one of a purely popular character, of any considerable importance, that ever existed."[22]

Calhoun discerned manifold application of the principle of concurrent voice in the existing system of government in the United States. There had been important American experience with the principle even before the establishment of the federal system in 1789. Thus the Articles of Confederation were adopted by unanimous agreement of all the States. The increased majorities required, in the Congress of the Confederation, for the adoption of resolutions or the proposal of amendments made it possible for a minority of the population to defeat them. This was government by concurrent majority. The practice of voting by States in the convention that framed the Constitution also afforded some protection of the interests of a minority reckoned by population. Likewise, the requirement of ratification of the Constitution by nine of the States was an important instance of the use of the principle. He found after some scrutiny of the census figures of 1790 that a federal population of only three hundred and thirty-six thousand out of a total of three million, three hundred and ninety-four thousand could have prevented its adoption. Thus it appeared that "the numerical majority of the population had no agency whatever in the process of forming and adopting the Constitution; and that neither this, nor a majority of the States, constituted an element in its ratification and adoption."[23]

Calhoun was impressed with the great consideration that the Founding Fathers gave to the interests of minorities. There could be no greater error than to suppose that the government they established, although resting on a popular basis, was one of an absolute, or numerical, majority of either people or States. Rather, it was "the States, regarded in their corporate character, and the population of the States, estimated in federal numbers," that constituted the two elements of which the federal government was exclusively composed. "It was the object of the framers of the Constitution, in organizing the government, to give these two elements . . . separate, but concurrent action, and consequently a veto on each other whenever the organization of the department, or the nature of the power would admit; and, when this could not be done, so to blend the two, as to make as near an approach to it in effect as possible."[24] The whole system of separation of powers and checks and balances in the structure of the federal government itself and also in the federal system of relationships between it and the States secured government based on the principle of concurrent majority.

The roots of Calhoun's theory of the concurrent majority go far back into history. The general idea that a government of superior excellence resulted from the establishment of checks and balances between the various parts of its structure, one element in the theory of the con-

142 THE POLITICAL THEORY OF JOHN C. CALHOUN

current majority, was an old one in political thought. In the second century B. C., Polybius, Greek historian, held as hostage in Rome, attributed the greatness of his captor country to the mixed constitution that gave its government stability and soundness. The constitution established checks and balances between three parts of the government, representing respectively the principles of kingship, aristocracy, and democracy; and there resulted a hardiness and a capacity to withstand the tendency, characteristic of the simple forms of government, to decay into corrupt counterparts.[25] Many years later in the eighteenth century A. D., the Englishmen, Bollingbroke and Hume, found the same kind of salutary equilibrium in the government of their own country. Shortly afterward, however, the Frenchman, Montesquieu, set forth what has become a more famous theory of separation of powers and checks and balances; and he did so in the belief that he was describing a peculiar excellence of the English government which Frenchmen of his time admired very much. His separation of the parts of the government, between which checks and balances should be provided, was upon the basis of governmental function—legislative, executive, and judicial. And the good attained through the mutual restraints imposed by the parts of the government upon one another was the protection of the liberty of the subjects of the government.[26] Although Polybius' work was read by some Americans, the influence of Montesquieu's work was predominant. The first American State constitutions gave formal statement to Montesquieu's theory, and in later modifications they gave it reality; and the Founding Fathers followed it in framing the federal Constitution.

Among Calhoun's predecessors in the State rights school, of course,[27] the idea had long obtained that some protection of minority rights should be secured through the proper organization of the government. This was one of the most generally accepted ideas among members of the Federal Convention; and a system of separation of powers and checks and balances was regarded as the proper method for giving effect to the idea. Madison was reiterating his earlier thought when he declared, in 1829, that "In republics, the great danger is that the majority may not sufficiently respect the rights of the minority. . . ." Neither conscience nor sense of fair play, or justice, was an adequate guarantee. "The only effectual safeguard to the rights of the minority must be laid in such a basis and structure of the government itself as may afford in a certain degree, directly or indirectly, a defensive authority in behalf of a minority having right on its side."[28] He had specifically in mind separation of executive, judicial, and legislative departments, and different bases of representation in the two legislative houses. Property rights of a minority would obtain the necessary security if the minority controlled one house of the legislature.

John Taylor had likewise recognized the value of separation of powers and checks and balances as a means of protecting private rights,[29] although he relied primarily upon the natural rights of individuals that limited the competence of all government. Calhoun, who had broken with the natural law and natural rights tradition, nevertheless carried on the tradition in regard for separation of powers and checks and balances, and he pointed out that in so far as these checks and balances enabled different interests to limit one another by way of self-protection they constituted an application of the principle of government by concurrent majority. The essential distinction to which checks and balances were to be applied, however, was not, in Calhoun's opinion, between legislature, executive, and judiciary, or between monarchical, aristocratic, and democratic principles of control, or even between central and local units of government, but between a majority and a minority differing in economic interest and geographical environment. The concurrent majority was above all a theory of minority protection. Compromise, mutual consideration, and a closer approximation of justice in the actions of the government—rather than the liberty posited by Montesquieu—were the immediate goods to be achieved. Robert Barnwell Rhett and Robert Y. Hayne, his fellow Carolinians, followed his lead in pointing out the protection afforded to minorities in various provisions of the Constitutions.[30] Rhett, impetuous and independent *enfant terrible* of South Carolina politics for years and later leader in secession, often accepted Calhoun's doctrine in his calmer moments. Thus he looked upon the constitutional system as a glorious extension of the veto principle.

The veto power, like the flaming sword in the garden of Eden, stands all around at every avenue of approach to guard the constitution. . . . Every constitutional limitation in a popular government is a limitation on the majority, but an enlargement of the power of all. Even in a matter clearly constitutional, mark in how many ways the Constitution clearly requires the sense of the people to be taken in order that a law should be the law of all. . . . But to make the will of *all* the law— by constitutional arrangements to protect the weak and enable the weak as well as the strong to rule themselves and thus secure the blessing of liberty and free government to all—that is the mighty problem which has puzzled the statesman and the patriot of all ages, and which has at last been so wonderfully solved in our Constitution. . . .Let the veto principle, on which the Constitution is built, be enlarged in order that great majorities—an increased number of wills—may be required to make laws for the people.[31]

Calhoun pointed out in a speech in the Senate in 1842 that the total effect of the operation of the various checks and balances in the federal government was to broaden the basis of the system, to increase the number of wills whose concurrence was necessary to the action of the government. These checks and balances were intended "to widen its basis and render it more popular, instead of less, by increasing the number necessary to put it in action,—and having for their object to prevent one portion of the community from aggrandizing and enriching itself at the expense of the other, and to restrict the whole to the sphere intended by the framers of the Constitution."[32] This was true of the veto power of the President, and of the review of legislation by the courts. In this wise Calhoun defended the presidential veto against the bitter attacks by Whigs in Congress, who were provoked by Tyler's persistent opposition to their pet measures. Tyler had vetoed two bank bills and two tariff bills. Probably the most important and effective check in the federal government was, according to Calhoun, the complete one possessed by each of the two houses of Congress on the adoption of all laws. Because States rather than population constituted the basis of representation in the Senate, the South, by its choice of at least half of the members of that body, had been able to maintain an effective check on all legislation.

The idea of sectional equilibrium in the Senate was probably first set forth by James Madison. In the Federal Convention he had observed that equal representation of the States in the upper chamber would establish a salutary balance between the five Southern States and the five Northern States (three States being neutral, perhaps). Moreover, as the South would grow faster than the North, he anticipated the achievement of a similar equilibrium in the lower house. This equilibrium would serve admirably to mitigate the clash of economic interests between North and South. Some Southerners later felt that the Missouri Compromise of 1820 had established the principle of the sectional equilibrium by setting the precedent for admitting new States only in pairs, one from the North and one from the South.[33] Certainly the principle of the sectional equilibrium was a generally recognized one. A. V. Brown, of Tennessee, reporting for the Committee on Territories in the House of Representatives in 1844, said: "The practice has . . . very properly become one of settled policy to preserve . . . in one of the branches of the Legislature of the Union that balance of power between two great divisions of the republic, which is so important to the harmony and security of the whole and to the permanency of the Union. It is right that every section of this happy and prosperous confederacy should not only be, but feel itself secure against any unjust or unequal action of the Federal Legislature upon those of their interests which may in some wise conflict with the interests, policy, or prejudices of other portions."[34]

But the delicately balanced political mechanism was incapable of withstanding the shock of the struggle for power between the industrial and commercial capitalism of the North and the agricultural regime of the South. The basic antagonism of interest, long recognized by the more perspicacious statesmen of both sections, was constantly aggravated by the dynamics of westward territorial expansion, that offered the opportunity to the faster-growing North to seize political dominance. The impulse to seize power, temporarily stemmed by the Missouri Compromise of 1820, was heightened by the emotional extravagance of the fight between the abolitionists and the pro-slavery advocates. The impulse broke forth in the proposal to exclude slavery from the territory gained as a result of the war with Mexico. Out of the stormy controversy over the Wilmot Proviso came the compromise solution of 1850, proposing (in part) the admission of California as a free State. This meant sixteen free States as compared with fifteen slave States. To many Southerners, this was not a compromise, but a destruction of the sectional equilibrium in the Senate. The threatened abandonment of this cardinal principle of Southern policy called forth re-assertion and defense of the principle by Calhoun, David L. Yules, Jefferson Davis, and other Southern leaders.[35] They felt that with the loss of equal representation with the North in the Senate, the South had lost an indispensable means of self-protection—its concurrent voice in the ordinary operation of the federal government. Calhoun contended that the principle of the sectional equilibrium had been embodied in the Constitution by the framers and accepted by ratification. The South had come to be outweighed by the North in every department of the federal government save in the Senate where there was an exact balance. The destruction of that balance, he felt, would mean civil war. The South had always been the conservative portion of the Union, and its possession of a due check on the rest was essential to the preservation of "this glorious Union of ours." On the verge of death, Calhoun grimly warned that "if we are to be reduced to a mere handful—if we are to become a mere ball to play the presidential game with—to count something in the Baltimore caucus—if this is to be the result—wo! wo! I say to this Union!"[36]

In still another way had various Southern statesmen and politicians sought to secure something of a balance between the sections—through political parties. It was believed that if organization of political parties along sectional lines could be prevented, competition of two great national parties for support of the South in the presidential elections would compel them to have tender regard for the interests of the South. It was necessary, therefore, for Southern States to maintain strength in both parties, varying the bulk of their support to suit the circumstances. This was but a specific application of Madison's old idea, expressed several times in *The Federalist,* that political parties arising in a large country would include such a variety and number of factions and interests that compromise, moderation, a nice balance of interests would of necessity characterize any party achieving a majority combination.[37] Thomas L. Clingman, Jefferson Davis, Alexander H. Stephens, Howell Cobb, and Robert Toombs all felt that the surest protection for Southern interests lay in the maintenance of such a party alignment, the latter three clinging to the idea right down to the outbreak of the Civil War.[38] Calhoun recognized the validity of their aims,[39] but soon came to believe their efforts futile. He had early noted the ability of separate geographical interests and of their representatives to unite for selfish ends regardless of party lines. Moreover, the abolitionists in the North were having great influence in participating in the same game of playing off one party against the other. The Democrats of the North were not to be trusted when they were willing to cater to abolitionist sentiment for the sake of support in the presidential election. He came to feel that the best course for the South was a united stand in a single party.[40]

Rather than an effective means of securing a concurrent voice for the South in the activities of the federal government, political parties had achieved majorities that had been able to break down one of the checks and balances of the federal system. The expectations of some of the framers of the Constitution that officers of the federal and State governments would check each other were upset by the formation of majorities that controlled federal government and many State governments at the same time, uniting at its command both delegated and reserved powers. The mutual State-federal veto, by which John Taylor had proposed that the States protect their rights,[41] had thus been subverted for many States. Calhoun be-

lieved with Taylor that where the two governments differed as to the extent of their powers a mutual negative
should be the consequence; and to Calhoun this would
have been another application of the principle of the concurrent voice. But political parties and the assertion and
enforcement of the jurisdiction of the federal Supreme
Court over State courts had weakened, if they had not
destroyed, this application of the check and balance principle. One of the methods for enforcing the federal division of powers between the State and central government
had been rendered nugatory.[42]

The application *par excellence* of the principle of the
concurrent majority in the federal system was to be found,
according to Calhoun, in the process of amending the Constitution. His whole theory of nullification was but an attempt to make the increased majority found there the effective sanction for the powers exercised by the government of the Union. The checks and balances embodied in
the structure of the federal government itself had not
proven sufficient protection for the interests of a large
minority section. More attention should be attracted to the
"creating voice," the amending power which required
ratification by three-fourths of the States, acting through
conventions or legislatures.[43] Furthermore, the federal
government was one of specifically delegated powers, and
presumably it was to exercise no other powers save by
amendment of the Constitution. Three-fourths of the
States was a sufficiently large majority to enable any important minority to check a delegation of power. In other
words, the principle of the Constitution was one of decentralization as well as of union.[44] Calhoun believed that
it could be "laid down as a principle that the power and
action of the Union, instead of being increased ought to be
diminished with the increase of its extent and population."
The greater the size of the country and its population, the

greater is the diversity of interests, the less is the mutual knowledge, understanding, and sympathy among the several parts. "The same principle, according to which it was provided that there should not be more closeness of union than three-fourths should agree to, equally applies in all stages of the growth and progress of the country; to wit: that there should not be at any time more than the same proportion would agree."[45] In thus championing decentralization, Calhoun was plainly opposing the current trend to political "consolidation," which he and his followers in the State rights school looked upon with apprehension. They saw nothing inexorable in the trend, however. They discerned no futility in their efforts to maintain, or even to increase, the political autonomy of Southern civilization.

Calhoun's view of the basic importance of the amendment process seemed a fair interpretation of the very words of the Constitution itself. But there was the remaining problem of how to invoke this "Deity of our political system." The Constitution provided that amendments should be proposed by a two-thirds majority in both houses of Congress, or by a convention called by Congress at the instance of two-thirds of the State legislatures. A minority certainly could not meet these requirements and propose an amendment of a decentralizing character. Moreover, if a numerical majority in the federal government were exercising powers beyond its constitutional competence, a minority was incapable of checking it by invoking the amendment process for a test on the powers in question. In a word, were there no other way for making the three-fourths majority requirement effective, the principle of government by concurrent majority embodied in the amendment provision would be destroyed and government by numerical majority would hold sway.[46] To meet this problem, Calhoun resorted to the doctrines of State sovereignty and State interposition, which are necessary to complete his theory of nullification. Treatment of these ideas is reserved for later chapters.[47]

C. VALUE AND PRACTICABILITY OF THE PRINCIPLE

Calhoun maintained consistently that government by concurrent majority, or by concurrent voice in non-popular forms, was superior to any absolute government, whether popular or not. The great merit of government according to this principle was the mutual consideration, toleration, and forebearance it required of the different interests in the community. Government would impose common restraints upon their interests only to the extent of a mutually recognized common ground, for constitutional government demanded for its successful operation agreement upon fundamentals of the political order. The existence of irreconcilables, as in governments by the numerical majority, would lead inevitably to the appeal to arms in revolution. In government of the concurrent majority, the ruling principle was compromise; and, no matter how high the increased majority requirement might be, the fear of anarchy was sufficient to insure that some compromise would be reached. "The voice of the people," he solemnly declared, "uttered under the necessity of avoiding the greatest of calamities, through the organs of a government so constructed as to suppress the expression of all partial and selfish interests, and to give a full and faithful utterance to the sense of the whole community in reference to its common welfare, may without impiety be called the voice of God. To call any other so would be impious."[48]

Certainly in a government so constructed that oppression and abuse of power became relatively improbable, if not impossible, the confidence of the people in their rulers and their loyalty to the existing regime would be raised to a higher pitch. Stability would be one of the most striking characteristics of such a government. The party strife and factitious spirit prevalent elsewhere would be largely nonexistent. This was true because "in governments of the concurrent majority individual feelings are from its organism necessarily enlisted on the side of the social and made to unite with them in promoting the separate interests of each; while in those of the numerical majority the social are necessarily enlisted on the side of the individual and made to contribute to the interests of parties regardless of that of the whole."[49] Probably not without some pride of discovery did Calhoun aver that the establishment of a government of the concurrent majority, in which "the individual feelings" were enlisted on the side of the social, was the greatest possible achievement of the science of government. Only under such stable and orderly government could liberty have a secure and durable existence. Government would be restrained from exceeding its proper limits; the liberty of the individual to strive to better his condition and the security of his acquisitions would rest upon a more solid foundation. The resulting material prosperity would enhance the physical power of the community—and so its military strength, whether for offense or defense. History, he believed, shows that greater material resources, power, and progress are enjoyed where liberty is the "largest and best secured."[50]

Calhoun argued persuasively that the stability, security, and liberty provided by his ideal form of government would produce not only greater material welfare but also higher moral qualities among a people. The liberty they experience develops self-reliance, energy, and enthusiasm. The constant necessity of sympathetic regard for the interests of others would lead various sections to choose its most intelligent, high-minded, and patriotic leaders to fill public office; and confidence in such officials and in the mutual good will of the sections would elicit a courageous and noble order of patriotism. The resulting harmony, even unanimity, and devotion to country would mean the elevation not only of public, but of private morals. Calhoun was impressed by the close alliance between the two spheres of morality. Where the rules of the game put a premium upon hypocrisy, fraud, artifice, slander, breach of faith, etc., for political preferment, the same indecent practises are carried over into men's dealings in private life. "That which corrupts and debases the community politically must also corrupt and debase it morally."[51] Wisdom, experience, and a high sense of honor would be the qualities favored in the politics of a government by concurrent majority; and the high plane of political ethics would inevitably exert a "powerful influence towards purifying and elevating the character of the government and the people morally as well as politically." In a word, government by concurrent majority was better adapted than other kinds to secure the ends for which all government existed, the preservation and protection of the community.[52]

Calhoun recognized only two important objections that could be urged against government by concurrent majority. The first was the extreme difficulty of attaining such a government; Calhoun readily admitted that for many peoples it was probably beyond reach. But for people of superior political ability to reject it on that ground was a kind of defeatism that he would not countenance. The difficulty of construction was not a valid objection against efforts to approach to some extent the ideal of government by concurrent majority. The second general objection was the difficulty of operation. Some critics who admitted the possibility of such a government pointed out the slowness and cumbersomeness with which it must operate. Calhoun again admitted the force of the objection, recognizing that it would not have the energy and dispatch of consolidated and absolute government. But it was worth the price. Some critics believed that concurrence among the diverse interests of the community was so difficult to obtain that anarchy or very poor government would be the result. This was true of Webster and the other opponents of nullification, which was Calhoun's application of government by concurrent majority to the American federal system.[53] Calhoun's reply to this argument was that fear of anarchy was a sanction powerful enough to insure that all parties would be predisposed to compromise and that concurrence would, therefore, be achieved. What those critics really feared, he believed, was not anarchy, but a government in which a selfish majority combination of interests could not readily enforce its will in exploitation of the rest of the community.

History showed that a government of the concurrent majority could not only work, but was usually of a very superior order. In addition to the instances of the working of the principle in various actual governments (noted above[54]) he pointed out its operation in the practice of jury systems. "In these, twelve individuals, selected without discrimination, must unanimously concur in opinion,— under the obligation of an oath to find a true verdict according to the law and evidence; and this too not infrequently under such great difficulty and doubt that the ablest and most experienced judges and advocates differ in opinion after careful examination. And yet, as impracticable as this mode of trial would seem to the superficial observer, it is found in practice not only to succeed, but to be the safest, the wisest and the best that human ingenuity has ever devised."[55] The argument that rule by concurrent majority actually would mean government by a recalci-

trant minority was an absurd one. It was true that a minority might check a mere numerical majority, but this was
not governing. The minority could do nothing in a positive
way. No one claimed, for example, that one house of Congress ruled the other simply because each had a complete
check on all acts passed by the other.[56] Such a government
might be relatively inactive, but this was no weakness in
his view.

D. CLASSIFICATION OF GOVERNMENTS

To Calhoun, the most important basis for the classification of governments was, of course, the principle of the
concurrent majority. Governments organized on that principle in such a way as to enable the important interests into
which the community was divided to protect themselves,
were constitutional governments; all others were absolute
governments. The principle of the former was compromise; of the latter, force. "The object of a constitution
is to restrain the government, as that of laws is to restrain
individuals."[57] And the mere existence of a written document, imposing limits on the government and called a constitution, did not make constitutional government. The
limits of a written constitution might well be destroyed by
governors, if there were no agency to enforce them. The
restraint must be real; and this was to be secured only by
such an "organism" of government as operated on the
principle of the concurrent voice. Constitutional government, then, was limited government only in this sense—
that its action was predicated upon comparatively widespread agreement among the members of the community.[58]
Calhoun accepted the traditional classification of governments into monarchy, aristocracy, and democracy as
the rule of one, the few, and the many; and any of these

traditional forms might be either constitutional or absolute. Constitutional democracy was the best form. Of aristocracy as a form of government he had little to say except that its conversion from the absolute to the constitutional form was probably easier than in the case of democracy, the absolute form of which was the most difficult of transition to constitutional government. His exact attitude toward absolute democracy was not entirely clear. It would seem that he should have preferred it to either monarchy or aristocracy, for government of a numerical majority affords a better check for the varying "natural" interests than that supplied by any numerical minority. In general he accepted democracy as the achievement of the American Revolution. However, he bitterly complained of the oppression of the minority by a numerical majority and regarded the tyranny of an absolute democracy as the most harsh and oppressive of all. This coupled with some expressions of admiration for monarchy, lends some doubt as to his actual preference between absolute democracy and constitutional monarchy. Monarchy was in his day the most prevalent form of government; and it was usually, in his opinion, the most durable, for three reasons: its military efficiency; its greater administrative capacity for the government of large expanses of territory; its greater susceptibility of improvement. However it may have originated, monarchy usually assumed the form of an hereditary regime. Its hereditary character tended, Calhoun believed, to identify the interests of the ruler with those of his subjects; and there naturally arose mutual feelings of paternity and loyalty. The privileges of the hereditary nobility came gradually to be recognized as "fixed rules of action" which limited the monarch. The transformation of monarchy into a constitutional government was to be expected in the course of things.[59]

Calhoun had no theory of a cycle of governments or

of a necessary succession of the different forms. He was aware that political regimes were constantly changing; and to some extent he was aware of the influence of material causes of these changes. It was the struggles between interests that gave instability to a regime; and he identified these interests generally with economic interests. However he was no determinist. He believed that at critical moments in these struggles human effort might bring about the necessary compromises and thereby establish constitutional government. Constitutional forms are the more stable, but they tend to degenerate into absolute forms. Governments, then, are in a constant state of flux. The government of a particular country sometimes improves, and sometimes degenerates. Nevertheless, although much error, confusion, and evil may be suffered on the way, it would be impious to be doubtful of progress in the long run. Political progress means an increase in the number of constitutional governments, and more especially of constitutional democracy.[60]

It may be noted here that Calhoun also made the distinction between confederacy, federal government, and "consolidated," or national, government. Briefly, the differences between them were that the first was a union of governments; the second, a union of sovereign states; the last, a single state. The first two differed in the organization and operation of a union between several units; the latter two differed in the relation of the units to the whole. Detailed discussion of the subject must follow treatment of the concept of sovereignty.[61]

NOTES

1. *Works,* Vol. I, p. 28; Vol. VI, p. 181.
2. *Works,* Vol. pp. 24-25, 26-27. Judge William Har-

per, Calhoun's fellow nullifier, gave expression to the same idea when he declared that "the only principle of free government" was that when there were great, distinct, and conflicting interests in the state, each must have the means of protecting itself. *Speech before the Charleston State Rights and Free Trade Ass'n.,* April 1, 1832, pamphlet (Charleston, 1832), p. 9.

3. *Works,* Vol. VI, pp. 181-193.
4. *Ibid.* Vol. VI, pp. 63-64.
5. *Works,* Vol. II, pp. 246-248.
6. *Ibid.,* Vol. II, p. 250. In the *Disquisition* he put it in different phrase, perhaps a little more clearly, when he wrote: "It is this mutual negative among its various conflicting interests which invests each with the power of protecting itself, and places the rights of each where only they can be securely placed—under its own guardianship. Without this there can be no systematic, peaceful, or effective resistance to the natural tendency of each to come into conflict with the others. . . ." *Ibid.,* Vol. I, p. 35.
7. William M. Meigs, *The Life of John Caldwell Calhoun,* 2 vols. (New York, 1917), Vol. II, pp. 95-96.
8. *Works,* Vol. II, p. 251.
9. *Ibid.,* Vol. VI, p. 65.
10. *Works,* Vol. II, pp. 251-252.
11. *Ibid.,* Vol. VI, pp. 65-66.
12. Madison, *The Federalist,* Ford ed. (New York, 1898), No. X.
13. *Works,* Vol. VI, pp. 182-183.
14. *Ibid.,* Vol. I, p. 393; Vol. VI, pp. 182-183. Athens was cited also; there one interest proposed and another enacted laws. *Idem.*
15. *Works,* Vol. I, pp. 392-396. See *supra.,* Ch. I.
16. He commented upon Roman institutions fairly often. See *Works,* Vol. I, pp. 73, 91-98, 271-272, 393: Vol. II, pp. 257-259; Vol. VI, pp. 183-184.
17. *Works,* Vol. I, pp. 71-72.
18. *Works,* Vol. I, pp. 72-73.
19. *Ibid.,* Vol. I, pp. 98-106.
20. *Works,* Vol. I, pp. 78-79. Elliott was mistaken when he wrote of Calhoun: "It is within the free judgment

of man to determine the external organization of the state. After his own free will he establishes the constitution and form of the state. The only way to an agreement of the wills of several men is by compact; by this method men create their constitution and their government, and it is ever within their power freely to change this constitution." "Die Staatslehre John C. Calhouns," *Staats-und volkerrechtliche Abhandlungen,* Vol. IV, No. 2 (1903), p. 22.

21. Calhoun, *Works,* Vol. I, pp. 79-83.

22. *Ibid.,* Vol. I, p. 80.

23. *Works,* Vol. I, pp. 167-171.

24. *Works,* Vol. I, pp. 181-182. Cf. James Madison, *The Federalist,* University ed. (New York, 1864), No. XXXVIII, pp. 265-266. See also Robert Y. Hayne, *Second Speech in Reply to Webster,* pamphlet (Washington ,1830), p. 12.

25. F. W. Coker, *Readings in Political Philosophy* (New York, 1914), pp. 113-117.

26. Montesquieu, *The Spirit of the Laws,* 2 vols. (London, 1777), Vol. I, Bk. XI, esp. Ch. VI.

27. See *supra.,* Ch. II.

28. *Debates in the Virginia Constitutional Convention,* 1829-1830 (Richmond, 1839), pp. 537-538. See also *supra.,* Ch. II.

29. See *supra.,* Ch. II. The theory of separation of powers and checks and balances was used to defend as well as to attack President Jackson's aggressive exercise of executive authority. See T. H. Hall, "Speech in the House, April 28, 1834," *Register of Debates in Congress,* 23rd Congress, 1st session, Vol. X, Part III, pp. 3824-3825; Felix Grundy, "Speech in Senate, Feb. 18, 1835," *Ibid.,* 23rd Congress, 2nd session, Vol. XI, Part I, pp. 528-529.

30. Rhett, "Speech in House of Representatives, July 1, 1842," *Congressional Globe,* 27th Congress, 2nd session, pp. 606-607 of Appendix: Hayne, *Oration before the State Rights and free Trade Party, etc., July 4, 1831,* pamphlet (Charleston, 1831), pp. 29-31.

31. Laura A. White, *Robert Barnwell Rhett: Father of Secession* (New York and London, 1931), p. 52.

32. *Works,* Vol. IV, pp. 88-89.
33. Madison, "Debates in the Federal Convention of 1787 as reported by James Madison," *Formation of Union Document,* 69th Congress, 1st session, House Document 398, pp. 381, 310-311, 369; D. L. Yulee, "Speech in the Senate, July 6, 1850," *Congressional Globe,* Appendix, Vol. XXII, Part II, 31st Congress, 1st session, p. 1162; J. F. Dowdell, "Speech in the House, July 28, 1856," *Congressional Globe,* Appendix, 34th Congress, 1st session, p. 1059.
34. *House Report* III, No. 557, 28th Congress, 1st session.
35. Yules, although only two years earlier he had renounced the Missouri Compromise, contended in 1850 that maintenance of the sectional equilibrium was the *quid pro quo* exacted for surrender of constitutional protection of slavery in all the territory of the Union. See *Remarks of Mr. Yules in the Senate of the United States, Feb.* 14, 15, *and* 17, 1848, etc., pamphlet (Washington, 1848), p. 2 and *passim; Congressional Globe,* 31st Congress, 1st session, pp. 1162-1163 of Appendix. See also R. M. H. Garnett, *The Union, Past and Future,* 4th ed. (Charleston, 1850), pp. 5-6; John Scott, *The Lost Principle, or the Sectional Equilibrium* (Richmond, 1860), pp. 11-17, 191-194, *passim;* William H. Trescott, *Position and Course of the South* (Charleston, 1850), pp. 6, 17; U. B. Phillips, *Life of Robert Toombs* (New York, 1913), pp. 75-76; Jefferson Davis, *Rise and Fall of the Confederate Government,* 2 vols. (New York, 1881), Vol. I, pp. 31-32, 47-48. To Alexander H. Stephens, the sectional equilibrium was not as important as the doctrine of State sovereignty. See his *Constitutional View of the War between the States,* 2 vols. (Philadelphia, 1868-1870), Vol. II, pp. 307-308.
36. *Works,* Vol. IV, pp. 341-343-344. 544. Calhoun pointed to the practice in his own State as a good example. There in one house of the legislature population was the basis of representation and the upper country of South Carolina controlled; in the other property was given more weight and the lower country controlled. Harmony between the sections and wise govern-

ment resulted. *Ibid.,* Vol. I, pp. 400-406. In the troubled days after the election of Lincoln and before the outbreak of Civil War, there were several suggestions put forward to restore the sectional equilibrium in the Senate and to create one in the federal chief executive and in the judiciary. See proposals of J. W. Noell, of Missouri, Andrew Johnson, of Tennessee, and Albert G. Jenkins and R. M. T. Hunter, of Virginia, *Congressional Globe,* 36th Congress, 2nd session, pp. 77, 78, 82-83. 329. William H. Seward probably derived from his "higher law" his complete rejection of any political equilibrium not based on a physical one of territory and of slaves and freemen. See *Congressional Globe,* 31st Congress, 1st session, p. 263.

37. *The Federalist,* Ford ed. (New York, 1898) Nos. 10 and 51.

38. One observer, writing in 1866, felt that Southern politicians had displayed "superior and consummate political skill" in maintaining a two-party system that largely straddled sectional issues for many years. E. A. Pollard, *The Lost Cause* (New York, 1866), p. 62. See Clingman's "Speech to the House in 1847," *Congressional Globe,* Appendix, 30th Congress, 1st session, pp. 45-47.

39. Calhoun declared in his speech on the slavery question on March 4, 1850: "The great mass of the people were divided, as in the other section, into Whigs and Democrats. The leaders and the presses of both parties in the South were very solicitous to prevent excitement and to preserve quiet; because it was seen that the effects of the former would necessarily tend to weaken, if not destroy, the political ties which united them with their respective parties in the other section." *Works,* Vol,. IV, p. 543.

40. *Correspondence,* pp. 250-251, 266-267, 634, 455-457, 460, 519-522, 556, 557, 664, 702-703.

41. *Tyranny Unmasked* (Washington, 1822), pp. 256-284.

42. *Works,* Vol. I, pp. 230, 266-272.

43. *Ibid.,* Vol. IV, pp. 89-93. Robert J. Turnbull, Calhoun's fellow Carolinian, was but reiterating the senti-

ment of various predecessors in the State rights school, Madison, John Taylor, Spencer Roane, Thomas Cooper and others, in enjoining Congress not to seize upon doubtful powers. If a desired power was not clearly granted, resort should be made only to the amendment process. Turnbull, *The Crisis* (Charleston, 1827), pp. 110-111.

44. *Work* , Vol. I, pp. 291, 295-296, 314; Vol. II, p. 255; Vol. IV, pp. 78-79; Vol. VI, pp. 172-176, 178-179.

45. *Ibid.,* Vol. I, p. 314.

46. *Works,* Vol. VI, p. 189.

47. See the next two chapters, VI and VII.

48. *Works,* Vol. I, p. 39.

49. *Works,* Vol. I, pp. 69-70.

50. *Ibid.,* Vol. I, p. 63. Calhoun also noted that one of the incidental advantages of government by concurrent voice was that it admitted with greater safety of very wide extension of the suffrage. The rich would have ample protection against the poor. *Ibid., Vol.* I, pp. 45-46.

51. *Works,* Vol. I, p. 49.

52. *Ibid.,* Vol. I, pp. 45-53, 59-64, 69-70, 89-91.

53. See Webster's speech in reply to Hayne, Jan. 26, 1830, *Register of Debates in Congress,* 21st Congress, 1st session, pp. 58-82, 92-93. Elliott attempted a *reductio ad absurdum* of Calhoun's theory. "If each interest group should have the right of veto, then it is not at all excluded that an individual can have his own interest opposed to legislation by the state and be thereby entitled to the right of veto. And if one possesses the right, why not several and finally all? Under this 'concurrent' majority it is possible either that no law prevails (which is nothing other than anarchy) or that those laws which are permitted do not bear equally upon all and fail therefore their goal." Elliott, "Die Staatslehre John C. Calhouns," p. 33. Cf. F. E. Chadwick, *Causes of the Civil War* (New York and London, 1906), pp. 39-40; John J. Lalor, ed., "Nullification," *Cyclopedia of Political Science,* Vol. II, p. 1051.

54. See *supra.,* this Chapter, Section B.

55. *Works,* Vol. I, pp. 65-66.

56. *Ibid.,* Vol. VI, pp. 54-55.

57. *Ibid.*, Vol. VI, p. 63.

58. *Works,* Vol. I, pp. 29-33.

59. *Works,* Vol. I, pp. 29-30, 35-36, 76-88. Calhoun in attributing identity of interest between ruler and subjects in hereditary monarchy apparently forgot for the moment his discussion of the experience of England, in which he had them directly opposed in interest. *Ibid.,* Vol. I, pp. 98-106. Judge Harper, perhaps Calhoun's ablest supporter in exposition of nullification, frankly distinguished two kinds of democracy: the Athenian (based on slavery) and that in which slave and master have equal voice in public affairs. Harper, "Memoir on Slavery," *Pro-Slavery Argument* (Philadelphia, 1853), p. 72. George Fitzhugh, sociological defender of the South, conceived the essence of democracy to be the equal distribution "according to capacity and ability" of social rights and obligations. Fitzhugh, *Cannibals All* (Richmond, 1857), p. 123.

60. Calhoun defined revolution as the transformation of "the organization and distribution of power" in a political society. *Works.* Vol. II, pp. 337-338; Vol. I. pp. 44-45, 88-91.

61. See *infra.*, Chapters VI and VII.

6

Sovereignty

A. SOVEREIGNTY BEFORE CALHOUN

THE CONCEPT of legal sovereignty had received considerable treatment in Europe before the time of Calhoun. It was essentially a modern doctrine, owing nothing to Greek philosophy and little more than phraseology to Roman jurisprudence. In the fourteenth century legalistic rationalization of the power of the national monarch in France gave expression to the idea. The transition from the pluralistic situation of the Middle Ages, in which the competing powers of Pope, Emperor, king, feudal lord, autonomous town, independent guild, and customary law divided the allegiance of individuals and produced the confusion of overlapping and often conflicting authorities, was marked by the growing independence of national monarchs from papal authority by their increasing dominance over lords, towns and guilds. By the latter sixteenth century this process had gone far enough to evoke the most notable of the early statements of the theory of sovereignty in Jean Bodin's *De Republica*. To Bodin, the state was "an association of families and their common affairs, governed by a highest power and by reason"; and he defined sovereignty as the "highest power over citizens and subjects, unrestrained by laws." Sovereignty was the power to give law to all citizens, both singly and collectively.[1]

It is true that despite his clear definition ascribing unlimited law-making authority to the sovereign, Bodin, in

other passages of the same work, admitted that the sovereign was limited by divine and natural laws as well as by
what he called "laws of the realm" (*leges imperii*). Commentators are not in agreement as to how to reconcile the
apparently contradictory statements. It seems clear, however, that the primary object of Bodin's discussion of sovereignty was to establish the point that although the pos-
sessor of sovereign authority ought not to regard himself
as free to violate natural, divine, or customary laws, there
was no human authority above him empowered to enforce
upon him the restraints embodied in these higher forms of
law; and by virtue of Bodin's original definition and analysis of the conception of sovereignty in the state, he came
subsequently to be regarded as founder of the modern
theory of legal sovereignty. Restatements and refinements
of his analysis appear in the writings of many of the most
celebrated modern political thinkers: notably, Thomas
Hobbes in the seventeenth century; Rousseau, Blackstone,
and Bentham in the eighteenth century; and (in Calhoun's
time and later) John Austin and the jurists of the nineteenth and twentieth century school of "Analytical Jurists." These writers have varied considerably in their
ideas on the location of sovereignty; but all of them have
tended to regard sovereignty as indivisible and inalienable
as well as legally illimitable.[2]

Blackstone was the chief source of English influence
on American thought on sovereignty in the middle period,
for his *Commentaries on the Laws of England* was then
part of the legal training which most American public men
received. Although definitely locating sovereignty for
England in Parliament, Blackstone took somewhat contradictory positions on sovereignty and law in general. On
the one hand, he recognized no legal limits on sovereignty;
for, he held, in every politically organized society there
was "a supreme, irresistible, absolute, uncontrolled au-

thority, in which the *jura summi imperii,* or rights of sovereignty, reside." On the other hand, he denied the validity of any human law, even though commanded by a sovereign, that transgressed natural or divine law, discoverable through the human reason.[3] This lack of definite consistency in Blackstone and the general sympathy of Americans for natural law doctrines probably contributed to the readiness with which they modified the concept of sovereignty to fit their own needs in the period of constitutional reformation. Bentham's scathing attack on Blackstone attempted to destroy all ideas of legal limits on sovereignty internally. In his zeal for legal reform, Bentham wanted to convince his generation in England that natural and traditional law, often cloaks for social wrong, offered no legal obstacles to reform by sovereign authority. The extent of "the supreme governor's authority" was "indefinite," i. e., without limit. The authority should be used, without fear, for the general social welfare. He did acknowledge one limit to sovereignty, and that was in the case of limitation by express convention. One state might submit to government by another upon terms, or "the governing bodies of a number of states might agree to take directions in specified cases from some body . . . distinct from all of them, consisting of members, for instance, appointed out of each."[4] This idea of limited sovereignty, given scant notice by Bentham, may well have contributed to the development of the American concept of divided sovereignty.

In American political thought before the time of Calhoun, the concept of sovereignty had not been very carefully defined. The term had been seldom used, and then generally to fix its location in the people rather than in any personal ruler: if sovereignty lay anywhere, it resided in the people. But the term "sovereign" was variously applied to the law-making power, to any power of government, to the power of the people to hold government responsible and to alter or abolish it; and sovereignty was variously located in the people of the Union as a whole or in the people organized separately in the States. This loose usage of the term was the result partly of the prevalence of a philosophy of natural rights of the individual, and partly of the difficulty of reconciling with the facts of the federal Union the old idea of sovereignty—as supreme and uncontrollable power, according to Blackstone's formula. It is significant that the term "sovereignty" was not used in either the Declaration of Independence or the Constitution. There was no place for such a concept of legal absolutism in a system of doctrine that held all governmental power to be limited by the natural rights of individuals. Likewise, it is probable that the Founding Fathers did not want to face the problem of locating sovereignty in the federal system; certainly they avoided it in framing our fundamental law.

The framers wanted to establish securely a strong central government, but they would not declare that the adoption of its Constitution would mark the creation of a national sovereignty. To do so would endanger its adoption. The particularistic opposition arising from the jealousy with which the States guarded their prestige and power was recognized as seriously threatening defeat to the work of the Founding Fathers. And defeat would mean the continuation of all the ills of the "critical period" which the Fathers hoped to escape—inept and weak government, inflation, and disastrous commercial rivalry among the States. As practical men in pursuit of practical ends, they felt it would be impolitic and unnecessary to risk wounding State pride by ascribing sovereignty to the proposed union. Key States, like Virginia, New York, and Massachusetts, might fail to ratify the Constitution.[5]

The federal Constitution did divide governmental

powers between the national government and the States.
A somewhat similar division of authority had, shortly before the American Revolution, been ascribed to the British constitutional system by Samuel Adams, John Dickinson, and others in their assertion of colonial rights; but it
was soon abandoned for the more revolutionary appeal
to natural law and natural rights.[6] James Madison was,
perhaps, the chief exponent of a newer concept of divided
sovereignty. To him, the federal Union presented a new
compound form of government that was without precedent, and therefore not to be explained in terms of old concepts. In the *Federalist*, no. 39, he explained that the Constitution was partly national and partly federal, for "were
it wholly national, the supreme and ultimate authority
would reside in the majority of the people of the Union.
. . ."[7] Patently the latter was not true. Federal jurisdiction
extended to certain limited objects only; and there was
left to the several States a residuary and inviolable sovereignty over all other objects .This was true even though a
tribunal established under the general government was to
decide disputes as to the boundaries between the two fields
of power. He declared of the Constitution: "In its foundation it is federal, not national; in the sources from which
the ordinary powers of government are drawn, it is partly
federal and partly national; in the operation of these
powers, it is national, not federal; in the extent of them,
again, it is federal, not national; and finally, in the authoritative mode of introducing amendments, it is neither
wholly federal nor wholly national."[8]

It was difficult for Madison to visualize such a system
save in terms of divided sovereignty. Of the possibility of
dividing sovereignty, he had no doubt. Shifting his ground
somewhat, he pointed out that the people of Virginia had
divided sovereignty by the separation of Kentucky from
Virginia, a creation of two sovereign societies where one

had existed before. The same was true of Massachusetts and Maine. Moreover, since it had been admittedly within the competence of the several States in their highest sovereign character "to surrender the whole sovereignty and form themselves into a consolidated state, so they might surrender a part and retain, as they have done, the other part, forming a mixed government with a division of its attributes as marked out in the Constitution."[9] In other words, he argued, if sovereignty was divisible in geographical extent, then it was also divisible in content. When a government was created by compact, and invested not only with a "moral power," but with a physical means of executing it, it had sovereignty, however much one might quibble over the mere word. To argue that sovereignty was not divisible, and had not in fact been divided, he wrote late in life, was to evince a fondness for the use of theoretical guides and technical language that showed little regard for realities.

It is true that Madison did refer to that ultimate authority, wherever the derivative might be found, which resided in the people alone. It was this authority which would determine in the long run the relative preponderance between the federal government and the State governments; but Madison remained conveniently vague in not specifying that he meant either the people of the Union as a unit or the several peoples of the separate States. Moreover, he did not identify this ultimate authority with sovereignty, for he too had ideas of a social compact and of the natural rights of individuals. Political power established by compact might do anything that could be rightfully done by the unanimous concurrence of the members of the society, but there remained certain reserved rights of individuals, as parties to the original compact, that were always "beyond the legitimate reach of sovereignty, wherever vested and however viewed." In other words, sovereignty was simply power of government, which was always limited and most certainly divisible.[10]

This idea of divided sovereignty was widely accepted in America prior to the time of Calhoun's attacks upon it. St. George Tucker and William Rawle had, in the first quarter of the nineteenth century, lent some support to the doctrine. The idea also found its way into decisions of the Supreme Court, and for many years was used in its opinions. Chief Justice Marshall, for example, in his famous opinion in *McCulloch v. Maryland* (in 1819), declared: "In America, the powers of sovereignty are divided between the government of the Union and those of the States. They are each sovereign, with respect to the objects committed to the other. . . . We cannot well comprehend the process of reasoning which maintains that a power appertaining to sovereignty cannot be connected with that vast portion of it which is granted to the general government. . . ."[11] Here again was not only the idea that sovereignty was divided, but that it designated merely governmental power.[12] Robert J. Turnbull, a contemporary of Calhoun, spoke of "the portion of sovereignty" which South Carolina gave up on entering the Union.[13] Even Daniel Webster, strong champion of the national cause, conceded a partial sovereignty to the States. In his famous reply to Hayne, Webster declared that the States were unquestionably sovereign in so far as their sovereignty had not been affected by the Constitution. Their authority was general and residuary.[14]

John Taylor's somewhat vacillating conception of sovereignty may be looked upon as a transition to Calhoun's doctrine. Taylor once wrote that sovereignty was "by nature a unit" and asserted that a division of sovereignty implied usurpation.[15] Moreover, as an advocate of complete State sovereignty, he saw the advantage of the doc-

trine of the indivisibility of sovereignty. Yet he was willing, on occasions, to concede, for the sake of argument,
that the States had yielded a portion of their sovereignty
on entering the Union, and to proceed from that point to
show that ultimately the States were still supreme in the
federal system. The people of each State had conveyed to
a federal authority a portion of State sovereign powers
and had retained a portion; but both the deputation and
the reservation were "bottomed" upon the sovereignty of
the States, and had to stand or fall with that principle.
Again he was disposed to ridicule the idea of divided sovereignty, declaring that it was almost as difficult to understand what was meant by the sovereignty of the spheres
as it was to hear the music of the spheres. Any political
authority was supreme within its sphere; and in this sense
the term might be applied to the king, lords, or commons
in England, without enlarging the actual power of any
one of them in least.[16]

Generally, however, Taylor disliked the term "sovereignty." He regarded it as an equivocal word which
"tickled the mind" with contemplation of unknown powers and ideas of supremacy. Its use was an ingenious strata-
gem for neutralizing constitutional restrictions by a single
word "as a new chemical ingredient will often change the
effects of a great mass of other matters." The psychological inadequacies of the term were so great that only
a love of mystery and obscurity could have prompted its
inclusion in our political language. He believed it best not
to use it. "The word being rejected by our constitutions,
cannot be correctly adopted for their construction; because
this unanimous rejection arose from its unfitness for the
design of defining and limiting powers. . . . Our constitutions . . . wisely rejected this indefinite word as a traitor
of civil rights, and endeavored to kill it dead by specifica-
tions and restrictions of power, that it might never again

be used in political disquisitions."[17] In short, the difficulty
for him lay in the incompatibility of absolute power with
the natural rights of individuals. He asserted that as a
matter of fact the term was sacrilegiously stolen from the
attributes of God and impiously assumed by kings; aristo-
cracies and republics later succeeded to the spoil. So originated, it embraced an absolute power over persons and
property that he could not accept. As noted above,[18] Taylor's theory of the social compact and the natural rights of
individuals would not admit legal absoluteness located
anywhere in the community. He would not subscribe to
any theory of sovereignty until it had been "chastened
down to the signification of a natural right in nations to
institute and limit their own governments. . . ."[19] The
"chastened" and limited sovereignty was located, according to his contention, in the people of the various States
of the Union, and was derived from the natural individual
right of self-government. This original right always remained superior to the sovereignty of a people and to the
authority of all government.

In sum, then, Taylor really supported no theory of
sovereignty at all. His individualism was of too extreme
a nature to countenance it. The limited power he found in
a community of people formed a unit, and remained distinct from and superior to the authority of any government instituted by the community.

B. THE NATURE AND LOCATION OF SOVEREIGNTY

Unlike Taylor, Calhoun was not handicapped in his
treatment of the concept of sovereignty by the philosophy
of natural rights. He rejected the whole theory of the social compact and all rights of individuals not sanctioned
by the politically organized community."[20] Sovereignty, to

him, was simply the highest law-making power within such a community. It expressed its will through law; and it logically followed, therefore, that the sovereign could not violate any law, constitutional or otherwise, by any valid expression of its will. The abrogation of a pre-existing law by a legal superior was not violation, but alteration. And it was obvious that there was no legal recourse above the sovereign, for such a possibility would be a contradiction of its legal supremacy.[21] Judge Harper, perhaps Calhoun's ablest theoretical ally in South Carolina, agreed that sovereignty was "the highest legal power," the "highest and ultimate authority" in a state. A state was simply inconceivable without it.[22] Some years later, Alexander H. Stephens added possibly a refinement of the concept, in declaring that "sovereignty . . . is that innate attribute of the Political Body so possessing it, which corresponds with the will and power of self-action in the personal body . . ."[23] Jefferson Davis contented himself with describing it as the power of commanding in the last resort in a civil society.[24]

It seemed obvious to Calhoun that sovereignty was a unit, for it was clearly impossible for two or more supremacies to be within the same community. "How sovereignty itself—the supreme power—can be divided," he wrote in his *Discourse,* "how the people of the several states can be partly sovereign, and partly not sovereign—partly supreme, and partly not supreme, it is impossible to conceive. Sovereignty is an entire thing;—to divide, is to destroy it."[25] He had previously declared, in his speech on the Force Bill in 1833: "In spite of all that has been said, I maintain that sovereignty is in its nature indivisible. It is the supreme power in a State, and we might just as well speak of half a square, or half a triangle, as of half a sovereignty."[26] Madison, Webster, Marshall, and the rest had simply been mistaken in positing a divided sovereignty. Their error had arisen, he believed, from their failure to distinguish between mere powers of government, which were limitable and divisible, and that supreme and ultimate legal authority, which it was logically impossible to divide. There was no difficulty in "understanding how powers appertaining to sovereignty may be divided; and the exercise of one portion delegated to one set of agents, and another portion to another."[27] On the other hand, however, it was a gross error to confuse the "exercise of sovereign powers" with sovereignty itself, or the "delegation of such powers with the surrender of them." A sovereign might delegate his powers to be exercised by as many agents as he thought proper, under such conditions and with such limitations as he cared to impose; but "to surrender any portion of his sovereignty to another is to annihilate the whole."[28] The power of taxation and the power over commerce were called sovereign powers not because they alone, or in conjunction with other like powers, constituted sovereignty; but because the legal competence of a sovereign always extended over them as over every other imaginable power or subject. These specific powers were simply emanations from a supreme legal competency; in his own words, they "appertained" to sovereignty.

Calhoun carried many of the Southern leaders along with him. Under his influence the whole State rights school came to distrust the doctrine of divided sovereignty as a stalking horse for centralization. Its continued acceptance would render practically impossible any effective opposition, as a matter of constitutional right, to an indefinite expansion of federal power. The fallacious doctrine must be discarded, and sovereignty more carefully conceived. Robert Barnwell Rhett and Judge Harper of South Carolina, Governor Troup of Georgia, and Calhoun's disciples, Alexander H. Stephens and Jefferson Davis, were probably more explicit on the point than the rest of the school. Troup declared: "This sovereignty, wherever it exists, is omnipotent; it is the same in one independent community as another, and is not susceptible of division, of increase, or diminution; it can only be destroyed by destroying the community in which it exists. Constitutions and governments are emanations from it, as light from the sun, which parts with it constantly, without itself being impaired, or wasted, or weakened."[29] Stephens maintained that although sovereign powers were divided into legislative, executive, and judicial, and into delegated and reserved, ultimate sovereignty remained unimpaired at the source. It was necessary to discriminate between powers of sovereignty and sovereignty itself, for "no political body can be absolutely sovereign for any purpose, and not be sovereign for all purposes. . . ."[30]

It should be noted here that, beginning with the work of the German emigré, Francis Lieber, the ideas of the unity and indivisibility of sovereignty were employed in justification of the national cause by Jameson, Brownson, Burgess, and others.[31] This process involved a modification of Calhoun's ideas on the subject in only one important respect, to be indicated presently.

Calhoun recognized, of course, that political power might be so organized and distributed in a community that legal supremacy might rest in a legislative body, or even in a single person, the monarch. In such case it might be difficult to perceive the distinction between sovereignty and ordinary power of government, for the two would be to some extent in the same hands. In America, however, the situation was different from that generally prevailing in Europe. Here sovereignty was vested in the people of a community, to whom the government remained subordinate. Calhoun repeatedly insisted upon the superiority of the people as a political aggregate over the government or its officials; and the characteristic manifestation of this superiority was the power to amend the constitution from which government derived all its power. This was no mere assertion of popular sovereignty in the sense that rulers are limited by and must always take account of the fixed attitudes and long-continuing desires of a people. The people to whom he referred comprised the members of a community as a collectivity and in its politically organized aspect. He was treating of the "political people," an entity identical with the state. As individuals the people stood below the constitution, as its subjects; but as a political unit, acting through representatives met in constituent convention, the people stood above the fundamental law of the land as its creator. The people in this latter capacity were in relation to government as principal to agent. It was in making and amending constitutions that the people exercised the legal supremacy that was sovereignty. Occasionally Calhoun lapsed into less exact usage of the term "sovereignty"; thus he wrote, in his *Disquisition*, that the election of public officials would make them responsible to the electorate and that thereby sovereignty would be retained in the community; here he was obviously not referring to legal sovereignty.[32] Jefferson Davis expressed nothing that would have been novel to Calhoun when he wrote: "There are but two modes of expressing their sovereign will known to the people of this country. One is by direct vote—the mode adopted by Rhode Island in 1788 . . . The other is the method . . . of acting by means of conventions of delegates elected expressly as representatives of the sovereignty of the people."[33]

Calhoun distinguished two aspects of sovereignty, the internal and external. The sovereignty of a state meant highest legal authority internally; and, externally, self-determination and complete freedom of will from other similar entities. Just as a sovereign could put formal limits on itself internally by the restraints included in a constitution, so also could it formally limit its complete freedom externally. It did this through treaties and compacts of union. However, such limitations were self-imposed, always requiring consent; and, consequently, they could be removed at will through the same procedure which imposed them. Entering into a federal compact with other states for the sake of the use of a single government as a joint agent for certain purposes, and even consenting to a modification of the usual mode of amendment of such a compact, does not in any way impair the sovereignty of a state. "It is an acknowledged principle that sovereigns may by compact modify or qualify the exercise of their power, without impairing their sovereignty, of which the confederacy existing at the time furnishes a striking illustration," he wrote.[34] In other words, the fact that three-fourths of the States might adopt an amendment of the federal compact was no evidence of an impairment of the sovereignty of any one of the States party to the compact. Each could withdraw its accession to the agreement; for as long as it remained sovereign it retained an absolute power of self-determination.[35]

Much of what Calhoun said on the subject of sovereignty was sound; and he occasionally buttressed his arguments with appeals to the authority of Burlamaqui and of Vattel, as did his allies in the controversy over the nature of the federal Union. The unity and indivisibility of sovereignty came to be generally accepted doctrine even when applied to a federal system of government. In the light of later sociological discussions, one notable deficiency marked his thinking on sovereignty. He apparently did not contemplate all the possibilities for a change of sovereignty, i. e., for the destruction of one state and the creation of another. He recognized revolution by force and violence as one method; and surrender through a constitutional compact as another. He often asserted that the federal Union was no single state; because, if the ratifying sovereign States had intended to create one by surrendering their own sovereignty, they would have so expressly stipulated in the federal Constitution.[36] In other words, short of an exercise of force a change of sovereignty was to be effected only by formal action of constitution-making authority. It is not that he did not consider the theory of sovereignty as description of fact. It is rather that his thinking on the subject was in legalistic rather than in sociological terms. He did recognize the psychological force of various social factors as bonds of union among a people; but he apparently did not seize upon the resulting sense of unity among a people as the determinant of the location of sovereignty; or at any rate he did not regard an expansion of the sense of unity among the people of a federal union as alone sufficient to effect a change in its location. Ties of a common origin, identity of language, similarity of race, religion, laws, customs, manners, commercial and social intercourse, common interests in foreign relations, a common sense of danger, and a "common glory"—all he recognized as bonds of union among a people.[37] Had he been confronted with the argument of later nationalists, that the strengthening of such bonds as these had created a sense of national unity among the whole people of the federal Union and thereby effected a change of sovereignty, he might have admitted the validity of the approach and still contested the conclusion as a matter of fact. It would have been a matter of judgment of the psychological state of the people living in the various States. But Calhoun did not consider this approach in terms of sociological forces; nor did his contemporaries generally. This was to be the work of Lieber and others who followed him.

NOTES

1. F. W. Coker, *Readings in Political Philosophy* (New York, 1914), pp. 226, 230-236.
2. See George H. Sabine and Walter J. Shepard, "Translators' Introduction," in H. Krabbe, *The Modern Idea of the State* (New York and London, 1922), esp. pp. xv-xxviii; Charles E. Merriam, *History of the Theory of Sovereignty since Rousseau* (New York, 1900), esp. Chs. I, VIII; Leon Duguit, *Law in the Modern State* (New York, 1919), Ch. I; F. W. Coker, *Recent Political Thought* (New York and London, 1934), pp. 498-503, 523-524.
3. William Blackstone, *Commentaries on the Laws of England*, Archbold ed., 4 vols. (Philadelphia, 1825), Vol. I, pp. 44, 33-56, and *passim*. Burlamaqui and Vattel, often quoted by Americans on the subject of sovereignty, also contemplated a sovereignty limited by natural law and by the fundamental law of the realm. J. J. Burlamaqui, *The Principles of Natural and Politic Law*, 2 vols., 6th ed., (Philadelphia, 1823), Vol. II, pp. 39, 41, 42-44, 46-49; M. D. Vattel, *The Law of Nations* (Northampton, Mass., 1820), pp. 72-73, 74-79.
4. Jeremy Bentham, *Fragment on Government*, Montague ed. (Oxford, 1891), p. 216 and *passim*.
5. A. C. McLaughlin, *Constitutional History of the United States*, Students ed., (New York and London, 1935), pp 199 ff.; Charles Warren, *The Making of the Constitution* (Boston, 1928), pp. 745-777.
6. See Samuel Adams, *The Writings of Samuel Adams*, 4 vols. (New York and London, 1904), Vol. I, pp. 13-23, 28-30; John Dickinson, *The Writings of John Dickinson* (Philadelphia, 1895), pp. 277-406; McLaughlin, *Constitutional History of the United States*, pp. 7-85; C. H. McIllwain, *The American Revolution* (New York, 1924), pp. 114-147.

7. *The Federalist,* Ford ed. (New York, 1898), pp. 251-252. See also J. Elliot, Ed., *Debates in the Several State Conventions on the Adoption of the Federal Constitution,* 5 vols., 2nd ed. (Philadelphia, 1888), Vol. III, pp. 94-95.

8. *The Federalist,* Ford ed., p. 252. Alexander Hamilton, Madison's collaborator on the *Federalist* papers, came to accept the doctrine of divided sovereignty when he sought to persuade the States to ratify the Constitution. See *Federalist,* University ed. (New York, 1864), No. 9, p. 54; No. 20, pp. 126-127; No. 31, pp. 198-199, 206-208; No. 32, pp. 208-209; No. 61, p. 430. This was a change from the view he expressed in the Federal Convention on opposing the New Jersey plan. "Two sovereignties cannot co-exist within the same limits." *Formation of the Union Document,* 69th Congress, 1st session, House Document 398, pp. 219-238.

9. *Writing,* 9 vols., Hunt ed. (New York and London, 1910), Vol. IX, pp. 568-569, 571-572.

10. Madison, *Writings,* Vol. IX, pp. 471-475, 511-512, 568-573; *The Federalist,* Ford ed., pp. 246-247, 249-252, 303-305, 311-312.

11. 4 *Law. Ed.* 602. See *supra.,* Ch.II, f.n.38.

12. Justice Strong gave voice to the same doctrine in *Tennessee v. Davis.* 25 *Law. Ed.* 650 (1879). And the Supreme Court apparently still holds to it to the present day. In 1922 Chief Justice Taft declared in *United States v. Lanza*: "We have here two sovereignties, deriving power from different sources, capable of dealing with the same subject-matter within the same territory. . . . Each government in determining what shall be an offense against its peace and dignity is exercising its own sovereignty, not that of the other." 67 *Law. Ed.* 314, 317. This double sovereignty was but a variation of the old idea of divided sovereignty. For other assertions of the doctrine by the Supreme Court, see *Collector v. Day,* 20 *Law. Ed.* 125, 126; *Flint v. Stone Tracy Co.,* 55 *Law. Ed.* 413-414; *Second Employers' Liability Case,* 56 *Law. Ed.* 349; *Bailey v. Drexel*

Furniture Co., 66 Law. Ed. 820; *Monaco v. Mississippi,* 78 *Law. Ed.* 1286.

13. Turnbull, *The Crisis, or Essays on the Usurpations of the Federal Government,* pamphlet (Charleston, 1827), p. 24. Howell Cobb as late as 1851 seems to have been thinking in terms of divided sovereignty in referring to the "reserved sovereignty of the states." U. B. Phillips, ed., "Correspondence of Robert Toombs, Alexander H. Stephens, and Howell Cobb," *Annual Report of the American Historical Association,* 1911. Vol. II, pp. 257-258.

14. *Register of Debates in Congress,* 21st Congress, 1st session, p. 74.

15. *Construction Construed* (Richmond, 1820), p. 27.

16. *Construction Construed,* pp. 99-104; *New Views of the Constitution of the United States* (Washington, 1823), pp. 171-177. Cf. Spencer Roane's criticism of Marshall's doctrine of the sovereignty "of the spheres" in *Branch Historical Papers,* Vol. II, p. 98.

17. *Construction Construed,* p. 26.

18. See *supra.,* Ch. II.

19. *Construction Construed,* pp. 25-28, 31-38; see also *Inquiry into the Principles and Policy of the Government of the United States* (Fredericksburg, 1814), pp. 424-425.

20. See *supra.,* Ch. II, Sec. B.

21. *Works,* Vol. I, pp. 139-140, 146, 277, 301; Vol. II, pp. 293, 381.

22. Harper, *Speech before the Charleston State Rights and Free Trade Association, April* 1, 1832, etc., pamphlet (Charleston, 1832), pp. 5-6.

23. Stephens, *Constitutional View of the Late War between the States,* 2 vols. (Philadelphia, 1868-1870), Vol. II, pp. 23-25.

24. Davis, *The Rise and Fall of the Confederate Government,* 2 vols. (New York, 1881), Vol. I, p. 41. Governor Troup of Georgia declared that sovereignty was omnipotent. "Hence it is that it makes and unmakes at pleasure, and knows no superior but Divinity, which is the law of right and justice." Troup, *Letter to a Gentle-*

man in Georgia, etc., pamphlet (Milledgeville, 1834), p. 4.

25. *Works,* Vol. I, p. 146.

26. *Ibid.,* Vol. II, pp. 231-232.

27. *Ibid.,* Vol. I, p. 146.

28. *Works,* Vol. II, pp. 231-232, Cf. Davis, *Rise and Fall of the Confederate Government,* Vol. I, pp. 142, 154.

29. Troup, *Letter to a Gentleman in Georgia,* p. 4.

30. Stephens, *Constitutional View of the War between the States,* Vol. II, pp. 23-24.

31. See Charles E. Merriam, Jr., *History of the Theory of Soveignty Since Rousseau* (New York, 1900), pp. 172-182.

32. *Works,* Vol. I, pp. 14, 274, 275-276, 302; Vol. II, pp. 291-292; Vol. VI, pp. 45, 146. Judge Harper was careful to use sovereignty in the exact sense. He declared that it might reside in a single individual, or in a single department. "If under our American constitutions, there were no provision for an appeal to the people in Convention, it might be said that sovereignty resided in the legislature, the executive, and the judiciary, since there would be no ulterior authority to control any act in which they concurred. But the sovereignty would, in effect, reside in the legislature, which might organize and modify the other departments at its pleasure. It would be in vain to talk of an abstract sovereignty residing in the people. A sovereignty which can never be called into action would be a nonentity. If under such a constitution, the people should assemble and modify the form of government, this would be revolution and force." *Speech before the State Rights. . . . Association, April* 1, 1832.

In 1840, Abel P. Upshur presented an interesting attempt at defining the state. He wrote: "We mean by it a political corporation, the members of which owe a common allegiance to a common sovereignty, and do not owe any allegiance which is not common; who are bound by no laws except such as that sovereignty may prescribe; who owe to one another reciprocal obligations; who possess common political interests; who

are liable to common political duties; and who can exert
no sovereign power except in the name of the whole.
Anything short of this would be an imperfect definition
of that political corporation which we call 'a people'. "
*Brief Enquiry into the True Nature and Character of
our Federal Government*, 2nd ed., (Philadelphia,
1863), pp. 14-15.
33. Davis, *Rise and Fall of the Confederate Government*, Vol. I, p. 153.
34. Calhoun, *Works*, Vol. I, pp. 139-140.
35. *Ibid.*, Vol. I, pp. 145, 148, 275, 295, 300-301; Vol.
II, pp. 132, 275, 286-289, 291-293, 615; Vol. IV, p.
20; Vol. VI, pp. 172-173; Cf. Alexander H. Stephens,
Constitutional View of the War between the States,
Vol. II, pp. 22-23.
36. Calhoun, *Works*, Vol. II, pp. 281-282; Vol. VI, pp.
107-108. Thomas Cooper, the versatile Carolinian professor, had already denied the second method recognized by Calhoun. "No independent sovereign state—
no nation—can alienate its sovereignty. It is an act
suicidal in its nature." Cooper, *Consolidation*, 2nd. ed.
Columbia, 1830), p. 35.
37. Calhoun, *Works*, Vol. I, pp. 189-190, 193, 200-201;
Vol. III, p. 379; Vol. IV, pp. 557-558; *Correspondence*,
p. 391.

7
The Nature of the Federal Union

A.   KINDS OF POLITICAL UNIONS

THE CONTROVERSY IN American political thought of the
middle period over the nature of the federal Union did
not draw directly upon earlier European discussions, for
there was no authoritative doctrine generally recognized
by the antagonists. It was thought that the federal Union
was a new political phenomenon, not to be confused with
earlier alliances and confederacies. Moreover, European
conceptions of sovereignty had been evolved largely out of
consideration of other political organization; the conceptions arose out of disputes over authority between king
and church, between king and people. In reference to
leagues, alliances, and confederations, European writers
on international law, including Grotius and Vattel, had
agreed in locating sovereignty in the members of the
union. They believed that common deliberation by the
members upon matters of common interest offered no real
impairment of the sovereignty of each. Yet to most of
these writers the concept of sovereignty was not entirely
definite. Handicapped by the prevalent loose theories of
natural law and social compact, Grotius, Pufendorf, and
Vattel contemplated a supreme authority that was nevertheless limitable and divisible.[1] In the eighteenth century,
Montesquieu, a writer of different interests, added little
clarity on this point, although his praise for confederation

as a means by which republics might combine the advantages of small size with the defensive might of monarchy became well known. His view of the nature of a confederation was essentially the same as that of Pufendorf. Pufendorf, a learned German professor of the late seventeenth century, maintained that the agreement of confederation required only that the parties refrain from specified actions "without the general consent of each other." He held that a single member could not be coerced by a majority of the others, even in regard to the matters of common concern for which the confederation had been formed; and that any member could voluntarily withdraw from the union, though it was designed to be "perpetual."[2]

The American controversialists accepted this generally approved conception of a confederacy, but were confident that the American federal Union was no confederation. It differed fundamentally from its immediate precursor (admittedly a confederation) in mode of formation, in organization, operation, and powers; its authority was more than that of a mere congress of ambassadors, as Pufendorf had called that of a confederation. The Founding Fathers thought that they were creating a new kind of government; James Madison asserted that it was partly federal and partly national. Recourse to the idea of governmental dualism was in part the result of the continuing influence of the argument of American revolutionary publicists, that there was an effectual division of authority between Great Britain and the American colonies and that the colonies possessed an internal authority or sovereignty which custom forbade the mother country to violate.[3] To Madison and his fellows the new American federal Union was somewhat similar; divided sovereignty was its essence. Calhoun and the State sovereignty school disagreed. Their interpretation made the federal Union what is today called a confederation, but one differing notably, they thought, from all earlier historical instances of the form.[4]

In the matter of the relation between the local and central units in a political union, Calhoun contemplated only three different forms: a confederacy, a federal union, and a national government. The first of these was simply a league between the governments of several independent states, one having, perhaps, more dignity than ordinary leagues because of the employment of a relatively permanent body to represent the union. Although this body and its agents were sometimes called a government, it was actually but a conference of diplomatic representatives of the members of the union. Calhoun agreed with the earlier view of Pufendorf that a confederacy was a league made by ambassadors, deriving its authority from an agreement between the governments of separate states. The people of each of these separate states, of course, remaining sovereign, could direct their agent, the government, to adhere to or withdraw from this union. Furthermore, the government of each state could, without specific direction from sovereign authority, repudiate the compact upon which the confederacy rested.[5]

In a federal union or government, Calhoun believed, the people of the separate states continued as sovereign entities; and in this respect the federal form resembled the confederacy. However, the central agency of a federal union constituted a real government with authority operating upon individual persons in all of the member states. The authority of a federal government was conferred upon it by the sovereign states according to the terms of an international agreement or compact; and its authority was made compulsory upon the inhabitants of each state only by the action of each of the sovereign member states. The agreement was one between principals, rather than one between agents, as in the case of the confederacy. To the extent of the authority granted by the agreement, the federal government was "as much a government as a national government itself"; and it possessed machinery to enforce its authority. It was this substitution of an actual government in lieu of a diplomatic congress that distinguished the federal union as a "new, peculiar, and unprecedented" form. Its superiority over the confederacy for the accomplishment of purposes common to the member states was patent. For its own peculiar ends, each of the member states had also its own government for an agent. The federal government and the state government were in the relation of equals and coordinates, both being agents of the state, one exclusively, the other shared with the other states of the union. The fact of its joint agency did not give the federal government any priority over the state government, for both stood in the same relation to the sovereign state—an agent to be ordered, changed, or abolished at will. Because the federal government was a joint agent of several states, however, modification would require the assent of all of them and abolition on the part of one state would not necessarily affect its continued existence. Calhoun saw nothing impossible in the use of a governmental organization as an international agency.[6]

A national government was the government of a single state, deriving its authority from the sovereign people of a single community, and operating directly upon the same people as individuals. There were no coordinate agencies, for local units of government were subject to the central government. That such a government might be organized in a manner much like that of a federal union, and that the local units might be given some formal protection by the constitution, or fundamental law, of such a system, Calhoun did not consider of much significance. The merits of the system, compared with a unitary organization of government, did not attract his attention, for in actual practice he thought there would be little difference between them.

Only a single sovereignty would be involved; and the choice of agents would be solely a matter of expediency. Whatever the organization might be, certainly the local units would have less protection against centralizing tendencies than in the case of a true federal union. In the possible case of the cession of sovereignty by several states in the creation of a new state, the semblance of a federal system might remain in the government structure, but none of the reality.[7]

Calhoun's classification admitted of no intermediate form between the federal union and the national, or consolidated, government. Implicitly he denied the possibility of the super-imposition on a union of sovereign states of a non-sovereign state, and likewise excluded the possibility of a large sovereign state composed of several non-sovereign states. There was no such thing as a non-sovereign state; such a term was self-contradictory, for sovereignty was the badge of the state. Explicitly he denied the possibility of a union partly federal and partly national, for to divide sovereignty was to destroy it.[8]

To Calhoun, the United States of America fitted only the description of the federal union. In a speech defending President Tyler in 1842, he seized the opportunity to lecture to the carping Whigs on the nature of the American Union. Tyler, a Southern Whig, had remained loyal to his State rights convictions and vetoed the Bank bill. Calhoun admonished Clay, Webster, and other Whig leaders not to expect their Congressional majority to enable them to rule the country as if it were a single state with a "consolidated" national government.

Ours is a union, not of individuals united by what is called a social compact—for that would make it a nation; nor of governments—for that would have formed a confederacy, like the one superseded by the present constitution; but a union of states, founded on a written, positive compact, forming a Federal Republic, with the same equality of rights among the states composing the union, as among the citizens composing the states themselves. Instead of a nation, we are in reality an assemblage of nations, or peoples . . ., united in their sovereign character immediately and directly by their own act, but without losing their separate and independent existence.[9]

Calhoun viewed the constitution generally as being of the nature of an international treaty; and, like sovereigns under international law, the member states under the terms of this compact were on a status of equality. With certain qualifications, he likened the federal union and the compact to a business partnership among several equal partners. For certain limited purposes the partners employed a common agent entirely subject to their control; any one of the partners was competent as an individual to use another agent for other purposes and to check unauthorized actions of either agent. For the control of foreign relations, the regulation of relations between the states, and certain incidental purposes, the States had entered into a union to the extent of employing a common agent, the federal government; as to all other purposes the States remained separate and distinct. The employment of this joint agent for certain purposes constituted no abrogation of the sovereignty of the individual states.[10]

B. THE SOVEREIGNTY OF THE STATES

In the middle period of American history, the constitutional doctrine of State sovereignty served various purposes; but it became increasingly the property of Southern leaders in their efforts to protect the minority rights and interests of their section. American economic development accentuated the differences between Northern and Southern civilizations, the one dominated by a rising commercial and industrial middle class, and the other by a landed squirearchy. Arising in part from the divergent economic interests of these two sections, there were other differences—in culture, habit, speech, tradition, and perhaps even temperament. As the consciousness of these differences, strengthened by the growing suspicions and fears engendered by abolitionism (which struck directly at an essential element of Southern economy), grew into deep sectional antagonism, Southern statesmen turned more and more to State sovereignty. The doctrine received its fullest elaboration at the hands of Calhoun and his followers. It would give legitimacy to the efforts of a minority to resist centralization and, if necessary, to sever the union. To maintain his case for the sovereignty of the States in the American federal Union, Calhoun had not only to dispose of Madison's theory of divided sovereignty, but also to meet the arguments of Webster and Story and the nationalistic school generally that the States were no longer solely sovereign and that sovereignty actually lay with the one people of the United States. For this purpose he resorted to interpretation of what historical evidence he had and to analysis of the very words and clauses of the Constitution itself. For Calhoun the dispute began in the dramatic nullification struggle of South Carolina against the federal protective tariff, and continued intermittently in connection with a variety of public questions—the tariff, the Bank, internal improvements, abolition petitions, territorial expansion, and admission of new States—until his death in 1850, after which the burden was assumed by others who followed him completely in their discussions of State sovereignty. In answering Webster and Story, he was aided by fellow Carolinians and by other Southern leaders, notably Turnbull, Upshur, Jefferson Davis, and Stephens.

The argument of Calhoun and his school was that the American States had always been separate and distinct political entities and still remained so. In the first stage of their existence as colonies subject to the British crown, they were united politically only through common subjection to the mother country. Their first loose union for resistance to England was one of distinct political communities; and, on declaring their independence to the world, they asserted themselves free and independent States. They became separate sovereign communities on maintaining their independence by force. When they formed the union of the old Confederation, they expressly affirmed the sovereignty, freedom, and independence of the several States. "When it was proposed to supersede the Articles of Confederation by the present Constitution, they met in convention as States, acted and voted as States; and the Constitution, when formed, was submitted for ratification to the people of the several States; it was ratified by them as States, each for itself; each by its ratification binding its own citizens; the parts thus separately binding themselves, and not the whole the parts. . . ."[11] The fact that a State refusing ratification would have remained as a foreign country outside the Union according to the terms of the Constitution itself revealed the compact nature of the Constitution and the creative power of the separate and independent States. Further, the Constitution purported to establish only a government of certain delegated powers, and made no reference at all to any cession of sovereignty by the ratifying States. The body of the Constitution throughout was federal, recognizing the existence of the States and invoking their assistance in choosing the legislative houses, the executive, and the judiciary, and in the procedure of amendment. To Calhoun, the conclusion was inevitable that the Constitution was the work of independent States, that the government it established was their agent, and that the federal Union was a union of States, not of individuals.[12]

Following Calhoun's line of argument, Abel P. Upshur, an able Virginian who became Secretary of State under Tyler, disputed Justice Story's thesis that one people or nation existed in the United States before the adoption of the Constitution. Story asserted in his *Commentaries on the Constitution of the United States* that even the American colonists were for many purposes one people. The colonists were fellow subjects of the British crown; they could inhabit other colonies, or inherit land in them; and their commerce was regulated by general laws of the empire. These facts, Upshur contended, were the result only of the relation between the colonies themselves. They could not act togther for any one function of government; they were not one people for any purpose involving allegiance on the one hand or protection on the other. Even Story admitted that the colonies had no direct political connection with one another. Then, argued Upshur, Story's assertions that the Continental Congresses were national governments organized with the consent of the people and that from the time of the Declaration of Independence the united colonies were a nation *de facto* were flatly mistaken. Many statements taken from public records of the time, Upshur showed, indicated that the States were regarded as sovereign; and this situation continued with the establishment of the Confederation. Story simply proceeded on the fallacious assumption that union for some purposes constituted union for all political purposes —the complete formation of a body politic.[13] Consequently, John Jay, John Marshall, and Justice Story himself, in several decisions of the federal Supreme Court, were guilty of taking their own wishful thinking for fact when they asserted that there had existed in the United States one people which could and did establish the Constitution. As Calhoun pointed out, the existence of cultural and psychological bonds and even of some political union was admitted by all; but the important question at issue was not whether there were any bonds of union, but what was the character of the existing political union.[14]

Both Story and Webster pointed to the words of the preamble of the Constitution as substantiating their argument for the existence of a single body politic: the establishment of the Constitution by "We, the people of the United States" could mean nothing else. Calhoun answered by pointing out that the words "United States" were plural and that "people" had been used only because there was no plural for the word. "The terms union, federal, united, all imply a combination of sovereignties, a confederation of States. They never applied to an association of individuals. Who ever heard of the United States of New York, of Massachusetts, of Virginia? Who ever heard the term federal or union applied to the aggregation of individuals into one community?"[15] And did not the Constitution read that treason was committed against *them?* Further the fact that any State refusing to ratify could have remained outside the constitutional Union showed that no single people established the Constitution. The nationalist argument, Turnbull contended, viewed in the light of the ratification procedure, presented the anomalous spectacle of the establishment of a government by the people of a nation as soon as a minority could agree, for the nine smallest States constituted a minority of the population.[16] Finally, the champions of State sovereignty joined Calhoun in pointing to the history of the preamble in the Federal Convention of 1787. The words "United States" had been substituted for the specific names of the several States only to obviate the embarrassment that might otherwise have arisen on the refusal of one or more of the States to ratify; the framers had no other purpose in the use of the term.[17]

Further attack upon the case for State sovereignty by the nationalists involved interpretation of the terms "constitution" and "government." Story declared that "There is nowhere found upon the face of the Constitution any clause, intimating it to be a compact, or in any wise providing for its interpretation as such."[18] Webster in his famous debates with Hayne and Calhoun denied that the Constitution was a compact, save perhaps in the sense of an executed contract. Both Webster and Story asserted that it was rather a fundamental law which had been "ordained and established," not a compact to which States "acceded." It created no league, but established a government. Webster argued: "The broad and clear difference between a government and a league or compact is that a government is a body politic; it has a will of its own; and it possesses powers and faculties to execute its own purposes. . . . A government executes its decisions by its own supreme authority."[19] In answer Calhoun exposed with rigorous logic Webster's evident confusion of terms, for a government was certainly no body politic, but the agent of the sovereign power which created it by establishing a constitution. Certainly the Constitution had been established as a fundamental law for the government created and for those subject to its authority, and yet that did not alter its character as a compact between the States ratifying it. The Constitution contained the precise words, "between the States." To the sovereign States, the Constitution was in the nature of a joint commission granting certain powers in trust to a common agent, the federal government. Webster himself, Calhoun cannily noted, had earlier called it the "constitutional compact"; and there was no real difficulty in regarding a compact as forming fundamental law. Here he appealed to the authority of Burlamaqui, and also cited instances of treaties of the United States and of compacts in the constitutional evolution of Great Britain. Further, if the Constitution were to be considered an executed contract, then it would be a "dead letter," having no binding effect. Moreover, the Virginia and Kentucky Resolutions of 1799, several of the ratifying conventions of the States, and many individuals prominent in public life had designated the Constitution as a compact.[20]

Several further difficulties confronted the case for State sovereignty. If the Constitution, laws of Congress, and treaties of the United States constituted the supreme law of the land to be enforced against contrary laws and constitutions of the States, then how could the States be sovereign? This was, of course, the best attack of Webster and the nationalists. Calhoun answered valiantly that this "supreme law of the land" was supreme only because it had been imposed on the federal government and its subjects and on the State government and its subjects by the highest law-making authority, the sovereign people, in each of the several States. Just as the sovereign had created the supreme law, so it might modify that law with the consent of the other parties to the compact, or abolish it so far as its own State was concerned. "The land" did not designate a single country, but rather the States of Virginia, New York, Massachusetts, etc., as the history of the phrase in the Federal Convention showed. The change from "several States and their citizens and inhabitants" to "land" had been made by the committee on style so that the law would extend to the territories as well as to the States; no other significance was to be attached to the change.[21] Moreover, as even Webster was forced to admit on contemplation of the Tenth Amendment, the federal Constitution and laws were supreme only within the sphere of the delegated powers; so also were the State constitution and laws supreme within the sphere of the reserved powers. Laws of Congress were supreme only if they were "in pursuance" of the Constitution, Calhoun noted; and Turnbull asserted the same was true of treaties. In case of conflict between federal law and State law, who was better to judge the dispute and change the one or the other than the high sovereign power that created them both? The fundamental principle of the superiority of the sovereign to the law it created must ever be observed.[22]

Certainly it was true that the Constitution provided for amendment on consent of three-fourths of the States; but that provision was really no evidence of loss of sovereignty by the States. The several States simply agreed for their mutual convenience and advantage to modify the exercise of their high sovereign power of creating constitutions as far as it related to the Constitution of the United States. But by this agreement they surely had no intention of divesting themselves of their sovereignty. "[It] is . . . clear that whatever modifications were made in the condition of the states under the present constitution, they extended only to the exercise of their powers by compact, and not to the sovereignty itself, and are such as sovereigns are competent to make; it being a conceded point that it is competent to them to stipulate to exercise their powers in a particular manner, or to abstain from their exercise altogether, or to delegate them to agents, without in any degree impairing sovereignty itself. . . ."[23] To clinch his argument, Calhoun insistently asserted that had so important a step as cession of sovereignty been intended, it must of necessity have been treated expressly in the Constitution. Silence could mean but maintenance of the *status quo* in this regard.[24]

Still other features of the existing system required some reconciliation with the views of the State sovereignty school. The question of the status of the new States, created out of a federal territory and admitted to the Union under the supervision of Congress, was an embarrassing one which Calhoun met courageously. Obviously they were not parties to the original compact, and apparently they were not sovereign any time before acquiring membership in the Union. However, Calhoun contended, these communities, on adopting constitutions under the sanction of an enabling act of Congress, actually became sovereign and independent States immediately and before admission into the federal Union. In administering the federal territory, the whole federal government was simply the joint agent of the member states of the Union; and the States had adopted the wise policy of permitting people in the territory to become independent, self-governing communities—sovereign States. Calhoun noted that the Constitution gave Congress power to admit to the Union only "states," not provinces. The facts that such a policy admitted of the legal possibility of a refusal to join the Union on the part of a State newly created out of territory, and that such refusal had never occurred, did not, Calhoun felt, appreciably weaken his position. Such a State simply acceded to the compact later than its original adoption by the member States.[25]

Calhoun and the State sovereignty school certainly regarded the theory of sovereignty as a statement of fact, and not as an ethical doctrine. They were describing what was, not what ought to be, the nature of the federal Union. Some political facts vitiated their case to some extent, and they were not insensible to them. Centralizing policies followed at various times jointly and severally by all three branches of the federal government tended to undermine the importance and dignity of the several States and to subvert their sovereignty. Certainly Jefferson, Madison, Taylor, Spencer Roane, Thomas Cooper, Turnbull, Calhoun, and others had decried and resisted "consolidation" for many years. Some of these centralizing policies had been abandoned or modified; but one that persisted, and one that was most important of all for its doctrinal implications, was the establishment and maintenance by the Supreme Court of the United States of its jurisdiction over the State courts on all constitutional federal questions. In the use of that jurisdiction in a number of important decisions, the work of the federal Supreme Court under the aegis of John Marshall had been highly nationalistic. Calhoun and his school admitted that the Supreme Court had the power to pass on constitutional questions, but not that it had the power to enforce its decisions on these questions upon the State courts in cases properly arising before the latter. The Court of Appeals of Virginia contended, in *Fairfax v. Hunter*, that such power was predicated upon the superiority of the federal judiciary over that of a State; whereas actually each was supreme in its own sphere. The two judiciaries were simply parts of coordinate governments, neither of which was superior. In a later case before the federal Supreme Court, *Cohens v. Virginia*, counsel for Virginia argued that it was contrary to the whole spirit of the Constitution to find only by unnecessary implication power of such consolidating effect.[26]

Calhoun could find no constitutional warrant for this assumption of power. The Judiciary Act of 1789 (providing for appeals from the State courts to the Supreme Court in cases involving federal questions) was unconstitutional, for its provision was not a necessary and proper means for carrying into execution any power or jurisdiction expressly given the Court by the Constitution. It was true that the jurisdiction of the Supreme Court extended to all cases arising under the Constitution and laws of the United States; but this jurisdiction extended only to "cases," a well-defined legal term. A case embraces only questions of a justiciable character, i. e., "questions in which the parties litigant are amenable to the process of the courts." There was no provision in the Constitution establishing that amenability on the part of the sovereign States; there was no clause in which the State governments had given their consent to cases involving questions of power between the federal government and the States. It was not to be implied from the clause extending Supreme Court jurisdiction to controversies to which the United States should be a party, for that only gave the consent of the federal government. There was less ground for such implication than that the States had given consent in cases of suits of individuals; and yet the States in the exercise of the sovereign power of amendment had rejected the latter construction.[27]

The decisions of the Supreme Court were not binding as between the United States and the several States, for neither could make the other defendant in any controversy between them. The Supreme Court must pass on the constitutionality of acts properly coming before it, just as the other branches of the federal government did; but so also must the courts and other branches of the governments of the States. Neither government was competent to enforce its decisions on the other; in cases of disagreement a mutual negative was the only legitimate result, save an appeal by either of the agents to the principal, the sovereign State. This mutual negative arose naturally out of the proper relationship between the federal government and the State government, according to old John Taylor; and Calhoun and the State sovereignty school heartily concurred in his conclusion. The claim, made by the nationalists, that the Supreme Court was the only body to judge in the last resort on questions of constitutional power, resulted from the mistaken conception that the federal government itself was a party to the federal compact. Hayne had fallen into this error in his great debate with Webster, and the latter had quickly made capital of it. But Calhoun corrected the position of his school, maintaining that an agent was not logically to be considered judge in the last resort of questions of power between itself and its principal. In the federal system such questions were political questions over which the court itself professed to have no jurisdiction. As in similar questions in the field of international law, declarations of sovereigns were conclusive on the courts. Moreover, it must be remembered that the Tenth Amendment to the Constitution protected the reserved powers not merely against invasion by Congress, but against the United States themselves, and against the whole federal government, including the judiciary as well as the other branches. Judge Harper, Governor Troup, and others reaffirmed Calhoun in this position.[28]

To Calhoun and his school, the work of Marshall and Story on the Supreme Court bench was certainly subversive of the sovereignty of the States; but their position was that the subversion was not yet completed. Any judgment on the location of sovereignty in the federal Union must take into account all of the political facts of the situation; and there were many facts indicative of the continuance of the sovereignty of the States. Calhoun enumerated the adoption of the Virginia and Kentucky Resolutions in 1798 and 1799, the decision of the Pennsylvania court in *Commonwealth v. Cobbett*, the successful defiance of the Supreme Court by the State of Georgia in the case of *Worcester v. Georgia*, and the successful nullification of the federal tariff law when his own State, South Carolina, put herself "on her sovereignty." Doctrines smacking strongly of State sovereignty had been expressed by New Englanders at the Hartford Convention during the War of 1812; and the personal liberty laws adopted by Northern States to aid runaway slaves constituted in effect nullification of federal law and even of part of the Constitution. In brief, although some encroachment had been made on the sovereignty of the States, that sovereignty remained the basic feature of the federal Union. If war were to carry the tendency to consolidation to its logical culmination, the process would be revolution. State sovereignty was the conservative position.[29]

C. NULLIFICATION AND SECESSION

Given his fundamental premise of State sovereignty, Calhoun's corollaries of nullification and secession followed with inexorable logic. In framing the Constitution, the Founding Fathers had, in the first place, divided the powers of government into the delegated and the reserved, the former to be exercised by the common government, the latter to be exercised by the governments of the States or retained by the people of the States. Secondly, this division of power was not to be changed save by amendments adopted by three-fourths of the States, the people of the States having agreed to modify the exercise of their sovereignty to that extent. Change in the division of powers was certainly not within the competence of the federal government, the mere agent of the sovereign States. Dispute as to the line of division between the federal government and a State government should properly result in a mutual negative, for each stood in the same relation to the sovereign State. However, if any member of the Union discerned an invasion of the reserved powers of the States on the part of the federal government, a palpable and dangerous infraction of the Constitution itself, it could assert its sovereignty and declare the action of the federal government null and void in so far as it affected the State itself or the citizens thereof. To act in its sovereign capacity, the State should hold a convention, which could decide whether the acts in question were unconstitutional. "The convention will then determine in what manner they ought to be declared null and void within the limits of the state; which solemn declaration . . . would be obligatory not only on her own citizens, but on the General Government itself; and thus place the violated rights of the State under the shield of the Constitution."[30] The nullification could be carried into practical effect through subsidiary legislation by the State legislature and through refusal of the State courts to send up a copy of the record to the federal courts in pertinent cases.[31]

This power of nullification, or interposition, by a State rested no more on mere inference than the Supreme Court's power of judicial review, which was not to be found in the written Constitution. It was a power reserved to the States, for certainly it had not been delegated or prohibited; and it was always within the competence of a sovereign to check unauthorized acts of its agent. With regard to the relation of the nullifying State to the other members of the Union, it was surely within the power of any of the States, Calhoun contended, to judge as to when the compact had been violated. This followed from the nature of any compact between equals over whom there was no superior competent to settle disputes. The case of a treaty between two sovereigns was strictly analogous. "No answer has ever been attempted," agreed Judge Harper, "to the common argument that if individuals enter into a compact, and have no arbiter, or superior authority, to interpret it for them, each must decide on its own interpretation, so far as respects the government of his own conduct; and if independent and sovereign states form a compact, each, not only may, but must of necessity determine the meaning of the compact, so far as it is to be carried into effect by itself, or within its own territory."[32] If a

State, through mistaken judgment or bad faith, were to nullify a law clearly and generally understood, when the constitutional compact was made, to be within federal competence, it would be guilty of a breach of moral obligation, Calhoun granted; but it would not be violating any law. For in the nature of things the States could not be under the dominion of law; being sovereign, they could violate no law.[33]

Calhoun and his school appealed to the Virginia and Kentucky Resolutions of 1798 and 1799 and to Madison's Report to the Virginia Legislature for support of their doctrine. The Kentucky Resolutions declared:

As in all other cases of compact among parties having no common judge, each party has an equal right to judge for itself, as well of infractions as of the mode and measure of redress. . . .

*   *   *

That the several states who formed that instrument being sovereign and independent, have the unquestionable right to judge of the infraction; and, that a nullification by those sovereignties of all unauthorized acts done under color of that instrument is the rightful remedy.[34]

Madison denied that either he or Virginia had intended to sanction anything like the doctrines of Calhoun, to which Calhoun replied that surely the language of the Virginia Resolutions, as strong as that of the Kentucky Resolutions save for the use of the word "nullification," was something more than a mere assertion of the right to protest and remonstrate. The latter right none denied, and it surely called for no such extraordinary elaboration. Further, Calhoun argued that the framers of the Constitution gave the States implicit sanction for the exercise of independent judgment of their obligations under the Constitution. For the Federal Convention rejected several proposals that would have given the federal government power to prevent such a State veto on its actions. The fact that these measures "were proposed and so urged, proves conclusively that it was believed, even by the most distinguished members of the national party, that the former had no right to enforce its measures against the latter, where they disagreed as to the extent of their respective powers—without some express provision to that effect; while the refusal of the convention to adopt any such provision, under the circumstances, proves equally conclusively that it was opposed to the delegation of such powers to the government, or any of its departments, legislative, executive, or judicial, in any form whatsoever."[35]

When a State presumed to nullify an act of the federal government, of course, three-fourths of the States, according to the constitutional agreement, might proceed by amendment of the compact to grant the disputed power to the federal government. If the amendment were within the limits of the amending power, the interposing State would at least be under the obligation of good faith to acquiesce. But, if the amendment were inconsistent with the character of the constitutional system and the ends for which it was established, the State would be entirely free to secede from the federal Union. "To refuse acquiescence, would be tantamount to secession; and place it as entirely in the relation of a foreign state to the other states, as would a positive act of secession. That a state, as a party to the constitutional compact, has the right to secede—acting in the same capacity in which it ratified the constitution—cannot with any show of reason be denied by any one who regards the constitution as a compact. . . ."[36] Nullification itself, however, was not secession; rather it was a means of conserving the Union in its original character. Secession was a withdrawal from an association of partners, whereas nullification was an assertion by a principal to an agent. Secession dissolved an association; nullification simply compelled an agent to fulfill the objects of an association, and thereby exercised a preservative influence. Both rested, however, on the firm foundation of State sovereignty.[37]

To Jefferson Davis and Alexander Stephens, who lived through the War between the States, the establishment of the legitimacy of secession was perhaps of more direct interest than to Calhoun. Consequently, they devoted more attention to it, although they followed generally the argument of their leader. Davis averred that the right of secession followed from the compact nature of the Constitution and the resulting partnership nature of the Union; precedent for it was seen in the dissolution of the old Confederation on the establishment of the new government in 1789. Secondly, he recognized secession as following as a matter of course from the sovereignty of the States. "Why was so obvious an attribute of sovereignty not expressly renounced if it was intended to surrender it?" The right of secession might be viewed as one of the reserved powers of the States, since it was neither delegated to the federal government nor denied to the States. Davis also joined Calhoun in finding support for the right in the statements of the ratifying conventions in Virginia, New York, and Rhode Island, that the State reserved the right to resume any of the delegated powers that might be abused. The other States recognized the principle on accepting these qualified ratifications. Moreover, the framers of the Constitution deliberately rejected a proposal for the coercion of the States; hence the federal government had no power to prevent secession. Secession was a legitimate right of the States, not a matter of revolution.[38]

Webster and the other champions of the national

cause believed the theory of nullification was anarchical doctrine. To recognize nullification as a constitutional principle, Webster declared, would be to make of the fundamental law of the Union "a rope of sand." Each State, in effect, would be given the power of initiating amendments; and jealous rivalry among the States would destroy the Union. This surely was directly contrary to the purpose of establishing the Constitution. In reply, Calhoun belittled prophecies of the dire results of nullification. The power was not one of abrogation of the Constitution, but of protection against another kind of destruction—consolidation. That it would be abused was improbable, because of the deliberateness of the mode of procedure, the pressure of public opinion, and the unlikelihood of provocation by the general government. Moreover, popular inertia would protect the federal government against undue decimation of its powers, for the people of a State would have to be aroused to act in their sovereign capacity in bringing about nullification.[39]

Frankly admitting, however, that recognition and use of nullification might mean loss of power and importance to the central government of the Union, Calhoun embraced the principle of decentralization and cherished it as superior to centralization. If the original nature of the Union must change, or if risk of such change must be assumed, consolidation, a proven danger, must be guarded against at all costs, even to the extent of risking decentralization. The latter would certainly incur less of the evils of anarchy than the former would of the ills of despotism. There was really little danger of anarchy anyway, according to Calhoun, for such a state was foreign to the nature of man. The issue was not of government or anarchy, but of what kind of government. Moreover, both from the general nature of the powers of the Union and from the method provided for amendment of the Constitution, Cal-

houn reasoned that the framers of the Constitution believed that no more power should be exercised by the
Union than that in which it was continuously supported
by three-fourths of the States. The people of the States
did not know, at the time when the Constitution was
framed, how the novel division of powers would work, and
frankly recognized it as an experiment. Conflict was expected, but the source was unknown; consequently, the
framers had to leave it to time and experience to reveal
the danger and furnish the remedy. The danger had appeared in consolidation for the ruthless oppression of minority rights; and nullification was the remedy most in
accord with the spirit of the Constitution. The only alternatives to nullification were consolidation or dissolution,
the danger of the latter being more real without than with
the recognition of nullification. In a word, as Calhoun affirmed many times, nullification was the conservative principle of the constitutional Union.[40]

If nullification were not to be recognized, the States
might well resume the powers which they had only delegated, and not surrendered. Several States, on ratifying the
Constitution, had asserted, and others had recognized,
their right to resume powers delegated to the federal government. If, on the other hand, nullification were to be
recognized, the division of powers would be provided with
a constitutional mechanism for its preservation. Just as the
authors of the *Federalist* papers had contended that something more than parchment barriers was requisite for the
maintenance of the separation of powers, so Calhoun
championed nullification as requisite to make real the
paper division of power. There would result from its
utilization a strong governmental system soundly ground-
ed in confidence; and there would be insured the safety
and respectability of the Union abroad and peace and harmony at home.[41]

D. INFLUENCE IN GERMANY

The American controversy over the location of sovereignty in a federal system found an interesting counterpart a generation later in Germany. There the antagonists were not so closely involved in the issues of practical politics. After the abortive culmination of the liberal movement in the Frankfort parliament in 1848,[42] the discussion moved on an academic plane, arising, as it did, out of the varying answers of scholars to the question of the location of sovereignty in the German federations of the latter half of the nineteenth century. The movement for the unification of Germany, under the guiding genius of Bismarck, supplanted the weak two-headed Confederation of 1815 with the North German Confederation in 1867, and the latter in turn with the new larger Reich of 1871. Writing earlier with an apparent interest in showing the importance of the political union of German states, Georg Waitz described the old German confederation as a *Bundesstaat,* a form characterized by divided sovereignty. He derived his ideas, in part at least, from the *Federalist* papers and from De Tocqueville's description of the American system. On the other hand, Max von Seydel, although he wrote after stronger unions had replaced the system Waitz had described, was the champion of indivisible sovereignty and of the sovereignty of the States in the German Reich. Von Seydel was certainly indebted to Calhoun for much of his thought on the subject; he had read much of Calhoun's work, cited and quoted from him with approval, and set forth the same doctrines, modified only as far as was necessary to meet the different facts of the German situation. Pufendorf may very well have been, as has been claimed, the German parent of Von Seydel's doctrine, but Pufendorf's influence was surely not so direct and apparent as that of Calhoun.[43]

Waitz, in his *Das Wesen des Bundesstaats,* which first appeared in 1853, found between the confederacy and the national, or unitary, state (*Staatenreich*) an intermediate form, the *Bundesstaat.* Its distinguishing characteristic was that sovereignty pertained not to the individual members of the union, nor to the union as a unit, but to both, the collective state and the individual states, "each within its own sphere." One of the prime requirements of a state was independence of every foreign power. In the *Bundesstaat* the collective state and the individual member states each had its special sphere of authority and its separate political organization; but each within its special sphere was as independent as the other. Each had a narrower sphere than the unitary state, and yet within that sphere its authority was not inferior (*schlechter*). This independence was called sovereignty. In the *Bundesstaat* only the extent and not the content of sovereignty was limited. This form was the ideal one where the fulfillment of a part of the political life of a nation required united action and the rest was better met by the separate activity of the various local units. The German Reich, he felt sure, was a *Bundesstaat,* and there was nothing in the concept of monarchy that stood in contradiction to the essence of that form.[44]

Von Seydel attacked Waitz' position directly by declaring the content of sovereignty to be precisely that it had no limits on its extent. He agreed with Waitz that the concept of a state included the idea of independence of all foreign power. But it should also be recognized that the state was the highest form of human society in the sense of possessing the superior will that must prevail over the wills of all other human associations within the same area. Not even the church paralleled the state in this respect, for in all external (as opposed to spiritual or inward) matters it was subject to the state. Conceptually it was necessary that the will of the state be single and indivisible, because where it was divided it lost its essence. Two highest wills repealed one another, and were therefore conceptually impossible. The highest and indivisible will was the power of the state, or sovereignty. This conception of sovereignty had the highest legal justification in logical necessity. Waitz correctly described sovereignty as independence from any higher power and asserted that each true state must be sovereign. But he failed to recognize sovereignty as the highest power in the state; and in that failure lay the inadequacy of his theory of federalism. Waitz' *Bundesstaatsbegriff* divided sovereignty by admitting a twofold supreme authority in each member state of the union, and limited sovereignty in giving to the single states, as to the collective state, only a certain number of the rights of supremacy. In a word, it contravened the two essential elements of sovereignty: indivisibility and illimitability.[45]

Von Seydel agreed with Calhoun that sovereignty knew no kinds or degrees. There was no such thing as divided, relative, or fragmentary sovereignty. Certainly various rights of sovereignty might be exercised by different agencies established for the purpose by the sovereign. But no one of these rights was to be identified with sovereignty, nor was even the sum of the individual rights of sovereignty to be so identified. Sovereignty was rather the single superior will which disposed of the individual rights, determined their exercise or their restraint, and transferred or withdrew them at discretion. Conceptually it was all the same whether this will arose from the working together of individual wills of the whole people, or of several people, or from the will of a single person.[46]

Having thus defined sovereignty and made it the indispensable and distinguishing mark of the state, Von

Seydel could well deny the possibility and logical tenability of the *Bundesstaat*. The attempt to conceive such a union, in which a single large state existed in the territory occupied at the same time by several small member states, logically depended upon either divided sovereignty or the concept of the non-sovereign state. Both of these were already excluded by the premises. Any given political system must be either a single state or a federation of several states. There was no middle ground. This position was essentially that of Calhoun, whose middle form, the federal union, was not an intermediate state-form, but a new kind of federation superior to older ones because of the employment of a stronger central agency. To both Calhoun and Von Seydel, the central agency was stronger because the member states as sovereigns had transferred to it some rights to be exercised in common even upon individuals within the states. The federal union or *staatsrechtliche Bund* came into being only when the sovereign member states made the content of the treaty of union between them at the same time law within the states. Only in this way could subjects be bound to obedience to the authority of the central agency. In this respect the constitution of the federal union differed from that of the older federation which rested solely on a treaty basis. Von Seydel further believed that the difference in political organization between the two forms was wider if princely government was involved. The old kind of federation might well permit a single monarch to exercise the external powers of sovereignty; but the federal union required, he argued, an assembly representative of the member states for the purpose. To Von Seydel, the German Reich was just such a monarchical *staatsrechtliche Bund* and the United States of America was a republican variety of the same federal form.[47]

It is interesting to find that despite his agreement with Calhoun on sovereignty and on the nature of a federal union, Von Seydel would not follow him to the doctrines of nullification or secession. He would not support these rights for the member states of either the German or the American system, both of which he recognized as federal unions and not as single states. Such rights, he continued, tend toward a dissolution of the organs of the union (*Bundesgewalt*) by organs of the member states. To avoid such dissolution had been the very purpose of the formation of the union in the first instance.[48] In such fashion Von Seydel presented the anomalous spectacle of throwing away in practical application the most significant part of his abstract doctrine. For he attempted to limit that which he had declared illimitable. To him, sovereignty was supreme legal authority, indivisible and illimitable, and in the federal union sovereignty was located in the member states; yet a member state could not withdraw from the union! He would have suffered short shrift at the hands of Calhoun.[49]

Later students of the German constitutional system accepted Von Seydel's view of sovereignty as an indivisible entity; and in this respect he completely supplanted Waitz in scholarly opinion. But none of these later students accepted Von Seydel's doctrine of the sovereignty of the member states in the union; all of them held that the power and importance of the German Reich fell nothing short of sovereignty. Yet most of them, under the influence of historical background and traditional usage, were unwilling to deny the statehood of the members of the union. Phillip Zorn, alone among Germans of the nineteenth century, attacked the view that the political subdivisions of the Reich were states. In this, Zorn shared Von Seydel's view of sovereignty as the indispensable criterion of the state. They were at one in abstract doctrine, although entirely opposed in their view of the particular nature of the German Reich.[50]

Other critics of Von Seydel, however, believing in the sovereignty of the Reich, and being unwilling to deprive the members of the Reich of the appellation "state", attempted variously to conceive a non-sovereign state. They proposed solving their dilemma by sustaining the old concept of the *Bundesstaat,* corrected to be sure, of its old mistakes. On analysis of the proposed criteria, Von Seydel found none of them adequate, not even the criteria offered by Georg Meyer, Paul Laband, and Jellinek. He dismissed as of minor importance the attempts of H. Rosin and S. Brie to distinguish between the sovereign state and the non-sovereign state by the different ends or goals of their activity. The efforts of Laband and Jellinek were of more significance. Laband found a criterion which, although less than sovereignty, distinguished a state from a mere province in "own right of rulership" (*offentlichrechtliche Herrschaft*). He contended that the non-sovereign state had the authority—by virtue of its own right and not on the basis of any delegation—to establish binding legal norms, to command free persons, and to compel obedience. This, asserted Von Seydel, included a contradiction within itself, for such authority must come from somewhere. It did come from the sovereign. Von Seydel pointed out that Laband himself confirmed this view when he declared that this "own right of rulership" must be exercised only within the limits which the sovereign had established. Von Seydel continued: "Every public power in the state must be able to point to the legal title of its investment, and for all these powers, high or low, there is only one highest end (*Schluss*), over which no further legal power is conceivable, and that is sovereignty. This latter power is *sui generis;* all others are dissimilar and show the common mark that they are subject to it. Whether it rests upon institution, forbearance (*Belassung*), or indulgence is of minor significance as compared with this deciding circumstance."[51]

Georg Jellinek, in his later position, accepted a criterion for the state practically identical with that of Laband. It was legally uncontrollable "own right" (*eigene Rechte*) to issue binding commands. But he tried to strengthen the case for the non-sovereign state by re-defining sovereignty as obligability only through one's own will. Von Seydel refuted the definition. Legal obligability (*Verpflichtbarkeit*), he declared, could exist only within a legal order, for only within a legal order was the obligation compulsory. The sovereign might bind itself, but it could also remove the bond at will. The distinctive mark of the sovereign was not that it might bind itself, but rather that it was in a position to oblige others over whom it ruled. "The sovereign as lawgiver is not legally obligable, because it creates and destroys the legal order; and that is the criterion of its sovereignty."[52]

In short, Von Seydel felt that the attempt to find a valid criterion for the non-sovereign state a fruitless undertaking. The measure of independence or autonomy which a state allowed its administrative districts could hardly serve as a basis for a new public-law concept. And with the failure of such attempt must fall also the concept of the *Bundesstaat*. With the appearance of new political systems in 1789, 1848, and 1871, the concept was created as a matter of convenience, for it permitted dispensing at once with a troublesome problem—the determination of whether the new systems remained federations or constituted new single states. The *Bundesstaatsbegriff* possessed the requisite elasticity only at the cost of obscurity and inconsistency. It could not provide a sharp distinction between state and part of a state. It lacked the scientific essential of definiteness and consequently was juristically untenable. The basic premises upon which Von Seydel reached this conclusion he shared with Calhoun, and probably derived them from him.

NOTES

1. Pufendorf stuck fairly consistently to the idea of the unity of sovereignty; but in some passages he wrote of "parts of sovereignty." He also viewed sovereignty as limited by the laws of nature, by custom, and by compact. However, in regard to these limitations, his position was to a great extent like that of Bodin: there was no human authority to enforce them. See Samuel L. Pufendorf, *The Law of Nature and of Nations*, 4th ed. (London, 1729), pp. 660, 661, 683, 624, and Bk. VIII, Ch. VI.
2. Pufendorf, *Law of Nature and of Nations*, Bk. VII, Chs. III-VI; Emmerich de Vattel, *The Law of Nations* (Northampton, Mass., 1820), pp. 57-59, 72-73; Montesquieu, *The Spirit of the Laws*, 2 vols., 11th ed. (London, 1777), Vol. I, Bk. IX, pp. 134-137.
3. See A. C. McLaughlin, *Constitutional History of the United States* (New York, 1935), pp. 43 ff., 70-73, 80-81, 85.
4. Madison, *The Federalist*, No. 39; Madison's remarks in the Virginia ratifying convention, J. Eliot, ed., *Debates in the Several State Conventions on the Adoption of the Federal Constitution*, 5 vols., 2nd ed. (Philadelphia, 1888), Vol. III, pp. 94-95; Calhoun, *Works*, Vol. I, p. 163. Alexander H. Stephens also claimed that the American federal system was a new form; it was neither a *Bundesstaat* nor a *Staatenbund*, although quite close to the latter form. See his *Constitutional View of the War between the States*, 2 vols. (Philadelphia, 1868-1870), Vol. II, pp. 18-21. Jefferson Davis apparently saw little difference between "federal republic" and "confederacy." Davis, *Rise and Fall of*

the *Confederate Government,* 2 vols. (New York, 1881), Vol. I, p. 145.

5. Calhoun, *Works,* Vol. I, pp. 156, 162-166; Vol. II, pp. 289-290.

6. *Works,* Vol. I, pp. 111, 163-167, 187, 197; Vol. II, pp. 289-293.

7. *Works,* Vol. I, pp. 162-166.

8. See *supra., Ch.* VI, Sec. B. Elliot was certainly correct when he wrote: "Since Calhoun denies the possibility of a non-sovereign state, he denies thereby the possibility generally of a *Bundesstaat,* the only logical foundation of which lies in the existence of a non-sovereign state." Elliott, "Die Staatslehre John C. Calhouns," *Staats-und volkerrechtliche Abhandlungen,* Vol. IV, no. 2 (1903), p. 40. See also C. E. Merriam *History of the Theory of Sovereignty Since Rousseau* (New York, 1900), p. 181.

9. Calhoun, *Works,* Vol. IV, pp. 80-81.

10. *Ibid.,* Vol. I, pp. 162, 186, 187-188, 200-207, 276; Vol. II, pp. 291-293; Vol. III ,pp. 30-31; Vol. IV, pp. 20-21; Vol. VI, pp. 73-74, 107, 112, 150. Cf. Stephens, *Constitutional View of the War between the States,* Vol. II, pp. 18-21; Davis, *Rise and Fall of the Confederate Government,* Vol. I, pp. 86-113.

11. Calhoun, *Works,* Vol. VI, pp. 147-148.

12. *Ibid.,* Vol. I, pp. 111-145; Vol. II, pp. 262-309; Vol. VI, pp. 106-112, 141-154. This was the conclusion, or the assumption, of the entire State sovereignty school. See the opinions of Justice Roger B. Taney in *Abelman v. Booth* (21 Howard 506) and *Dred Scott v. Sandford* (19 Howard 393). See also Abel P. Upshur, *A Brief Enquiry into the True Nature and Character of our Federal Government* (Philadelphia, 1863), reprint from the Petersburg edition of 1840; Stephens, *Constitution View of the War between the States, passim;* Davis, *Rise and Fall of the Confederate Government,* Vol. I, pt. II; Robert J. Turnbull, *The Crisis* (Charleston, 1827), especially pp. 16-17, 97-100.

13. Upshur, *True Nature and Character of Federal Government,* pp. 9-48; Story, *Commentaries on the Constitution of the United States,* 2 vols., 4th ed. (Boston,

1873), Vol. I, pp. 147-156. A logical extension of Story's line of reasoning in this regard found expression later in Lincoln's message to Congress in 1861, in which Lincoln declared that the Union was older than any of the States, and, in fact, created them as States. They had not, and never had, any political status save as members of the Union. Lincoln, *Complete Works*, 2 vols. (New York, 1902), Vol. II, p. 62.

14. Opinion of Jay in *Chisolm v. Georgia* (4 Dallas 419); Marshall in *McCulloch v. Maryland* (4 Wheaton 316) and in *Cohens v. Virginia* (6 Wheaton 264); Story in *Martin v. Hunter's Lessee* (1 Wheaton 304); Calhoun, *Works*, Vol. I, pp. 189-190, 193, 200-201; Vol. VI, pp. 107-108; Davis, *Rise and Fall of the Confederate Government*, Vol. I, pp. 114-134. Later Justice Chase in *Texas v. White* (7 Wallace 700) followed the nationalistic opinions with his doctrine of the "indestructible union" of "indestructible states."

15. Calhoun, *Works*, Vol. II, pp. 231-232.

17. Webster, *Speech in Reply to Hayne*, pamphlet (Washington, 1830), pp. 61-62; Webster, *Works*, 6 vols., 6th ed. (Boston, 1853), Vol. III, pp. 471-477; Calhoun, *Works*, Vol. VI, pp. 109, 149; Vol. I, pp. 128, 133; Vol. II, pp. 282-284. See also Upshur, *True Nature and Character of Federal Government*, pp. 50-61; Davis, *Rise and Fall of the Confederate Government*, Vol I., p. 153.

18. Story, *Commentaries on the Constitution*, Vol. I, p. 244. Also see pp. 243-263.

19. Webster, *Works*, Vol. III, p. 467. See also pp. 457-459, 464, 465-469.

20. Calhoun, *Works*, Vol. II, pp. 267-280, 283-284; Vol. I, pp. 248-251. Stephens claimed that no President from Jefferson to the time of Lincoln rejected the view of the Constitution as a compact. Also Stephens noted that Webster later in a speech in 1851 returned to the compact view of the Constitution. Stephens, *Constitutional View of the War between the States*, Vol. I. pp. 404-405, 441-446. See also Davis, *Rise and Fall of the Confederate Government*, Vol. I, pp. 134-140; E. B. Bryan, *The Rightful Remedy* (Charleston, 1850), pp. 148,

150; M. R. H. Garnett, *The Union, Past and Future,* pamphlet 4th ed. (Charleston, 1850), pp. 3-4.

21. Calhoun was correct as to the history of the verbal changes in the phrase, whatever may be made of his interpretation of motives. See "Debates in the Federal Convention of 1787 as reported by James Madison," *Formation of Union Document,* 69th Congress, 1st session, House Document 398, pp. 206-207, 391-392, 476, 603, 712.

22. Calhoun, *Works,* Vol. I, pp. 252-257; Vol. II, pp. 294-295, 381; Turnbull. *The Crisis,* p. 77; Story, *Commentaries,* pp. 119-133; Webster, *Reply to Hayne,* pp. 76-77, 94.

23. Calhoun, *Works,* Vol. II, p. 292.

24 *Works,* Vol. I, pp. 139-140, 274-275, 295; Vol. II, pp. 281-282. Calhoun seemed to assume that the States were at least competent to cede their sovereignty. However, Thomas Cooper, his fellow Carolinian, believed that no state or nation could alienate its sovereignty, for such was a suicidal act. Thomas Cooper, *Consolidation* 2nd ed. (Columbia, 1830), p. 35.

25. Calhoun, *Works,* Vol. II, pp. 586-596; Vol. IV, pp. 569-570.

26. *Fairfax v. Hunter* (14 Munford 1); see also Charles Warren, *The Supreme Court in United States History,* 3 vols. (Boston, 1922), Vol. II, pp. 8-9, for argument of counsel in *Cohens v. Virginia.*

27. Calhoun, *Works,* Vol. I, pp. 259-263, 320-326; Vol. II, pp. 201-204, 294-300.

28. Calhoun, *Works,* Vol. I, pp. 264-267; Vol. II, pp. 201- 204; Vol. VI, pp. 70, 73-74; Hayne, *Second Speech in Reply to Webster,* pamphlet (Washington, 1830), pp. 708; Webster, *Reply to Hayne,* p. 93; Harper, *Speech on Nullification,* pamphlet (Charleston, 1832), pp. 3-4; G. M. Troup, *Letter of the Rights of the States,* pamphlet (Milledgeville, 1834), p. 5.

29. Calhoun, *Works,* Vol. I, pp. 353-358, 364-367, 380; Vol. II, pp. 237, 614; Vol. II, pp. 272, 394; Vol. IV, p. 572; Vol. VI, p. 60; Calhoun, *Correspondence,* p. 468; Spencer Roane, "The Rights of the States and of the People," *Branch Historical Papers* 2:116-118; Hayne,

"Speech on Mr. Foot's Resolution," *Register of Debates in Congress,* 21st Congress, 1st session, Vol. VI, p. 55; Turnbull, *Oration before State Rights and Free Trade Party,* pamphlet (Charleston, 1832); Davis, *Rise and Fall of the Confederate Government,* pp. 144-145.
30. Calhoun, *Works,* Vol. VI, p. 45.
31. *Ibid.,* Vol. VI, pp. 34-44, 162-163; Vol. I, pp. 279-280; Vol. II, pp. 200, 221-222, 262-263. See also James Hamilton, Jr., *Speech on the Tariff and the Constitutional Means of Redressing Its Evils,* pamphlet (Charleston, 1828), pp. 15-20; Cooper, *Consolidation,* pp. 31-37; Harper, *Speech on Nullification,* pp. 7-10; Upshur, *True Nature and Character of Our Federal Government,* pp. 62-71; Stephens. *Constutional View of the War between the States,* Vol. I, pp. 389-476. Governor Troup was one of those who stoutly affirmed the sovereignty of the States, but who nevertheless refused to support nullification, seeing no real recourse save secession. Troup, *Letter on the Rights of the States,* pp. 2-5.
32. Harper, *Speech on Nullification,* p. 3.
33. *Works,* Vol. VI, pp. 46-52; Vol. I, pp. 277-278; Vol. II, p. 293.
34. *The Virginia and Kentucky Resolutions of 1798-'99; Jefferson's Original Draft Thereof; Madison's Report; Calhoun's Address; Resolutions of the Several States in Relation to States Rights,* pamphlet (Washington, 1832), pp. 15-16, 20.
35. Calhoun, *Works,* Vol. I, pp. 244-246, 267; Vol. II, p. 300; Vol. VI, pp. 154-155. For the proposals in the Federal Convention to adopt a federal negative on State laws, see "Debates in the Federal Convention of 1787 as reported by James Madison," pp. 130-131, 174-178, 201, 208, 211, 235, 242, 390-391.
36. *Works,* Vol. I, pp. 300-301.
37. *Ibid.,* Vol. VI, pp, 168-172. To Harper, nullification and secession were legal rights, not merely moral ones; they were not disguises for revolution. Harper, *Speech on Nullification,* pp. 2-7. Upshur distinguished between nullification and secession: "The nullifier contends only

for the right of a state to prevent the constitution from being violated by the general government, and not for the right either to repeal, abrogate, or suspend it. The seceder insists only that a state is competent to withdraw from the Union whenever it pleases; but does not assert that in so doing it can repeal, or abrogate, or suspend the constitution, as to the other states." Upshur, *True Nature and Character of Our Federal Government*, p. 66. Wiliam Seal Carpenter appears to have assumed *sub silentio* the complete validity of the nationalist argument on the location of sovereignty when he declared that his (Calhoun's) doctrine of secession involved a fatal confusion of ideas. "He sought nothing less than the establishment of the power of revolution as a constitutional right," Carpenter asserted. On the contrary, given the sovereignty of the States, for which Calhoun made a very strong case, secession certainly was not revolution; it was a right derived not from the Constitution, but from legal supremacy of the States over the Constitution. See Carpenter, *Development of American Political Thought* (Princeton, 1930), pp. 148-149.

38. Davis, *Rise and Fall of the Confederate Government*, pp. 168-184; Davis, Message to Confederate Congress, Jan. 12, 1863, *Messages and Papers of the Confederacy,*, 2 vols. (Nashville, 1905), Vol. I, pp. 278-279; Stephens, *Constitutional View of the War between the States*, Vol. I, pp. 477-544; Troup, *Letter on the Rights of the States*, pp. 8-9, 15-16. Yancey, Rhett, and other secessionists, it should be noted, occasionally spoke of secession as revolution. See W. G. Brown, *The Lower South in American History* (New York, 1903), Ch. II; L. A. White, *Robert Barnwell Rhett: Father of Secession* (New York and London, 1931), pp. 17, 24, 44-45.

39. Calhoun, *Works*, Vol. I, pp. 308-311; Vol. II, pp. 304-305; Vol. VI, pp. 46-52.

40. *Works*, Vol. I, pp. 238-239, 248-250, 314; Vol. II, pp. 296-297; Vol. V, p. 160.

41. *Works*, Vol. I, pp. 310-311; Vol. VI, pp. 140-141.

42. Some of the members of the Frankfort parliament seemed to have shown interest in Calhoun's suggestions

as to constitutional union for Germany made in a letter to Baron von Gerolt, Prussian Minister—resident in Washington. Calhoun found less homogeneity there than in the American States and advised against complete political unity for Germany. Believing that the proposed constitution gave too much power to the central government, he recommended only some strengthening of the old German Confederation. See Calhoun, "Letter to Baron von Gerolt, May 28, 1848," *American Historical Review* 40:477-478; and the prefatory note by M. E. Curti, *Ibid*, 40:476.

43. Von Seydel, "Der Bundesstaatsbegriff," *Staatsrechtliche und politische Abhandlungen* (Freiburg and Leipzig, 1893), pp. 15, 27-30, 38-40; *Commentar zur Verfassungsurkunde fur das deutsche Reich* (Freiburg and Leipzig, 1897), pp. 3, 20; "Der Bundesgedanke und der Staatsgedanke, in Deutschen Reiche," *Staatsrechtliche und politische Abhandlungen* (Freiberg and Leipzig, 1893), pp. 93, 95-96; "Verfassung und Verfassungsgeschichte der Vereinigten Staaten von America," *Staatsrechtliche und politische Abhandlungen*, Neue Folge (Tubingen and Leipzig, 1902), pp. 47-51. Hugo Preuss claimed that Pufendorf had some influence on Von Seydel. See Rupert Emerson, *State and Sovereignty in Modern Germany* (New Haven, 1928), p. 97. Professor Anton Dryoff of the University of Munich expressed the opinion that Von Seydel was not directly influenced by Calhoun's theory, and that the similarity of the two is rather due to similar historical developments in Germany and the United States. Letter to present writer of Professor Karl Loewenstein, Yale University, Oct. 18, 1935.

44. Waitz, "Das Wesen des Bundesstaats," *Grundzuge der Politik nelst einzelen Ausfuhrungen* (Kiel, 1862), pp. 162-170, 173-185, 209-216.

45. Von Seydel, "Der Bundesstaatsbergriff," pp. 4-6, 18-21; *Commentar*, pp. 3-4.

46. Von Seydel, "Der Bundesstaatsbegriff," pp. 5, 7, 9-10, 15.

47. Von Seydel, "Der Bundesstaatsbegriff," pp. 15, 18-21; *Commentar*, pp. 5-6. In distinguishing a kind of

federation in which the treaty of union between the states was also made binding upon individuals within the states, Von Seydel was going beyond Pufendorf's treatment of confederation to an idea already set forth by Calhoun. See Von Seydel, *Commentar*, p. 5; Calhoun, *Works*, Vol. I, pp. 156, 162-166; Vol. II pp. 292-293.

48. Von Seydel, "Der Bundesstaatsbegriff," pp. 95-97; "Verfassung und Verfassungsgeschicte der Vereinigten Staaten von Amerika," pp. 50-51.

49. Even after having agreed with Calhoun that the fact of amendment of the Constitution by three-fourths of the member States constituted no abrogation of the sovereignty of the States in the American Union. (*Commentar*, p. 20), Von Seydel wrote: "Nullification and secession do not suit the constitutional character, not merely of the state, but of a single proper federation. The mistake in the argument of the ingenious Calhoun lay in his belief that he might, without any direct support in the Constitution itself, derive such destructive rights as nullification and secession from the nature of the federation." Von Seydel, "Verfassung und Verfassungsgeschicte der Vereinigten Staaten von Amerika," p. 51.

50. Von Seydel, *Commentar*, p. 10. See also Emerson, *State and Sovereignty in Modern Germany*, pp. 112-113.

51. Von Seydel, *Commentar*, p. 9. See also *Ibid.*, pp. 7-9; Paul Laband, *Deutsches Reichsstaatsrecht* (Tubingen, 1907) ; Emerson, *State and Sovereignty in Modern Germany*, pp. 101-103, 103-106. An interesting similarity is to be found between Laband's conception of a nonsovereign state based upon "own right of rulership" and John Marshall's earlier view of the status of American Indian nations. Marshall declared: ". . . They are or may be deemed a state, though not a sovereign state, at least while they occupy a country within our limits . . . Their right of personal self-government has never been taken from them. . . ." *Cherokee Nation v. Georgia*, 8 *Law Ed.* 34 (1831).

52. Von Seydel, *Commentar*, pp. 9-10; Jellinek's earlier

view that the non-sovereign state was the creature of the sovereign center in the Reich, created by auto-limitation of the sovereign, is to be found in his *Die Lehre von den Staatenverbindungen* (Berlin, 1882); his later view is in his *Allgemeine Staatslehre* (Berlin, 1905), more especially pp. 490-497 and Ch. XXI.

8

Defense of Slavery

A. RACIAL INEQUALITY

IN THE CONTROVERSY over the nature of the federal Union, the cause of State sovereignty and its logical corollaries of nullification and secession provided for Calhoun and other Southerners a first line of defense for the institution of slavery. For the possession by the States of a sure check on the actions of the federal government, coupled with general recognition of the incompetence of the federal authority to deal with that institution, would leave slavery to the tender care of the States within which it existed. The Constitution recognized that it was a matter within the jurisdiction of the States. However, even in the early years of the constitutional Union, slavery itself required some justification for its continued existence to satisfy the doubtful within the slave States, if not to meet the criticisms of individuals in the North. Consequently, for many years it had been sufficient to point to the evils that would inevitably be incurred by emancipation. Jefferson had felt that slavery violated individual natural right to liberty, and had condemned the "boisterous passions" to which masters gave vent in punishing their slaves. Yet he believed that for the sake of self-preservation the South could not effect emancipation without colonization; it was a choice of evils, and holding the wolf's ears was the lesser.[1] St. George Tucker, on the other hand, was representative of a number of substantial Virginians who were of

the opinion that the inconsistency between slavery and
the professions of the Declaration of Independence should
be absolved by "total though gradual emancipation."[2]

Calhoun in the early part of his career apparently accepted slavery as a matter of course. In 1811, on assuring
the members of Congress that in the event of war with
Great Britain there was no danger of a slave insurrection,
he did not feel impelled to make any distinction between
the tenets of the Declaration of Independence and those
"French principles" whose "baneful influence" had not,
he asserted, touched the slaves. Yet in 1816 he felt shame
and confusion on having to discuss the slave trade, for
which his section bore a large share of the responsibility.
His attitude was probably very similar to that of Jefferson—that slavery was simply a necessary evil. The deep
agitation over the Missouri question, however, aroused
his concern; and by the early thirties he had reached the
conviction that the peculiar domestic institution of the
South marked the section as the intended victim of exploitation by Northern industrialism. He wrote to Francis
Pickens in 1834 that he saw in the schemes of the American
Colonization Society the early moves toward complete
emancipation.[3] Robert J. Turnbull had made the same
charge a few years earlier.[4] To men who believed that
the fate of the South was bound up in slavery, this could
but be alarming. Moreover, the vigorous and often hysteri-
cal attacks made by the abolitionists, beginning in the early
thirties, touched high-born Southern pride to the quick.
Property worth from nine hundred million to two billion
dollars, according to various estimates,[5] could not be as
bad as it was pictured. In 1836 and 1837 Calhoun struck
forth in speeches and reports in the Senate; he now no
longer excused slavery as a necessary evil, but rather defended it as "a positive good." He carried into the national
arena the fight that Thomas R. Dew had begun in the Vir-

ginia legislature a few years earlier.[6]

To Calhoun, as to most Southerners, slavery was the warp fabric of plantation society; the woof would fall apart without it.

The relation which now exists between the two races in the slave-holding states has existed for two centuries. It has grown with our growth, and strengthened with our strength. It has entered into and modified all our institutions, civil and political. None other can be substituted. We will not, cannot permit it to be destroyed. If we were base enough to do so, we would be traitors to our section, to ourselves, our families, and to posterity. It is our anxious desire to protect and preserve this relation by the joint action of this government and the Confederate States of the Union. . . .[7]

Dew, Calhoun, Harper, Hammond, William Gilmore Simms, and others who took up their cudgels in a more positive defense of slavery never ceased to reiterate that abolition would mean social catastrophe for the South. To them, as to Jefferson, this alone was sufficient reason for the continuance of the institution. Harper believed that the inevitable result of emancipation would be a war of extermination between the races which would endanger all life and property. Turnbull felt that it would mean a surrender of their lands to the "beasts of the field and the wild men of the forest." Calhoun feared that in case of emancipation the Negroes might, with the aid of the fanatics of the North, virtually enslave the Southern whites. Certainly poverty and desolation of the section and degradation of both races would ensue. The only other alternatives he could envision were the expulsion or the extirpation of one race or the other. A condition of political and social equality between blacks and whites was beyond the realm of possibility. Dew pointed a warning finger to the sad experiences of other peoples with emancipation in Santo

Domingo, Colombia, Guatemala, Poland, and Livonia.[8] In addition to conjuring up the nightmares of tragedy and chaos, Calhoun and his fellow slavocrats turned to ever more insistent affirmation of the intrinsic worth of the institution of slavery.

The major premise upon which they erected this positive case for slavery was the inferiority of the Negro race. The Negro was physically, mentally, and morally inferior to the white; he was a creature unfit for liberty. Calhoun and others probably derived this argument in part from Aristotle. That ancient Greek philosopher had contended that some persons were slaves by nature, for from birth they were physically strong and mentally weak. They had capacity enough to perceive reason, but not to use it. In the inherently necessary subordination of some persons to others in the task of procuring subsistence, these inferior persons were the natural slaves of their intellectual superiors.[9] Defenders of the Southern regime found Negroes to be such "natural" slaves. So deeply imbedded in the minds of the people was the consciousness of the diversity between the races, Calhoun felt, that slavery, real or nominal, was the only relation between the races tolerable to the whites; for racial feelings were among the strongest in human nature. Moreover, the experience of the whole of humanity demonstrated the inferiority of the colored races. He noted the remarkable fact that " . . . in the whole history of man . . . there is no instance whatever of any civilized colored race of any shade being found equal to the establishment and maintenance of free government, although by far the largest portion of the human family is composed of them; and even in the savage state we rarely find them anywhere with such governments. . . ."[10] The instance of Latin America he thought an illuminating one. There it had been the superior intelligence and ability of the Spanish, or white, race that had enabled the various countries to throw off the yoke of the old world. They had committed the fatal error of placing the colored race on an equality with the white; the consequent mixing of bloods brought on the social instability and disorder which threatened to destroy their civilization.[11]

Other champions of slavery offered more details of the Negro's inferiority. They argued that in Africa and other native habitations he lived a poor, miserable, savage life, characterized, in many instances, by brutal enslavement to his fellows, polygamy, "heathen worship," and even cannibalism. He was indolent, filthy, and diseased— utterly degraded. Ethnologists and anthropologists by the score were cited and quoted to show that scientific opinion held him in low esteem, his inferiority being marked in every respect save in the capacity to endure hot climate. His peculiar and repugnant odor was another badge of his low estate. After an examination of the pertinent scientific literature, one John Campbell declared that these men, with woolly heads, flat noses, and thick and protruding lips, had never of their own efforts emerged from barbarism to even a semi-civilized state anywhere. He confidently averred that "there is as much difference between the lowest tribe of negroes and the white Frenchman, Englishman, or American, as there is between the monkey and the negro."[12] Harper expressed the general view when he said that nature had stamped "slave" upon the Negro's very countenance. He was a characterless creature of his appetites who could bear very little moral responsibility and who had very little moral courage.[13]

Further proof of the actual inferiority of the Negro, it was believed, was furnished by the degraded conditions prevailing among the free Negroes living in the North. In gaining their freedom, they succumbed to their natural shiftlessness and laziness; they became poor, and then turned to vice and crime. This was Nathaniel Macon's im-

pression in 1820; and in 1844 Calhoun seized upon the
official census figures to show that the proportion of deaf,
dumb, blind, idiot, and insane was much higher among the
free Negroes than among the slaves. Professor R. L. Dabney confirmed this conclusion with figures from the following census (1850). Thomas R. Dew earlier and David
Christy later found the free Negro much more criminal
than his slave cousin. The irrefragable proof of experience
on the American continent established the inferiority of
the Negro race. It was inescapable fact.[14]

Social institutions could not ignore hard facts to do
obeisance to ephemeral theories; and to deprive such an
inferior being of his liberty was not to violate his natural
rights. Calhoun, as has been noted,[15] had wholly rejected
the doctrine of natural rights and had posited the general
good of the community as the criterion for the rights of
individuals. These rights were neither natural or inalienable, and were wholly conditioned upon the common welfare. Almost all of his fellow defenders of slavery followed him in abandoning the "anarchical" philosophy of
the Declaration of Independence. Restraint was as natural
in the social relationship as liberty, and was, in fact, the
only means of securing it. Communities had generally
long recognized that the degree of restraint should vary
with the differences in character and ability of the several
categories of people. Women had for many ages enjoyed
fewer privileges than men without being regarded as deprived of their natural rights. Prisoners, soldiers, and
sailors had been subjected to various degrees of restraint;
and so also had wards, children, and apprentices, in many
cases being controlled by the wills of personal superiors
just as arbitrary as those of slave masters, if not more so.
The restraints imposed upon the Negro by the institution
of slavery were not different in essence from these others
which were generally accepted, for in each case the judg-

ment and experience of the community immediately concerned approved the restraint as conducive to the best interests of all. That restraints upon the Negro were more
numerous and of longer duration was justified by his natural inferiority. Peculiar character required the restraint
of the peculiar institution of slavery. This was the reasoning of Calhoun, Harper, Simms, Fitzhugh, Hundley, Albert Taylor Bledsoe, and others.[16]

B. THEORY OF EXPLOITATION

The subordinate status of the Negro slave was further
justified by a theory of progress through exploitation. The
thesis was set forth by Calhoun and his fellow defenders
of slavery that throughout the history of mankind the
progress of civilization had rested upon the exploitation of
a laboring class in the community by a ruling or master
class. Through the appropriation of a goodly share of the
fruits of the toil of the working people, the dominant
group had to a great extent freed itself from the necessity
of daily labor. It had the leisure and the means for the
pursuit of culture; and its achievements had lifted man
from savagery to the higher levels of civilized life. The
"mudsills" of society performed the less elevating, but no
less necessary, tasks of common labor; they were the substratum upon which was erected the structure of civilization. Aristotle, of course, had recognized that slavery
contributed to the necessary leisure of Greek citizens for
the pursuit of the good life; and Pufendorf in late seventeenth-century Germany produced the interesting idea that
slavery was socially desirable, because by reducing the
number of idle men it also reduced vagrancy and crime. In
France in the early and middle nineteenth century, St.
Simon and his followers maintained that slavery was

simply a primitive form of universal class exploitation, which had characterized the whole past history of mankind; their own purpose was to abolish that exploitation peacefully. Southerners accepted the charge that slavery was exploitation, but asserted also that all human exploitation was in essence slavery. Slavery had, therefore, a longer history than the St. Simonians recognized. Moreover, it was an ineradicable characteristic of civilization, not always evil, but often productive of much good. Calhoun, in a speech delivered in the Senate in 1837, said:

There never has yet existed a wealthy and civilized society in which one portion of the community did not, in point of fact, live on the labor of the other. Broad and general as is this assertion, it is borne out by history. This is not the proper occasion, but if it were, it would not be difficult to trace the various devices by which the wealth of all civilized communities has been so unequally divided, and to show by what labor it was produced, and so large a share given to the non-producing classes. The devices are almost innumerable, from the brute force and gross superstition of ancient times to the subtle and artful fiscal contrivances of modern. I might well challenge a comparison between them and the more direct, simple, and patriarchial mode by which the labor of the African race is among us commanded by the European. . . .[17]

Thomas R. Dew had contended a few years earlier that domestic slavery had been one of the greatest of civilizing instruments, because it had provided the means of fixing the savage wanderer to the soil despite his migratory instincts and habits. It had made settled existence possible. As a substitute for the practice of murdering captives, it had mitigated the horrors of war. To argue, as Rousseau had, that the conqueror had no right to kill, and therefore none to enslave, his captive, was absurd because it placed the hostile parties on a plane of equality. Moreover, slavery had alleviated the lot of women. Slavery of some sort had been the fate of a large portion of humanity since ancient times; even in the nineteenth century slaves constituted the greater part of the human race. Finally, slavery arose from a sort of law of necessity; for it was in fact, if not in name, the inevitable result of the accumulation of private property in the hands of a limited number of the community. "It may with truth be affirmed that the exclusive owners of property ever have been, ever will, and perhaps ever ought to be the virtual rulers of mankind. If, then, in any age or nation, there should be but one species of property, and that should be exclusively owned by a portion of citizens, that portion would become inevitably the masters of the residue."[18] This was as true of the owners of industrial capital as of the feudal landlords of the Middle Ages. Power followed property. Domestic slavery was one form of property that history showed to have been of inestimable value to mankind. The advocates of its abolition should recognize the impossibility of eradicating exploitation in that manner.[19]

Calhoun added some refinement of the idea of universal exploitation by mustering into service the labor theory of value, possibly borrowed from the classical economists. Labor, he declared, was the only source of wealth; yet in all old and civilized countries, even in the best governed, only a relatively small portion of the wealth was left to those by whose labor it was created. With very few exceptions, laborers everywhere had as little volition or agency in the question of the distribution of wealth as the African in the slave-holding States had in the distribution of the proceeds of his labor. Here Calhoun recognized implicitly that the nominal liberty of the laborer, including his liberty to contract, was of little worth in actual economic life; agreeing with Dew, he believed that economic fact was of much greater significance to the worker than legal right. The oppression or exploitation was not mitigated one jot by the fact that distribution was effected through rules enforced by the government rather than through the will of a master. If one mode of distribution was an evil, so was the other. The only difference was in the amount and mode of "exaction" and in the agency by which it was effected. The laborer, the producer of wealth, did not control its distribution.[20]

George Fitzhugh elaborated this idea in a way that clearly showed his debt to early English socialists as well as to Proudhon, Fourier, and St. Simon—a debt which he gladly acknowledged, declaring that the works of the socialists, viewed correctly, contained the true defense of slavery. He agreed with Calhoun that labor was the source of all value. He was almost Marxian in his exposition of the theory of labor as the source of value, of profits as exactions from the product of labor by means of command of capital or skills, and of wages as the residue after the exactions were made. The laborer did not receive what he produced; and to that extent he was the subject of exploitation "Labor makes values, and wit exploitates [sic] and accumulates them."[21] Ignoring the possibility that "wit" contributed to the creation of wealth and thus deserved economic reward, Fitzhugh reached the conclusion that this process of exactions was moral cannibalism. "All good and respectable people are 'cannibals all', who do not labor, or who are successfully trying to live without labor, on the unrequited labor of other people. . . ."[22] The capitalist, retaining his capital and never laboring, lived in luxury on the labor of others. Capital commanded labor, as the master did the slave; neither paid for labor. Yet this cannibalism, this living off one's fellow man, was the inevitable and normal condition of civilized society. Exploitation was eternal; only its form could be modified. Slavery was the most humane, the most beneficent, of all social substructures, for (paradoxically enough) slavery identified the interests of the rich and the poor, master and slave, and begat domestic affection on the one side, and loyalty and respect on the other.[23]

Further, the defenders of slavery argued, because it was to the interest of the owner to keep him productively efficient, and therefore strong and healthy, the lot of the slave in the Southern States was a happy one. By comparison with the condition of laborers elsewhere, it was obviously a superior status. Chancellor Harper pointed out that the slave was given a most desirable security, saved from anxiety concerning the future support of himself and his children; he was amply supplied to meet his natural wants; he mated when physically ready; he was supported in sickness and in old age without labor; he never had to beg; had no temptation or opportunity for great crimes or the more destructive vices; was temperate of necessity; and was required to engage in regular and healthful, though not excessive, labor. The authority of the master protected wives from their husbands, and children from their parents. Fitzhugh pointed out that the economic security of the slave was of a permanent sort, for the failure of this master's enterprise meant, not unemployment and want, but simply transfer to another concern. Calhoun believed that the happiness and well-being of the Negro slaves was attested by their rapid growth in numbers; and he felt no uncertainty in asserting that few laborers received so much of earthly goods and of kind attention in sickness and in the infirmities of age as the American Negro slave.[24]

The relative excellence of the peculiar institution of Southern slavery was immediately manifest, these defenders claimed, in a comparison of their condition with that of emancipated Negroes in the North or of working classes everywhere. Calhoun challenged abolitionists to make the comparison, and found in the official census figures concrete evidence of the superiority of slavery over freedom for Negroes in America.[25] Hammond in his "Letters on Slavery," which were commended by Calhoun, attacked what he deemed the hypocritical philanthropy of English advocates of abolition. The Englishmen bore very poorly their responsibility for their poor and laboring classes, a responsibility incumbent upon men in independent circumstances throughout the world. The poor in England were more miserable, more degraded physically and morally, than ever were American slaves. To substantiate these assertions, Hammond quoted at length from official reports of Parliamentary investigating commissions. British sufferance of such wretchedness, at home and among people of their own race, was the strongest sort of evidence that commercial profit—not humanitarian zeal— was the motive of their crusade for abolition throughout the world. The British had used slavery in their colonies as long as it was profitable; then they had substituted a system of apprenticeship, for long terms and under harsh regulations, because it became more profitable to do so; the change relieved employers of certain legal obligations they had borne as masters. "For the condition of your wretched laborers," he solemnly asserted, "you, and every Briton who is not one of them, are responsible before God and man. If you are really humane, philanthropic, and charitable, here are objects for you. Relieve them. Raise them from the condition of brutes to the level of human beings —of American slaves at least. Do not for an instant suppose that the name of being free men is the slightest comfort to them. . . ."[26]

Chancellor Harper, William Gilmore Simms, Hundley, Professor Dabney, and others pushed the comparison between slave society and Yankee and English free society into many ramifications. The comparison was a sure and most telling rejoinder to every attack made on slavery. Some illicit sex relations between masters and their female slaves, although not to be condoned, were surely no worse than the widespread prostitution in the North, in England, France, and elsewhere. The wayward slave Negress rarely became a prostitute, and never suffered the harsh lot of prostitutes elsewhere. Further mitigation of the situation was to be found in the superior chastity and virtue of the white womanhood of the South. It was confidently asserted that vice and crime as well as poverty had been reduced to a minimum in the South; and that, despite charges of sexual licentiousness made by several neurotic individuals, there were in the South fewer cases of divorce, separation, criminal conduct, seduction, rape, and bastardy than among any other five million people on earth.[27]

Moreover, it was denied that slavery was a source of military weakness, or the cause of the persistence of dueling, or the reason for the repudiation of the public debt. Had not free States repudiated some of their obligations? But, more important, it was denied that the relations between master and slave was one of brutal tyranny on the one hand or of abasement and fear on the other. Harper felt that the relation was naturally one of kindness, for it was not "the common nature of man . . . to delight in witnessing pain."[28] Also, as many were quick to point out, good treatment of the slave was to the economic interest of the master; so powerful was the protection that it had not been found necessary to extend to the slave the manifold protection by law that was provided for free men. However, critics often erred in proceeding to the conclusion that the American Negro slave had no rights under the law. He was not the mere property of his master, subject to unlimited disposition. The laws forbade tyranny and cruelty, and confined punishment within limits. The owner could not kill, maim, overwork, or refuse to feed and clothe his slave. If the laws also forbade teaching the slave to read, the responsibility, Hammond asserted, belonged largely to the abolitionists. As a matter of fact, Simms believed, masters as a class had come to feel it a grave dishonor to treat slaves brutally. Mrs. Stowe's *Uncle Tom's Cabin* pictured the exceptional situation and misrepresented the really satisfactory lot of most slaves in the South. Alexander Stephens later echoed their arguments.[29]

The excellence of the institution of slavery was further attested, in the minds of these men, by what they believed were the superior virtues of the master class. The leisure and power of this class constituted at once a responsibility and an opportunity, and both had been met with admirable completeness. Slave owners were an educated group of superior refinement, grace of manner, courteous bearing, gentle deportment, studious forbearance and unobtrusiveness, marked generosity, strict probity, high pride of character, and strong sense of honor; in a word, they were gentlemen of quality. In politics, in industry, and in war they approached the chivalric ideal of Sir Walter Scott and the doughty courage and integrity of Carlyle's heroes. They were fit leaders in the progress of civilization. Wealth and leisure served them merely as tools, their enjoyment of leisure never degenerating into indolence, their love of wealth never becoming exaggerated to the extent of obliterating or warping their devotion to the state. With unmistakable sincerity, Hammond declared:

The American slaveholders, collectively or individually, ask no favors of any man or race who tread the earth. In none of the attributes of men, mental or physical, do they acknowledge or fear superiority elsewhere. They stand in the broadest light of knowledge, civilization, and improvement of the age, as much favored of heaven as any of the sons of Adam. Exacting nothing undue, they yield nothing but justice and courtesy, even to royal blood. They cannot be flattered, duped, nor bullied out of their rights or their propriety. They smile with contempt at servility and vaporing beyond the seas, and they turn their backs upon it as "irresponsible"; but insolence that ventures to look them in the face will never fail to be chastised.[30]

The composite picture of the virtues they claimed for slaveholders presented, of course, unbelievable excellence, and possibly appeared the work of arrogant boasting. And yet these slavocrats knew that people elsewhere had noted and remarked upon the gracious manner and high order of character and ability among the Southerners. They also knew other people by observation. And they were firmly convinced that their aristocratic pride was not a false one.[31]

In Southern society, then, a superior race governed and directed the labors of an inferior people for the best moral and material welfare of both. In any complete society a variety of skills and abilities of low and high degree were essential to its efficient functioning. The caste organization of Southern society resting upon the social subordination of the Negro slaves afforded the necessary variety; and, further, it met the requirements of morality by distributing social privilege according to power, knowledge, and virtue. Something of the Platonic conception of justice was included in the emphasis that Dabney, Hammond, and Simms placed upon the necessity of order and rank in society and their identification of them with justice when distributed properly. "Each in his place" made for justice, order, stability, the progress of civilization. The harmony, happiness, and resulting stability of this society were especially impressive to Calhoun and Fitzhugh. The latter claimed, apparently taking his cue from Calhoun, that the Southern farm was a joint concern in which slave consumed more of the coarse products than the master and was far happier; it was the "beau ideal" of communism. It was a favorite idea of Calhoun that the Southern plantation was simply an extension to the community of the family regime, communistic and benevolently paternal. "The Southern States," he declared, "are an aggregate, in fact, of communities, not of individuals. Every plantation is a little community with the master at its head who concentrates in himself the united interests of capital and labor, of which he is the common representative. These small communities aggregated make the state in all, while action, labor, and capital is equally represented and perfectly harmonized. Hence the harmony, the union, and stability . . ." of the South.[32] Other societies might well envy the South's freedom from "mere oppugnancy."

C. ECONOMIC ARGUMENT

The defenders of Negro slavery also answered the often repeated charge that slave labor was economically inefficient. According to the critics, slave labor produced less than free labor. This argument was in accord with the doctrine of classical economy; for the slave lacked the incentive of private profit. Moreover, slavery attached a stigma to labor in the whole community. The use of slave labor was economically possible only through the employment of inefficient methods that rapidly exhausted the soil and rendered it unfit for further cultivation. The planter was led to expend too much capital in merely acquiring property in man and not enough in conserving the land and making capital improvements upon it. All of this meant economic backwardness for the South and the retardation of the growth of its population (an index of progress to the classical economy of the period.)[33]

Thomas Cooper in 1826 had apparently admitted the charge, and excused the use of slaves, nevertheless, on the ground that white men could not do hard physical labor in the almost tropical climate of the South. He seemed unaware that his excuse was really direct refutation. If white men could not work in the hot climate then Negro labor in that climate was more productive. William Harper set this point straight, identifying free labor with white labor, slave with Negro labor. Moreover, the comparison between free white labor and Negro slave labor was hardly a fair one, as Dabney pointed out, for free Negro labor was the only possible alternative for the planter. In addition, he believed that the reputed exhaustion of the soil was more apparent than real.[34]

Further it was answered that self-interest was less a motive among free laborers than among slaves. In conformity with their whole picture of the lot of laboring populations elsewhere, the defenders of slavery asserted that it was not so much desire for profit as fear of starvation that moved most free laborers to work. Self-interest rarely impelled a wage-earner to work harder than he was compelled to by the close supervision of foremen and managers; and idleness frequently triumphed over the desire to accumulate. Slaves, on the other hand, were free of the fear of starvation and were subject to no stricter supervision of their labor. They often consciously identified their own interest with that of the plantation, and they felt a pride of ownership that gave energy to their work. No stigma attached to labor in the South, observed Calhoun, save to that of menial and body servants. Slave owners often worked with the slaves in the fields. If slave labor yielded a smaller return to masters than free labor yielded to employers, the result was due to the larger real wages paid to the slaves, not to the inferior productivity of their labor. All of these men argued, in effect, that the rate of return to the employer was not the only index to the productivity of labor. Slave labor received more food, clothing, shelter, and care in sickness and old age; and what was lost to the master thereby was gained for society and humanity. Certainly the community, Hammond asserted, was not burdened with the cost of wasteful pauper systems in use elsewhere. Not slavery but the unequal operation of the policies of the federal government had depressed the South and caused it to lag behind the North in increase in wealth and population.[35] This argument was without doubt the best answer to the charge of economic inefficiency.

David Christy claimed that actual experience with free Negro labor in Jamaica, Haiti, and other islands of the West Indies proved that Negro slave labor was the most efficient for the production of cotton. If and when free white labor became more productive, the planter would certainly use it. Their own economic doctrine should teach the critics, E. B. Bryan pointed out, that slavery would come to an end when free labor became cheaper. Moreover, Christy argued, the economic justification of slavery rested firmly on the economic dependence of other sections of the country and other parts of the world on the cotton-growing South. The slave-owning, cotton-raising section furnished essential raw materials for industry elsewhere; and it provided a market indispensable to the prosperity of both the agricultural and industrial North. So interdependent were the various sections, so entwined was their prosperity with that of the South, that the economic interest of the rest of the country required the use of slave labor in the South. The key position held by the cotton South made it indispensable to world economy and rendered it secure from all attacks on its peculiar labor supply. "Cotton is King."[36] William Harper had anticipated some of this argument, but had not pushed it to such sanguine conclusions. However, in 1858, Hammond, who had become a Senator from South Carolina, pushed this argument further in his defiant rejection of Seward's assertion that the South was a conquered province which the North would rule. England and the whole civilized world, he argued, were dependent upon the continued production of cotton in the South and could not permit a war against the South. "No, you dare not make war upon cotton. No power on earth dares to make war upon it. Cotton is King." Hammond and other Southerners retained until the outbreak of the Civil War this confidence of aid from foreign intervention.[37]

D. OTHER ARGUMENTS

To the abolitionist charge that slavery was sinful, the defenders replied with an appeal to the Bible. They referred to both the Old and New Testaments to show (much in the fashion of Saint Augustine) that slavery had the approval of God as a punishment for sin and as a means of preparing degraded beings for a higher way of life. Howell Cobb contended that slavery of Negroes had its origin in the punishment of Ham and his posterity for Ham's sin in viewing the nakedness of his father, Noah. Simms added that God had placed even the Israelites, his chosen people, in slavery for their own good. Hammond, Harper, Fitzhugh, and others claimed divine approval of slavery in the words of the tenth commandment and in the action of Saint Paul in apprehending and sending back a runaway slave. Moreover, God had apparently approved the enslavement of the Gideonites by the Israelites, the former serving the latter as "hewer of wood and drawers of water."[38]

Thomas R. Dew employed the additional argument, seldom used by other Southerners, that slavery was a just commutation of the right to kill in war. To enslave was to inflict the lesser punishment, and was consequently humane. To deny this right, and thus to place victor and vanquished on a plane of equality, was absurd, for victors in war have long demanded and received compensation. Homer and Aristotle approved such enslavement; and Grotius, Rutherford, Vattel, and Locke recognized the right to enslave captives of war.[39] The lack of immediate applicability of this argument to Negro slavery in the South probably deterred other Southerners from following Dew in its use.

In sum, Dew, Calhoun, Harper, Hammond, Bryan, Christy, and other Southerners defended slavery as an essential element of the agrarian economy of their section upon various grounds: the racial inferiority of the Negro; a theory of progress through exploitation; a comparison of the Southern slave system with labor systems in other sections and other countries; the economic soundness of the institution; and biblical authority. In this manner they sought to justify an institution that was attacked, and, in their opinion, grossly misrepresented by fanatics in the North in the name of liberty and equality. They wanted to preserve it as the necessary alternative to social catastrophe and as the necessary basis for the plantation economy which determined the character of Southern civilization.

NOTES

1. Jefferson, *Notes on Virginia*, 3rd American ed. (New York, 1801), pp. 240-242; Jefferson, *The Writings of Jefferson*, 10 vols., Washington ed. (Washington, 1854), Vol. VII, pp. 148, 159-160. Calhoun was careful to note that Jefferson was anything but an abolitionist. Calhoun, *Works*, Vol. IV, pp. 492-493. Certainly Jefferson was no doctrinnaire egalitarian, a fact which constitutes a serious qualification of the view expressed

by Parrington that Jeffersonianism was in essence a compound of egalitarianism and humanitarianism. See V. L. Parrington, *Main Currents in American Thought,* 3 vols. (New York, 1927-1930), Vol. II, p. 70.

2. Tucker, Appendix to Vol. I, Pt. II, of Blackstone's *Commentaries,* pp. 31, 32, 41, 54.

3. *Works,* Vol. II, pp. 8, 133; Vol. VI, p. 132; *Correspondence,* pp. 181, 327. See also *supra.,* Ch. I.

4. Turnbull, *The Crisis* (Charleston, 1827), pp. 124-125.

5. Calhoun estimated the value of slave property at nine hundred and fifty million dollars; Clay, at one billion two hundred million; Hammond, at two billion. See Calhoun, *Works,* Vol. V, p. 204; Albert Taylor Bledsoe, *Essay on Liberty and Slavery* (Philadelphia, 1856), p. 285, quoting Clay; Hammond, "Letters on Slavery," *Pro-Slavery Argument* (Philadelphia, 1853), p. 141.

6. There was some earlier intermittent pro-slavery argument in America, but the thirties marked definitely the burgeoning forth of the great body of this doctrine in the South. See W. S. Jenkins, *Pro-Slavery Thought in the Old South* (Chapel Hill, 1935), pp. 65-66, 69, 81-82, 89. See Calhoun, *Correspondence,* p. 369; *Works,* Vol. II, pp. 483-489; 629-633; Vol. V. pp. 201-202.

7. *Works,* Vol. II, p. 488. Similar statement on Vol. II, p. 630. Compare with statement of Robert J. Turnbull, *The Crisis,* p. 124. See also the speech of Nathaniel Macon on Jan. 20, 1820, *Abridgement of the Debates of Congress,* 16th Congress, 1st session, Vol. VI, pp. 415-416.

8. Harper, "Memoir of Slavery, *"Pro-Slavery Argument,* pp. 89-90; Turnbull, *The Crisis,* p. 124; Calhoun, *Works,* Vol. II, p. 633; Vol. IV, p. 552; Vol. V, pp. 204-205; Dew, "Review of the Debate in the Virginia Legislature, 1831-'32," *Political Register* (Washington), Oct. 16, 1833, pp. 769, 815-817.

9. Aristotle, *Politics,* Everyman ed. (London and New York, 1912), Bk. I, Chs. IV-VII.

10. *Works,* Vol. IV, p. 411.

11. *Ibid.,* Vol. V, pp. 204-205; Vol.IV, pp. 315, 405, 410-411, 472. Cf. E. B. Bryan, *The Rightful Remedy* (Charleston, 1850), pp. 32-34.

12. John Campbell, *Negro-Mania: being an Examination of the Falsely Assumed Equality of the Various Races of Men* (Philadelphia, 1851), pp. 6-7, 10, 161.

13. Harper, "Memoir on Slavery," pp. 39-73. See also Simms, "The Morals of Slavery," *Pro-Slavery Argument,* pp. 178-179, 207, 214, 269, 273; Bledsoe, *Essay on Liberty and Slavery,* pp. 292-300; Howell Cobb, *A Scriptural Examination of Slavery* (Georgia, 1856), pp. 49-75; D. R. Hundley, *Social Relations in Our Southern States* (New York, 1860), pp. 311-313. See an account of fourteen different novels that appeared after, and in reply to, Mrs. Stowe's *Uncle Tom's Cabin* (1851). One of their two constant themes was the inferiority of the Negro. J. R. Tandy, "Pro-Slavery Propaganda in American Fiction in the Fifties," *South Atlantic Quarterly* 21: 41-51, 170-179 (January and April, 1922). Hinton Rowan Helper, after a rather scurrilous attack on slavery in his *The Impending Crisis of the South: How to Meet It* (New York, 1857), incontinently attacked the Negro for his inferiority, and hoped to see him ultimately exterminated from the earth. See his *Nojoque: A Question for a Continent* (New York, 1867), pp. v-vi, 14-16, 16-62, 65, 66-80. In his opinion in the Dred Scott case, Chief Justice Taney insisted that at the time of the adoption of the Constitution the inferiority of the Negro was universally accepted "as an axiom in morals as well as in politics"; this axiom became one of the underlying principles of the constitutional system. *Dred Scott v. Sandford,* 19 Howard 407-421.

14. Macon, *Abridgement of the Debates of Congress,* Vol. VI, p. 415; Calhoun, *Works,* Vol. V, pp. 336-339, 459-461; Dabney, *A Defence of Virginia* (New York, 1867), pp. 343-344; Simms, "The Morals of Slavery," pp. 225-228; Dew, "Review of the Debate in the Virginia Legislature, 1831-'32," pp. 810-814; Christy, *Cotton is King* (New York, 1856), pp. 200-209. See also

Hundley, *Social Relations in Our Southern States*, pp. 300-301; Robert Y. Hayne, "Speech . . . On Mr. Foot's Resolution, Jan. 21, 1830," *Register of Debates in Congress*, 1st session, Vol. VI, pp. 45-47.

15. *See supra*, Ch. III, Secs. C and D.

16. Calhoun, *Works*, Vol. I, pp. 54-57; Harper, "Memoir on Slavery," pp. 6-7, 10-11, 13-15; Simms, "The Morals of Slavery," pp. 259-260; George Fitzhugh, *Cannibals All! or Slaves Without Masters* (Richmond, 1857), pp. 115-116, 120; Hundley, *Social Relations in Our Southern States*, pp. 326-327; Bledsoe, *Essay on Liberty and Slavery*, pp. 34-39; W. A. Dunning, *Political Theories from Rousseau to Spencer* (New York, 1920), pp. 359-360; Pufendorf, *The Law of Nature and of Nations*, 4th ed. (London, 1729), Bk. VI, Ch. III.

17. Calhoun, *Works*, Vol. II, pp. 631-632. Cf. the later argument of James H. Hammond in the Senate, *Congressional Globe*, 35th Congress, 1st session, Vol. XXVI, Pt. I, p. 962.

18. Dew, "Review of the Debate in the Virginia Legislature, 1831-'32," p. 776.

19. Dew, "Review of the Debate in the Virginia Legislature, 1831-'32," pp. 771-774, 776, 781, 784-785, 789.

20. Calhoun, *Works*, Vol. V, pp. 207-208.

21. Fitzhugh, *Cannibals All!* p. ix.

22. *Ibid.*, pp. 26-27.

23. *Cannibals All!* pp. 25, 28-29, 34, 48, 61; also his *Sociology for the South, or the Failure of Free Society* (Richmond, 1854), pp. 43, 248.

24. Harper, "Memoir on Slavery," pp. 49-50, 31-32; Fitzhugh, *Sociology*, pp. 245-246; Calhoun, *Works*, Vol. II, pp. 631-632; Vol. V, p. 204.

25. *Works*, Vol. II, pp. 631-632; Vol. V, pp. 333-339, 458-461.

26. Hammond, "Letters on Slavery," pp. 134-138, 145-149, 161-163, 171, 139. William J. Grayson made a similar defense of slavery by contrasting the lot of the wage slave with that of the bond slave. See his poem, *The Hireling and the Slave* (Charleston, 1856).

27. Harper, "Memoir on Slavery," pp. 41-45, 65-67;

Simms, "The Morals of Slavery," pp. 229-230; Dabney, *A Defense of Virginia*, pp. 276-282; Hammond, "Letters on Slavery," pp. 117-120.

28. Harper, "Memoir on Slavery," pp. 29-31, 32-33.
29. Hammond, "Letters on Slavery," pp. 112, 113-115, 123-124; Dabney, *A Defence of Virginia*, pp. 260-261; Simms, "The Morals of Slavery," pp. 215-217, 229. Alexander Stephens presented a similar view somewhat later when he wrote: "The slave, so-called, was not in law regarded entirely as a chattel, as has been erroneously represented. He was by no means subject to the absolute dominion of his master. He had important personal rights, secured by law. His service due according to the law, it is true, was considered property, and so in all countries is considered the service of all persons, who according to law are bound to another or others for a term, however long or short. So is the legal rights of parents to the service of their minor children . . ." Stephens, *Constitutional View of the War between the States*, 2 vols. (Philadelphia, 1868-1870), Vol. II, pp. 24-25. Thomas Dew asserted Jefferson was wrong in characterizing slave masters as a class to be of boisterous passions. Dew, "Review of the Debate in the Virginia Legislature, 1831-'32," p. 20. For an authoritative summary of the legal status of the American Negro slave, see U. B. Phillips, *Life and Labor in the Old South* (Boston, 1929), pp. 161-163.
30. Hammond, "Letters on Slavery," p. 151.
31. Harper, "Memoirs on Slavery," pp. 35, 61-62; Simms, "The Morals of Slavery," pp. 185, 220, 244; Dabney, *A Defence of Virginia*, pp. 283-287; Dew, "Review of the Debate of the Virginia Legislature," pp. 820-821. Southerners read both Scott and Carlyle a great deal. See William E. Dodd, *The Cotton Kingdom* (New Haven, 1921), pp. 62-63.
32. Calhoun, *Works*, Vol. III, p. 180; Dabney, *A Defence of Virginia*, pp. 255-256; Hammond, "Letters on Slavery," pp. 110-111; Simms, "Morals of Slavery," pp. 258, 262; Fitzhugh, *Sociology for the South*, pp. 245-246. According to Simms, true liberty was the enjoyment of the peace in society for which one was fit;

this constituted true equality for Dabney. Simms, "Morals of Slavery," 'p. 258; Dabney, *A Defence of Virginia,* pp. 255-256.
33. See U. B. Phillips, *American Negro Slavery* (New York and London, 1918), Ch. XVIII; Helper, *The Impending Crisis* (New York, 1857), Ch. I and *passim;* Edmund Ruffin, *Political Economy of Slavery* (Richmond, 1857).
34. Cooper, *Lectures on the Elements of Political Economy* (Columbia, 1826), pp. 94, 95; Harper, "Memoir on Slavery," pp. 67, 72; Dabney, *Defence of Virginia,* pp. 334-335.
35. Hammond, "Letters on Slavery," pp. 122, 161-163; Dabney, *A Defence of Virginia,* pp. 317-331; Dew, "Review of the Debate in the Virginia Legislature, 1831-'32," pp. 829-831; Calhoun, *Works,* Vol. IV, p. 505.
36. Christy, *Cotton Is King* (New York ,1856), pp. 27, 62-70, 180-199, and *passim;* E. B. Bryan, *The Rightful Remedy,* pp. 101-102.
37. Hammond, Speech in Senate, Mar. 4, 1858, *Congressional Globe,* 35th Congress, 1st session, Vol. XXVI, Pt. I, p. 961. See William H. Russell, *My Diary North and South,* 2 vols. (London, 1863), Vol. I, pp. 142-143, 152, 170-171, 178.
38. Cobb, *A Scriptural Examination of Slavery,* pp. 3, 25-27, 36, 41-42, 92, 95-96; Simms, "Morals of Slavery," p. 263; Hammond, "Letters on Slavery," pp. 105-108, 155-159; Harper, "Memoir on Slavery," p. 16; Fitzhugh, *Cannibals All!* p. 296; Dabney, *A Defence of Virginia,* pp. 153-155, 185-192; Bledsoe, *Essay on Liberty and Slavery,* Ch. III; M. T. Wheat, *Philosophy of slavery,* 2nd ed. (Louisville, 1862); John H. Hopkins, *Bible View of Slavery,* pamphlet (New York, 1863); John Fletcher, *Studies on Slavery* (Natchez, 1852).
39. Dew, "Review of the Debate in the Virginia Legislature, 1831-'32," pp. 775-776.

Part IV

Summation and Appraisal

9

Conclusion

THE POLITICAL THEORY of John C. Calhoun was born of
the pangs of conflict between two great sections having
divergent interests and ways of life. The differences between the North and the South were recognized from the
very beginning of the political union under the Constitution. In the Federal Convention of 1787, James Madison
described the fundamental character of the cleavage
arising from differences of climate, pursuits, and labor
systems; to him and others, the greatest danger to the
Union of two distinct regimes lay in the opposition of
economic interests. However, this opposition was not
deemed prohibitive of much real cooperation for the common good; the Founding Fathers met the situation in a
practical spirit of accommodation, by establishing a Union
government of definitely limited competence and by agreeing upon a sectional balance in its structure. Equal representation of the States in the Senate secured an equilibrium
in the control of the common government, for the two
sections were evenly balanced in the number of States and
in all probability would remain so. It was even considered
possible that the South through a faster growing population might attain equality in the popularly representative branch of the federal legislature. This sectional equilibrium was clearly understood and was given tacit expression in the Constitution. It was the means of removing
the danger that one section might seriously encroach upon

the interests of the other. For one generation no serious danger appeared.

The coming of the industrial revolution in the North with the opening years of the nineteenth century accentuated the differences between the two civilizations. The invention of the cotton gin and the growth of textile factories resulted in a tremendous increase in the demand for cotton and a firm intrenchment of plantation economy in the South. The Northern States grew rapidly in population and wealth under the aegis of an industrial and commercial capitalism which in time sought also the reins of political power. Its attempts to write its claims into public policy were met by the opposition of the agricultural community led largely by Southern statesmen. In the realm of practical politics there were the conflicts over the protective tariffs, the internal improvements financed by the federal government, the bounties on fish, navigation laws and other burdens on commerce, and the Bank of the United States which reputedly aided the concentration of financial resources in the North. Bound to a colonial economy through a system of exchanging raw agricultural products for imported manufactures, the South felt irritation over the tribute exacted for dependence on Northern capital and industry; yet politically the section remained competent for some time to protect itself within the framework of the Union. For a time also events seemed to justify Madison's belief in the beneficent working of the party system over a large territory. During the middle period it was generally true that national party success depended on support in all three sections, North, South, and the new West. As long as success depended partially upon appreciable support from the South, whether Whig or Democratic, this section had some security for its interests. Only an alliance owing no political debt to a section would completely ignore its welfare.

In the rivalry of the dominant groups in the two older sections for the political support of the ever new West, the South proved somewhat successful during the middle period. The South and the West shared the agrarian distrust of the creditor North, and their politicians generally achieved satisfactory compromises between their divergent interests. But the increasing economic dependence of the West upon the North furnished the basis of alliance between these two. Railroads and canals and the trade flowing over them bound the two sections closer together. The North provided capital for economic development in the West; the East was a more important market for Western products than the South. Moreover, the great majority of the settlers of the West were emigrants from the East. However, it was only with the injection of the slavery issue into the struggle that the South was completely segregated from the rest of the country and threatened with dire exploitation. When, to the growth of economic bonds between the free agrarian West and the dominant capitalism of the North, there was added slavery in the guise of a moral issue, the South was faced with sectional isolation. Then arose the specter of subjection to a hostile majority party in control of the federal government, whose powers the Supreme Court threatened to make alarmingly expansible. There ensued the well-known struggle over the admission to the Union of new States from the West as free or slave. Thus the dynamics of territorial expansion and economic growth destroyed the original political balance; and the passions and prejudices engendered by the struggle for power led to the trial by combat. In the eyes of Southerners, the industrial and commercial capitalism of the North found complete exploitation of the agrarian South possible only with the aid of the sword.

Calhoun, pre-eminently the representative of the

agrarian civilization of the South, early discerned the danger to his section. While participating in the broils of practical politics, he observed the movement of the main stream resulting cumulatively from the meeting of small currents. He saw clearly the fundamental conflict of economic interests between the North and the South, which Madison had feared earlier and which John Quincy Adams affirmed in his own time. Following the Missouri Compromise of 1820, Calhoun began to suspect that antipathy to slavery was to be made the cement for an alliance of North and West hostile to the South. To meet the danger, it was not sufficient to employ the tactics of ordinary party warfare. Calhoun set himself to the task of finding adequate means of self-protection for the South as a minority in the federal Union. The South as a whole was conscious of its minority position from the time of the formation of the Union, but deemed it of little importance until abolitionism raised its hydra head in the North in the thirties. By then Calhoun had anticipated the danger to the South and had sought defense in his doctrines of State sovereignty, nullification, and secession. In the "South Carolina Exposition" (1828) he set forth his constitutional theory and began its philosophic justification. This was written in the thick of the political fight against the high protective tariffs, but Calhoun was not unaware of its relation to other issues and to the inchoate sectional isolation of the South. During the remainder of his life, he devoted himself to perfecting his juristic and philosophic ideas and to waging defensive political warfare against protective tariffs, expensive internal improvements, abolitionism, and exclusion of slavery from the territories.

Calhoun was well qualified by his life and character to be a doughty champion of his native region. He was born and bred on the Southern plantation, grew to know and appreciate the general quality of its existence, and loved it always. Personally proud, ambitious, and even of passionate temperament, he was schooled in its virtues of self-respect, good breeding, pride of family, and sense of public responsibility. He enjoyed the leisure of its way of life, the means for travel and study, and the courage and confidence of individual independence. He proved a devoted husband and an exemplary father, ever solicitous of the welfare of his wife and children. Although not of a deeply religious nature, he faithfully observed family prayer and church attendance, for he valued religion as a conserver of moral and social standards. Toward his Negro slaves, he was kind and forbearing by custom, but a strict disciplinarian when the occasion required. His personal wants were few, and his tastes simple; but he was also known as a bounteous host. To his friends and associates he was a Southern gentleman, courteous and amiable, lively in conversation, respectful of ability and culture, and cordially hospitable. The prestige and power which he achieved in public life, he accepted as the reward of merit; but to the discharge of his public functions he was impelled by a stern and uncompromising sense of duty. To the service of the Southern regime of which he was so much a part, he devoted himself with unswerving loyalty. He conceived of himself as a later-day fulfillment of the Roman ideal of a statesman who feels that his superior virtues impose upon him the obligation to lead his community to its highest good, stoically sacrificing whatever of personal welfare might be necessary.

To the task of rational defense of the South, Calhoun brought a mind of unusual power, logical acumen, and historical insight—a mind which on occasion struck the spark of originality. His native mental strength was sharpened by a self-imposed, rigid intellectual discipline. Although his specific political theory arose out of a partisan defense of Southern interests, he was no mere advocate seizing upon any winning argument, but rather a seeker after philosophical truth. His intellectual honesty drove him in zealous quest of more universally and eternally valid reasons for his conviction that the way of life in the South was good and deserving of control over its own destiny. He strove with such vigor that he came to dominate the State rights school as the successor of Thomas Jefferson and John Taylor and as the leader of Hammond, Harper, Dew, Upshur, Jefferson Davis, Stephens, and others. He produced a body of doctrine that confounded his contemporary antagonists, and that, within the same frame of reference, remains unanswerable today.

It has been suggested that his intellectual might was due to the rigorous logic with which he built an argument, like an inverted pyramid, upon a single premise.[1] It should also be noted that his strength was due to the very careful selection of the basic premises upon which he relied. His capacity for selecting ideas generally accepted, even by his antagonists when used in another context, and adapting them to his own use, rendered almost invulnerable the "inverted-pyramid" structure of his argument. For example, the basic assumption of the "economic man," derived from Adam Smith and the classical economists, was generally accepted in America as a valid part of the economics of individualism; and this fact made Calhoun's utilization of the same idea unimpeachable in his time. The assumption is no longer generally accepted as entirely valid. Therein lies the weakness of most generalizations of social theory. Calhoun's method had the virtue of an attempt to achieve philosophical validity by founding his political doctrine on the most nearly inductive ideas of his time.

In defense of slavery, the focus of most attacks on Southern policy, Calhoun drew from Aristotle the idea of natural inequality of individual men, added the idea of race inequality, and combined these with the German concept of progress through exploitation.[2] Even though he accepted generally the American democratic doctrine, he made subtle exception of Negro slaves. He showed with clarity that this exception did not differ in essence from other exceptions recognized widely by democratic communities. His picture of the good life pursued in democratic fashion by a superior white race, sustained by the labor of an inferior race, was something of a reincarnation of the Greek ideal of social order and stability achieved through a hierarchy of groups.

Calhoun's doctrine of the inevitability of social exploitation was a notable anticipation of an element in Marx's philosophy of history. Further, subsequent history seems to have borne out Calhoun's judgment as to the incompatibility of whites and blacks; two races of different color and culture living side by side would not mingle on a plane of equality. His argument, and that of all his fellow defenders of slavery, that the Negro was inferior by nature does not receive scientific sanction today, although, given the particular environment, general inferiority of the Negro seems well established by experience. His prophecy that abolition of slavery would not alter the status of the Negro as a class, but merely change the form of his economic vassalage, has generally come to pass. To the modern complaint that Calhoun's mistake was not in refusing equal status to the Negro, but in denying him the right to be considered as a human being, Calhoun's reply would be that political and civil rights are not the "natural" inheritance of men and are only bestowed by the judgment of the community, and that the Negro slaves did have legal rights more substantial in actual effect than the nominal liberty of the laborer in other regions.

To protect the South from political attack, Calhoun

and his school propounded the theory of State sovereignty within the federal Union and derived as corollaries the doctrines of nullification and secession. To establish State sovereignty, Calhoun sought to show that its very nature as ultimate legal supremacy was one and indivisible, and that sovereignty in the United States was originally possessed by the individual States and had never been surrendered by them. The right of secession from the Union followed directly from State sovereignty. Nullification was a somewhat more complex doctrine; it required also the utilization of the three-fourths majority of the States which was the amending power of the federal Constitution. In questions over the federal division of power, the presumption was in favor of the individual States. The power of the central government could not be increased save by agreement of three-fourths of the members. In fact, the present "closeness of union" depended upon continuous accord of this three-fourths majority. Calhoun supplied philosophical justification for this interpretation in his theory of the concurrent majority. This theory represented an attempt to establish the principle of consent in a union of political units having definite self-consciousness and awareness of divergence of interests; the concurrent majority would give any substantial minority the power of self-protection.[3]

Basically, Calhoun devoted himself to the task of justifying autonomy and practically complete self-determination for the South, which to him and to many of his contemporaries represented a more genuine unity of interest and culture than the larger and politically articulated union of the United States. The particular form of his political and constitutional theory was largely determined by the fact that the South as such had no political organization and could, therefore, be distinguished from the North only by making the States the significant political entities. However, Calhoun was also motivated by an honest interest in the protection of minorities and by a belief in the efficacy of decentralization in government. If he could have divorced the term "nationalism" from its connotation of complete political unity and centralization, he could well have called himself a Southern nationalist. He worked for a "solid South" during the last twenty or more years of his life.

His theory of the concurrent majority was remarkably ingenious and persuasive; and it is not at all certain that its working in the American political system would have been too cumbersome. Its operation would not necessarily have been any slower than that of our present system of judicial review of legislation. It would have made for decentralization. The opinion has been expressed that it would have been an anachronism in the Western world of the nineteenth century, because it would have somehow been in the way of inexorable forces of manifest destiny. Calhoun, it was said, was championing decentralization in an era of nationalistic unification.[4] However, it should be noted that whatever nationalism there was in the South was more Southern than American, and that the decentralizing effect of Calhoun's scheme would have made possible the preservation of that inchoate Southern nationalism. The opposing force was not merely the Dr. Jekyll of American nationalism, but the Mr. Hyde of imperialistic conquest. The opinion also assumes too much certainty for the full tidal sweep of historical forces. There are cross-currents and counterflows. Decentralization has found striking expression in the development, beginning in the nineteenth century and continuing into the twentieth century, of the "autonomous nationhood" of some of the more important Dominions of the British Empire. Calhoun's scheme might in the long run have worked out a similar decentralization of the American system. Who can be certain as to the superiority of the present system to the one that might have been—save upon the consoling faith that what happens is always progress?

Later juristic theory has accepted Calhoun's doctrine that sovereignty could not have been divided between the individual States and a single national state in America. The Founding Fathers in framing the Constitution avoided the issue of the location of sovereignty; and the various adherents of the doctrine of divided sovereignty, from the time of the *Federalist* papers down to the Civil War, were but pushing the evasion one step further by refusing to consider the ultimate location of legal supremacy in case of conflict of the two authorities, each acting within its constitutional sphere. Some referred vaguely to the people behind and above the Constitution; but that left undetermined whether the issue was referred to the people collectively as a single nation or to the people of the separate States as distinct entities. Story and Webster, although doing obeisance to the theory of divided sovereignty, nevertheless contended that ultimate determination of conflicts of governmental authority lay only with the people collectively of a single nation. Thus somewhat clumsily they arrived at maintaining national sovereignty. Calhoun started with the unity and indivisibility of sovereignty and consequently proceeded with more logical dispatch to upholding the sovereignty of the separate individual States. In the clash of interpretation of the phrases of the Constitution, Calhoun maintained his case with brilliance. And his historical argument, from the facts of the origin of the American federal Union, was never met effectively by his opponents.

Several American historians have acknowledged that Calhoun was correct in his premise that sovereignty lay in the several States at the beginning of the federal Union under the present Constitution.[5] Some, however, challenge his assumption that sovereignty had to continue in the possession of the several States. They contend that his logical brilliance led him astray, and that he overlooked the nationalizing forces at work during his own lifetime. Professors Merriam and Parrington charge, in effect, that Calhoun's logical brilliance was counterbalanced by a dullness in his sense of social history.[6] Calhoun, however, did not assume that sovereignty must remain forever with the several States simply because it was there at the beginning of the federal Union. He did believe that acceptance of his historical premise established a presumption in favor of sovereignty remaining where the work of the Founding Fathers left it, until another political reorganization explicitly changed its location. The burden of proof rested upon those who would contend that the situs of sovereignty had been changed.

Calhoun was well aware of certain nationalizing forces operating within the Union: influence of common blood, language, and historical experience; the economic bonds of an expanding capitalist economy; and various precedents set in united political activity. But he also recognized certain events that revealed a strong counter-current of resistance to nationalism; the protest of the Virginia and Kentucky Resolutions; the threat of nullification and secession by New Englanders during the War of 1812; Georgia's defiance of the Supreme Court in 1831-1832; the nullification episode in South Carolina in 1832-1833; and the nullification of the federal fugitive slave law by Northern States through their "personal liberty" laws. Certainly from this confusing scene of conflicting facts the conclusion that the movement of events had changed the location of sovereignty could not be clearly drawn.

Calhoun could not have failed to see the forces of nationalism, for he was constantly decrying them. As early as the nullification controversy, he declared, in a letter to

Richard K. Cralle, that the real issue at stake was not tariff protection but political centralization or "consolidation." During the same episode he denounced the Force Bill, intended to coerce a State, because such an assumption of power by the central government tended strongly to destroy the original state. Throughout the rest of his life he opposed expansion of federal power for the same reason, and in speech and in writing exposed a persistent nationalizing trend which he traced back to the Hamiltonian legislative program of the first Congress. He clearly discerned the economic and sectional impulsion behind the trend, and fully appreciated the support given it by "so many ties, political, social, and commercial." "The cords that bind the States together are not only many, but various in character. Some are spiritual or ecclesiastical; some political; others social. Some appertain to the benefits conferred by the Union, and others to the feeling of duty and obligation."[7] Only in the sense that Calhoun did not regard these nationalizing forces as inevitably destined for triumph could it be said that he overlooked them. That his estimate of the considerable strength of resistance to centralization was not entirely "unhistorical" is attested by the four years of civil war that proved necessary to overcome that resistance. He predicted that unless nullification succeeded the South would either secede or would be subjected to exploitation. Secession failed, and the quickened industrial development of the North exploited the agrarian South as a dependent region of colonial economy. Calhoun was acutely sensitive to the forces making for change and of the direction of the change. He can hardly be charged with a lack of historical perspective, merely because he did not regard these forces as inexorable or believe that their direction could not be changed by deliberate human effort.

As a theorist, Calhoun followed the American tradition in espousing the principles of government by consent and representative democracy, even though he employed new criteria for his appraisal of those principles. He accepted also the idea of progress, which was then gaining popular currency. He followed American tradition in approving governmental checks and balances for the protection of liberty; his most significant contribution to political theory was built upon this general idea. By relating political checks and balances to economic forces, he showed the value of political decentralization. The distribution of governmental powers and the equipoise among the parts was to be applied territorially as well as functionally; and this led to his theory of the concurrent majority and his doctrine of nullification. Calhoun followed a substantial American tradition, represented notably by Jefferson and John Taylor, in his preference for an agrarian way of life. He could not match these distinguished Southerners in their enthusiasm for life on the soil; but he went further than they did in elaborating a rational justification of Southern agrarianism.

Calhoun's political theory revealed certain influence of both ancient Greek philosophy and modern European thought. He was particularly influenced by Aristotle, the English utilitarians, and Edmund Burke. Aristotle was, of course, of great assistance in the defense of slavery. To the Greek philosopher he also owed a sounder comprehension of the origin and nature of government than his American background could provide. He acquired the empirical outlook which rejected the *a priori* rationalism then current in American political thought. And he probably derived from Aristotle the organic view of the relation between the state and the individual. Thus, from the political thinker whom he regarded as "among the best,"[8] he received the impulse for a surer approach to the age-old problem of the conflict of liberty and authority; and he achieved in this regard a philosophical position that appears more valid to the modern world than that of the old social compact school of natural law and natural rights. It should be recognized that Calhoun's use of the organic conception of the nature of political society was pioneering in America. It represented a definite break with his predecessors in both the nationalist and State rights schools.[9] Calhoun may have been indebted in part to Greek philosophy as well as to English thought for his thorough appreciation of the economic basis of politics. He recognized the economic foundations of political power; and his basic assumption as to human nature was a compound of the utilitarian concept of the economic man and Aristotle's political animal. Further influence of English utilitarianism was revealed in his use of classical economic doctrine to support his preference for political individualism. Calhoun also drew inspiration from Burke, whom he regarded as "the wisest of modern statesmen", and as having "the keenest and deepest glance into futurity."[10] Calhoun appreciated Burke's conservative sense of historical continuity with the past, his rejection of aggressive and radical social innovation, and his perception of the proof of worth in the survival of existing institutions. In Burke also he found gratifying confirmation of the Tory attitude of *noblesse oblige.*

The scope of Calhoun's theory was somewhat limited by the concentration of his attention upon political problems of immediate practical importance. This was but natural for one who was no mere philosopher, but also a statesman and a man of affairs. Yet his theory suffered the limitations of an abstraction that seems the price of all philosophy. He lacked the relativistic, pluralistic outlook that characterizes later political and social thought. At times he seems to have confused philosophy and science and to have attributed to philosophic generalizations the validity of scientific laws. This confusion led him, in some instances, into a too dogmatic assurance. It should be added that his own personal position and stake in the existing order doubtless interfered with his attempt to set forth a really objective system of thought. Yet his system was not the work of a mere partisan who availed himself of any argument that promised immediate practical advantage. He did attempt to set forth a social philosophy that was internally consistent and universally valid. His intellectual independence is revealed in his complete break with the American tradition of natural law and natural rights. In juristic theory, his attack on the theory of divided sovereignty retrieved and adapted for America the best of European thought on the subject. His doctrine of the unity and indivisibility of sovereignty came to be generally accepted—even by the nationalistic followers of Webster; although John Taylor had made some feeble motion in this direction, it was Calhoun who really made a place for the doctrine in American juristic thought. He would certainly have been among the first to reject the current effort among American advocates of world government to revive the old conception of divided sovereignty[11]; however noble the cause, the Madisonian concept founders upon the question of ultimate supremacy.

The theory of Calhoun was perhaps the most significant contribution in the whole field of American political thought before the Civil War. Its adaptability to the needs of the South won for it enthusiastic support in that section and its brilliance commanded respect in other regions. It came to dominate the State rights school—Harper, Hamilton, Hayne, Hammond, Rhett, Yancey, Jefferson Davis, Stephens, and others. It remained the official apology of the South even after the Civil War. The political theory of Calhoun was a fusion, original in some respects, of elements drawn from Greek philosophy, modern European and English thought, and earlier American theory.

One aspect of Calhoun's political theory, of considerable significance for modern thought, is that involved in the concept of the concurrent majority and its constitutional counterpart, nullification. These constituted for him the vehicle for attaining his ideal of a political system suffused with the spirit of rational toleration and respect for differences of opinion and interest. His theory of the concurrent majority was an attempt to enlarge the element of consent in government. In this effort Calhoun comes within a respectable tradition of political thought and possibly offers something of value to more modern seekers after political justice. The gist of his thought on the subject is that each significant minority interest should have some check upon the majority, and that the completeness of the check should vary directly with the degree of difference between the conflicting interests and the extent of possible exploitation. Stated thus abstractly, his ideas might furnish some suggestion even for advocates of functional representation and functional devolution. Pluralists, guild socialists, and others who seek more self-government in industry share at least a broad general aspiration with Calhoun. His more specific aim was for a flexible federalism in which even distinct social orders might exist in peace and harmony. Geographical decentralization was an essential part of it. Although in his time Calhoun did not directly concern himself with world federation to keep the peace, his doctrine would clearly insist that ambitious present-day projects in orchestration of world community be wary of building power structures without assuming full responsibility for federal devolution to preserve enduring national interests and ways of life.

In a world in which economic and political realities seem to impel increasing governmental centralization, there remains the constant necessity for some decentralization for the sake of efficiency. Those who cherish the value of individual human personality maintain also a persistent concern for conserving the democratic ideal of consent of the governed. Political integration into larger units must be accompanied by a loosening up of internal relationships, whether functionally, or territorially, or both. Only superficially are the centripetal and centrifugal forces contradictory; they may be made to achieve a satisfactory balance. A growing unity in affairs really and fundamentally of common concern may be reconciled with a transcending diversity in affairs designated individual, local, or regional by nature, if the end is pursued with patience and intelligence. Steps in the right direction may be found in the cultural autonomy permitted the national groups in Soviet Russia and in the principle of national self-determination followed in the reconstruction of Central Europe after World War I. Regionalism in France, a movement of lasting vitality, purports to give natural geographic-economic units, largely coincident with the historical provinces, governmental power for the independent conduct of affairs in cases where local variation would not harm the national welfare. In the United States, proposals occasionally put forth for a somewhat similar organization of regional unities, based on common and vital economic and social interests,[12] might lead to the creation of a Southern region conforming essentially to Calhoun's picture of the section.

The most striking development of decentralization in the modern political world has been the growing autonomy of the British Dominions of Canada, Ireland, Australia, New Zealand, and South Africa. In this instance, members of a single political system have increasingly taken their fates into their own hands generally without much restraint by the central government. Powers reserved to the central government can be exercised over any Dominion only with the full consent of that Dominion. The result is that each Dominion has the capacity to protect itself against any action of Great Britain which it deems detrimental to its interest. This is what Calhoun believed ought to have been possible in the American Union through nullification. Any minority of American States in a group comparable in size and importance to one or more of the present British Dominions would have had the capacity to protect its interests by staying the action of the general government and possibly even by diminishing its competence. And just as Calhoun argued for the members of the American Union, some authorities maintain that each Dominion has a legal right of secession from the British Commonwealth of Nations.[13]

Some of the structural differences between the constitution of the Commonwealth of Nations and Calhoun's scheme are less important than they appear at first sight. The Commonwealth has no central legislature; but there are occasional Imperial Conferences and frequent consultations among several Dominions' executive agencies; and the Dominions use the executive agencies of the central government for certain purposes. Corresponding to the Crown as the object of loyalty for citizens of all units of the British Commonwealth, there is in Calhoun's system the federal Constitution, to which citizens of the several States would owe a common allegiance. Thus the British Commonwealth of Nations achieves the sort of political union that Calhoun advocated for the United States. Perhaps the satisfactory working of the British union affords some proof of the correctness of Calhoun's claim that a decentralized political union was workable and desirable in the United States. There cannot easily be any economic exploitation of one of the members of the British union by any combination of the others; and their voluntary cooperation is made possible by the democratic procedure of the conferences.

Calhoun's theory of the concurrent majority may offer the solution of urban-rural conflict in modern politics. Especially in the American States has the clash of interest between city and country become pronounced, and to some extent the cleavage impinges upon national party politics. As Professor Holcombe has pointed out,[14] there is a fundamental division between city-dweller and country-man in their attitudes toward government. Their conception of governmental organization and work are different, and their demands for public services differ. Urban population has steadily grown into a larger part of the whole, but static constitutional provisions on representation in legislatures have failed to give cities proportional representation. In almost every State in the Union large cities are under-represented. The New England States have, perhaps, the most serious rotten borough situation, although there presently emerges a growing awareness of the gravity of the situation in the South.[15] In both regions reform has generally been blocked by rural opposition arising out of an appreciation of the serious divergence of interest between urban and rural areas. Application of Calhoun's theory would mean adjustment of representation so that rural elements predominate in one house of the legislature and urban elements in the other. In Connecticut there is frank recognition that such a balance has been achieved, and in New York there is a tendency in the same direction. To Calhoun, this balance would mean insurance of justice in legislation affecting both groups. Some writers on American State government have considered the idea (apparently without concern as to its origin) and summarily rejected it as conducive to deadlocks and disruption of party responsibility. However, such an application of Calhoun's concurrent majority would give some real significance to the continuance of bicameralism. And in view of recent emphasis upon the importance of the urban-rural problem, the idea may have unsuspected validity for modern American government.

Although agriculture remains the most important economic pursuit in the South, the old order has changed. To many Southerners, the change presages the complete annihilation of all that was peculiarly Southern. Some of them welcome this new South—which will be more American than Southern.[16] But there has persisted among others the self-consciousness of a defeated minority section which does not apologize for the past and strives to preserve its integrity. Their efforts go beyond respect for the historical tradition and aspiration for cultural autonomy, and have even economic aspects. Not long ago, a group of some twelve Southern intellectuals, including John Crowe Ransom, Donald Davidson, Stark Young, and others, put forth a manifesto inveighing against making the South an industrialized society and declaring for the preservation or revival of much of the good in the old agrarian South. In their book, *I'll Take My Stand*,[17] they point out the ills of industrial life elsewhere, describe the virtues of agrarian ways, and plead that Southerners recognize the desirability of achieving at least a balanced economy. The South should accept the increased productive power and material benefits of industrial progress only so far as is compatible with the preservation of human values. These have been sacrificed elsewhere to industrialism.

They make the familiar indictment of industrialism: pointing to the fluctuations of the business cycle, the increasing economic insecurity, and the increasing inequality in the distribution of wealth. Pursuit of profits leads to incessant expansion. Constant technological change leads to unemployment and to exploitation of consumers and workers. More important are the moral and aesthetic evils of industrialism: the absorption of the mind in economic affairs, rendering one unfit for higher intellectual and artistic pursuits. Life in an industrial community, they believe, is hurried, greedy, imitative, dull. The arts are divorced from nature and continue only a desperate existence of escape or rebellion. Munificently endowed education accomplishes little more than the training of the gosling in the goose-step. The amenities of life—good manners and intelligent conversation, hospitality and neighborly sympathy, family life and romantic love—are sacrificed in imitative and competitive display-consumption and in devotion to the fetishes of speed and efficiency.

These "Neo-Confederates," as they have been called, prefer an agrarian society, i. e., one in which "agriculture is the leading vocation, whether for wealth, for pleasure, or for prestige—a form of labor that is pursued with intelligence and leisure, and that becomes the model to which other forms approach as well as they may."[18] They want the conditions of a life that affords more leisure, more security, more stability of established institutions, social habits more conducive to devotion to cultural pursuits, and a climate of opinion fostering more intelligence and individuality in the practice of the arts of living. In the fashion of Jefferson and Taylor, they believe that the culture of the soil is the "best and most sensitive of vocations," and that it will develop human beings of superior virtue. To them, love of soil is fundamental in human nature. They admire the patriarchial ideal of community responsibility for the well-being of the neighborhood, which Calhoun claimed for the plantation regime. They share also with the earlier agrarians much of the specific criticism of industrial society; and, like Calhoun, they feel that an agrarian regime offers more social harmony and stability. Although these agrarians make no plea for slavery, they hold the aristocratic attitude of Calhoun, Harper, and Hammond on many questions of social re-

272 THE POLITICAL THEORY OF JOHN C. CALHOUN

lationships. Education, they say, should be confined to
superior children; or for the masses it should be limited
mainly to vocational training. Nevertheless, these modern
agrarians accept political democracy, as did their predecessors in this tradition. Indeed, they believe that an agrarian basis would make democracy less of a mockery than it
proves to be in industrial society.

Some of this group, led by John Crowe Ransom, de-
part considerably from the tradition represented by Calhoun in favoring public policies to discourage commercial-
ized agriculture, or agricultural capitalism; they want to
foster a simple and more democratic agricultural regime
of small farmers who are largely self-sufficing. Further,
Calhoun in his attitude toward industrialism differed from
the modern Southern agrarians in several important respects. He enjoyed the agrarian life of his section and
thought it had certain superior virtues, but he applauded
also the industrial development of the North. "I am no
enemy of the manufacturing interest. On the contrary, . . .
according to my conception, the great advance made in the
arts by mechanical and chemical inventions and discoveries
in the last three or four generations has done more for
civilization and the elevation of the human race than all
other causes combined in the same period."[19] He hoped to
see Northern industry rival that of Great Britain. Industrialism contributed the wealth necessary to the enjoyment
of leisure and the pursuit of culture. It produced a leisure
class that shared with the Southern aristocracy a superior
way of life marked by high responsibility, power, and
prestige. Unlike these later Southern critics of industrialism, he viewed the masses as destined to a life of labor
which largely rendered them incapable of attaining the
standards of the dominant classes. They were the "mudsills" of society. Calhoun's opposition to Northern industrialism was not a direct attack, but rather a compara-

tive defense of the Southern regime and a plea for toleration. He sought Northern respect for what he deemed fair demands for Southern political and economic self-determination. Occasionally he showed antipathy to industrial development in the South, but this was primarily due to fear of a divided stand on the protective tariff.

There is no doubt that the modern attempt to revitalize the Southern agrarian tradition is of much potential value. It may well be looked upon as the antithesis called forth by the uncritical exaggeration in American society of the thesis of industrialism. From the conflict of the two, to continue with dialectic logic, might well arise a superior synthesis in both thought and action. The antithesis, presented by *I'll Take My Stand,* has certainly its doubtful aspects. Love of the soil is not a proved innate human characteristic. The position that agriculture is a pursuit closer to nature than industrial activity rests upon the questionable assumption that the mechanical works of man are not "natural." The attack on democratized education contains only partial truth; and surely the cultural benefits of the great wealth of industrial society have been underestimated. That industrialism of itself destroys intelligent use of the leisure it begets is clearly overstatement. Further, the lack of individual discrimination in tastes and pursuits on the part of large numbers of people may well be made only more apparent and not actually fostered by an industrial regime; certainly this is the view that the more aristocratic attitude of Calhoun would support. Finally, the opinion that industrialism leads inevitably to socialism and then to communism and that any form of collectivism is necessarily bad appears both superficial and second-hand.

However, the antithesis contains certain elements which would contribute to a fruitful synthesis. It is something more than a mere repetition of certain faults in

American industrial society. The sum total of human happiness would probably be increased if some effective social technique could be devised to eliminate the unemployment caused by technological improvements. It might be wise to slow down the rate of technological change if we could thereby promote the economic security of labor as well as protect the investor from losses suffered in the destruction of obsolescent machinery. And the South, which is still predominantly agricultural, has the opportunity to restrain its industrial development within the bounds of satisfactory human adjustment, by enacting laws to prohibit child labor, fix minimum wages and maximum hours, provide unemployment insurance and old-age pensions, limit the charges and earnings of financial management in the public interest. In such wise a better balance between industry and agriculture might be secured in the South for some time, with the probable result that agriculture would remain the dominant economic pursuit. The cause of balanced economy would also be promoted within agriculture itself, as others have pointed out,[20] by progress of subsistence homesteads to improve the lot of tenants and share-croppers, crop diversification and control, soil conservation, reforestation, flood control, and orderly utilization of the new technology for cultivation and cooperative technique for marketing. A complete program for the South would include also the demand made by Peter Molyneaux and Professor Claudius T. Murchison to abandon economic nationalism, reduce tariffs, and encourage foreign trade; nothing could be more directly within the Calhoun tradition. If by such means the South could attain a stable and balanced economy in which agriculture still remains predominant, the people of the South would have a splendid material basis for happiness and a rich cultural life. The development of a provincial or regional literature, destined to receive some conscious and deliberate encouragement anyway, would proceed apace in such a favorable environment. Whatever loss in horsepower or dollars might be sustained would be compensated by gain in human values. The resulting harmony and stability in society, so prized by Calhoun, would facilitate good living without any sacrifice of genuine progress.

NOTES

1. B. F. Wright, *American Interpretations of Natural Law* (Cambridge, 1931), p. 272.
2. The German doctrine had been imported to America by Thomas Dew, it has been claimed. See W. E. Dodd, *The Cotton Kingdom* (New Haven, 1921), pp. 49-50.
3. D. F. Houston makes the mistaken claim that Robert J. Turnbull originated the theory of nullification in his "Crisis" essays. See Houston, *Nullification in South Carolina* (New York, 1908), pp. 72-73, 80. A careful examination of *The Crisis* (Charleston, 1827) reveals only a very few of the elements of nullification and nothing at all of its rationale. The theory was the work of Calhoun without serious doubt.
4. C. E. Merriam, "The Political Philosophy of John C. Calhoun," *Studies in Southern History and Politics* New York, 1914), pp. 337-338. Merriam's reading of history recalls Becker's definition of history as the tricks that historians play on the dead. He argues, for example. as though it had been predestined that "if conflict were precipitated, the one and indivisible sovereignty would fall to the nation." Military experts cannot bear him out that the triumph of the North in the Civil War was inexorable.
5. C. F. Adams, *Studies Military and Diplomatic, 1775-1865* (New York, 1911), pp. 203-227; C. A. and Mary R. Beard, *Rise of American Civilization*, 1 vol. ed., (New York, 1930), Bk. II, pp. 47-51; H. C. Lodge, *Daniel Webster*, 5th ed. (Boston, 1885), pp. 176-177; C. E. Merriam, *History of American Political Theo-*

ries (New York, 1903), pp. 287-288; Goldwin Smith, "England and the War of Secession," *Atlantic Monthly,* March, 1902, p. 305.

6. This is Merriam's judgment. See his "Political Phillosophy of John C. Calhoun," pp. 335, 337-338. This is also apparently Parrington's view, as he writes of the almost tragic self-deception in Calhoun's opposition to economic forces. V. L. Parrington, *Main Currents in American Thought,* 3 vols. (New York, 1927-1930), Vol. II, p. 81.

7. Calhoun, *Works,* Vol. IV, pp. 557-558. See also Calhoun, *Correspondence,* pp. 321, 391, 624-625; Calhoun, *Works,* Vol. I, pp. 239, 255, 317 ff.; Vol. II, pp. 200, 260, 337-338, 383-394; 637; Vol. III, pp. 30-31, 379; Vol. VI, pp. 141-143.

8. Calhoun, *Correspondence,* p. 469.

9. In his summary exposition of Calhoun's theory, Merriam necessarily treats the conception, but he fails to note the innovating character of Calhoun's use of it. See C. E. Merriam, "The Political Philosophy of John C. Calhoun", *Studies in Southern History of American Political Theories* (New York, 1903), pp. 267-284. Parrington also neglects this aspect of Calhoun's theory, although he emphasizes other points of Calhoun's discontinuity with Jeffersonian thought. V. L. Parrington, *Main Currents in American Thought,* Vol. II, pp. 70 ff.

10. Calhoun, *Works,* Vol. III, p. 591.

11. Emery Reves, *The Anatomy of Peace* (New York, 1945), pp. 126-144; Cord Meyer, Jr., *Peace Or Anarchy* (Boston, 1947), p. 151; Vernon Nash, *The World Must Be Governed* (New York, 1949), pp. xiii-xv, 36.

12. W. B. Munro, *The Invisible Government* (New York, 1928), Ch. VI; W. Y. Elliott, *The Need for Constitutional Reform* (New York, 1935), Ch. IX; H. W. Odum, "The Case for Regional-National Social Planning," *Social Forces* 13:43-50 (October, 1934).

13. See P. J. Noel Baker, *The Present Juridical Status of the British Dominions in International Law* (London, 1929), pp. 34, 63, 267-268, 370-372, and *passim;* W.

Y. Elliott, *The New British Empire* (New York and London, 1932), Chs. I-II, VIII; Arthur B. Keith, *The Dominions As Sovereign States* (London, 1938), Part I, esp. pp. 100-148.

14. A. N. Holcombe, *The New Party Politics* (New York, 1933), pp. 126-131 and *passim*.

15. H. C. Nixon, "Southern Regionalism Limited," *The Virginia Quarterly Review* 26: 161-170 (April, 1950). Cf. V. O. Key, Jr., *Southern Politics* (New York, 1949) pp. 115-129; 669-675, and *passim*.

16. This is the attitude quite widely held by modern commentators. See W. C. Ramsdell, "The Southern Heritage," *Culture in the South* (Chapel Hill, 1934), p. 23; Broadus Mitchell, "A Survey of Industry," *Culture in the South*, pp. 80-82; Gerald W. Johnson, "No More Excuses," *Harper's Monthly* 162: 331-337, Feb., 1931; J. W. Garner, "Southern Politics since the Civil War," *Studies in Southern History and Politics*, esp. pp. 367, 385-387; Holland Thompson, *The New South* (New Haven, 1919), Ch. IX.

17. *I'll Take My Stand, the South and the Agrarian Tradition* (New York and London, 1930) by "Twelve Southerners." Some of these "Nashville agrarians" give further expression to their ideas in chapters contributed to *Who Owns America?* (Boston and New York, 1936), edited by Herbert Agar and Allen Tate. T. J. Cauley, who belongs essentially to the same group, has set forth his thought on the subject in *Agrarianism* (Chapel Hill, 1935). Cf. Francis B. Simkins, *The South Old and New* (New York, 1947), pp. 7-9, 352-355, and *passim*.

18. *I'll Take My Stand,* p. xix; Cauley, *Agrarianism,* p. 3. H. C. Nixon, one of the original "twelve Southerners," seems to have shifted somewhat away from Southern agrarianism in his "Southern Regionalism Limited," cited above; cf. John Temple Graves, "Revolution in the South," *Virginia Quarterly Review* 26: 190-203 (April, 1950).

19. Calhoun, *Works*, Vol. IV, pp. 183-184; Calhoun, *Correspondence*, pp. 654-656. See also "John C. Calhoun and the Presidential Campaign of 1824: Some Un-

published Calhoun Letters, I," *American Historical Review* 40: 82-96 at p. 90.
20. See W. T. Couch, ed., *Culture in the South* (Chapel Hill, 1934), especially the chapter "Southern Agriculture" by A. E. Parkins, the chapter "Depression and the Future of Business" by Claudius T. Murchison, and the chapter "The Profile of Southern Culture" by Rupert B. Vance; B. B. Kendrick and A. M. Arnett, *The South Looks at its Past* (Chapel Hill, 1935), especially Ch. IV.

Bibliography

WRITINGS AND SPEECHES OF CALHOUN

The Works of John C. Calhoun, edited by Richard K. Crallé, 6 vols. (New York, 1851-1867). Vol. I contains the "Disquisition on Government" and the "Discourse on the Constitution and Government of the United States."

Address in the Senate of the United States on Slavery, March 4, 1850, pamphlet (Washington, 1850)

"Calhoun—Gouverneur Correspondence, 1823-1836," *New York Public Library Bulletin,* 3: 324-333 (1899).

The Calhoun Textbook (New York and Philadelphia, 1843).

Constitutional Doctrines of Webster, Hayne, and Calhoun, pamphlet (New York, 1896).

Correspondence between General Andrew Jackson and John C. Calhoun . . . on the course of the latter in the deliberations of the cabinet of Mr. Monroe on the occurrences in the Seminole War, pamphlet (Washington, 1831).

Correspondence between Governor Hamilton and John C. Calhoun, Vice President of the U. S. on Subject of State Interposition, pamphlet (Charleston, 1832).

"Correspondence of John C. Calhoun," *American Historical Association Annual Report,* 1899, Vol. II, edited by J. F. Jameson (Washington, 1900).

Extracts from his *Works* in *Library of World's Best Literature,* edited by C. D. Warner (New York, 1896-1899), Vol. VI, pp. 3071-3100.

"The Government of the United States from 'Discourse on the Constitution and Government of the United States' " *Old South Leaflets,* Vol. V (Boston, 1900), pp. 117-140.

"John C. Calhoun and the Presidential Campaign of 1824: some unpublished Calhoun Letters, I and II," *American Historical Review* 40: 82-96, 287-300 (1934-1935).

"Letter of John C. Calhoun, 1847," *American Historical Review* I: 314 (1896).

"Letter on the Seminole Question," *Niles' Register* 39: 447; 40: 11, 37, 70 (1831).

"Letter to Baron von Gerolt, May 28, 1848," *American Historical Review* 40: 477-478 (April, 1935).

Life of John C. Calhoun, presenting a Condensed History of Political Events from 1811 to 1843 (New York, 1843).

Mr. Calhoun's Resolutions Relative to the Constitutional Rights of the South on the Abolition Question, pamphlet (Philadelphia, 1838).

Noted Speeches of Calhoun, Briggs ed. (New York, 1912).

Papers of Patrick Noble, containing some letters of John C. Calhoun.

Remarks of the Hon. John C. Calhoun delivered in the Senate of the United States, Jan. 13, 1834, on the Subject of the Removal of Deposits from the Bank of the United States, pamphlet (Washington, 1834).

Remarks of the Hon. John C. Calhoun delivered in the Senate of the United States on Mar. 21, 1834, on the Motion of Mr. Webster for Leave to Introduce a Bill to Continue the Charter of the Bank of the United States for Six Years after Expiration of the present Charter, pamphlet (Washington, 1834).

Remarks delivered in the Senate of the United States, May 6, 1834, on the President's Protest, pamphlet (Washington, 1834).

Remarks on the Bill to Regulate Deposits of Public Money, June, 1836, pamphlet (Washington, 1836).

Remarks of Mr. Calhoun on the Bill Authorizing an Issue of Treasury Notes, delivered in the Senate of the

United States, Sept. 19, 1837, pamphlet (Washington, 1837).

"Report on Incendiary Publications," *Niles' Register* 49: 408 (1836).

"Speech on Nullification," *Niles' Register* 43: Supplement 155, 221 (1833).

"Speech on Jackson's Protest," *Niles' Register* 46: 213 (1834).

Speech of the Honorable John C. Calhoun, of South Carolina on the Abolition Petitions, . . . Mar. 9, 1836, pamphlet (Washington, 1836).

Speech of the Honorable John C. Calhoun on His Amendment to Separate the Government from the Banks, . . . Oct. 3, 1837, pamphlet (Washington, 1837).

Speech of Mr. Calhoun, of South Carolina, on the Subtreasury Bill, delivered in the Senate of the United States, Feb. 15, 1838, pamphlet (Washington, 1838).

Speech delivered in the Senate, Feb. 5, 1840, *on Grundy's Report in relation to Assumption of State Debts by the Federal Government,* pamphlet (Worcester, 1840).

Speech of Mr. Calhoun, of South Carolina, in the Senate, Mar. 13, 1840, pamphlet (Washington, 1840).

Speech on the Bill to Distribute the Proceeds of the Public Lands, . . . Jan. 23, 1841, pamphlet (Washington, 1841).

Speech in Reply to Webster and Clay on Crittenden's Amendment to the Redemption Bill . . . Jan. 30, 1841, pamphlet (Washington, 1841).

Speech of the Honorable John C. Calhoun in Support of the Veto Power . . . Feb. 28, 1842, pamphlet (Washington, 1842).

Speech of the Honorable John C. Calhoun, of South Carolina, on Mr. Clay's Resolutions in Relation to the Revenues and Expenditures of the Government, delivered in the Senate of the United States, Mar. 16, 1842, pamphlet (Washington, 1842).

Speech of Mr. Calhoun of South Carolina, on Resolutions

giving Notice to Great Britain of the abrogation of the Convention of Joint Occupancy, delivered in the Senate of the United States, Mar. 16, 1846, pamphlet (Washington, 1846).

Speech of Mr. Calhoun, of South Carolina, on the Appropriation Bill for the War with Mexico . . . Feb. 9, 1847, pamphlet (Washington, 1847).

Speech of Mr. Calhoun, of South Carolina, in Reply to Mr. Turney of Tennessee, delivered in the Senate of the United States, Feb. 12, 1847, pamphlet (Washington, 1847).

Speech of Mr. Calhoun, of South Carolina, on His Resolutions in Reference to the War with Mexico, delivered in the Senate of the United States, Jan. 4, 1848, pamphlet (Washington, 1848).

Speech on the Oregon Bill delivered in the Senate, June 27, 1848, pamphlet (Washington, 1848).

Speech of Mr. Calhoun, of South Carolina, on the Slavery Question, delivered in the Senate of the United States, Mar. 4, 1850, pamphlet (Washington, 1850).

Speeches delivered in the Senate on the Enforcing Bill, pamphlet (Boston, 1833). By Calhoun and Webster.

Speeches of John C. Calhoun, delivered in the Congress of the United States from 1811 *to the present Time* (New York, 1843).

Speeches of Mr. Calhoun, of South Carolina, on the Ten Regiment Bill in Reply to Mr. Davis of Mississippi and Mr. Cass, delivered in the Senate, Mr. 16 *and* 17, 1848, pamphlet (Washington, 1848).

Speeches on Slavery in the Senate of the United States, March, 1850, pamphlet (New York, 1850).

OTHER PRIMARY MATERIALS

Ames, Herman V., *State Documents on Federal Relations: the States and the United States,* 6 vols. (Philadelphia, 1900-1906).

Anonymous, "Calhoun and Daniel Webster," *DeBow's Review* 32 : 20 ff.

——————, "Charges against John C. Calhoun While Secretary of War," *Niles' Reigster* 31 : 292-387; 32 : 1 (1827).

——————, "Efforts of John C. Calhoun against General Jackson," *Niles' Register* 41 : 141 (1832) ; 43 : 79, 90 (1833).

——————, *John C. Calhoun in his Personal, Moral, and Intellectual Traits of Character* (New York, ——).

——————, *Measures, Not Men, illustrated by some Remarks upon the Public Conduct and Character of John C. Calhoun, Collected principally from Public Documents.* By a citizen of New York. Pamphlet (New York, 1823).

——————, *Memoir of John C. Calhoun,* pamphlet (New York, 1850).

Baldwin, Henry, *General View of the Origin and Nature of the Constitution and Government of the United States* (Philadelphia, 1837).

Bledsoe, Albert Taylor, *Is Davis a Traitor; or Was Secession a Constitutional Right previous to the War of 1861?*

——————, *An Essay on Liberty and Slavery* (Philadelphia, 1856).

Boucher, C. S., and R. P. Brooks, ed., "Correspondence Addressed to John C. Calhoun, 1837-1849," *American Historical Association Annual Report,* 1929 (Washington, 1930), pp. 125-551.

Bryan, Edward B., *The Rightful Remedy, addressed to the Slave-holders of the South* (Charleston, 1850).

Chandler, Daniel, *Address on the Rights and Remedies of the States, delivered before the State Rights Association of Wilkes County, June 3, 1834,* pamphlet (Washington, Georgia, 1834).

Cheves, Langdon, *Speech of the Honorable Langdon Cheves, delivered before the Delegates of the Nash-*

ville Convention, on Friday, Nov. 13, 1850, pamphlet (Columbia, 1850).

Christy, David, *Cotton Is King: or the Culture of Cotton, and its Relation to Agriculture, Manufactures, and Commerce; and also to the Free Colored People of the United States, and to those who hold that slavery is in itself sinful,* 2nd ed. (New York, 1856).

Cooper, Thomas, *Consolidation: an Account of Parties of the United States from the Convention of* 1787 *to the Present Period,* pamphlet, 2nd ed. (Columbia, 1830).

————, *Lectures on the Elements of Political Economy* (Columbia, 1826).

————, *Manual of Political Economy* (Washington, 1833).

————, *Memoirs of a Nullifier, With a Historical Sketch of Nullification in* 1832-1833 (New York, 1860).

————, "Speech at Columbia, July 2, 1827," *Niles' Register* 33: 28-32.

————, *Two Tracts on the Proposed Alteration of the Tariff* (Charleston, 1823).

Dabney, Robert L., *A Defence of Virginia and through her of the South in recent and pending Contests against the Sectional Party* (New York, 1867).

Davis, Jefferson, "Farewell Speech to the Senate, Jan. 21, 1861," *Congressional Globe,* 36th Congress, 2nd Session, pp. 487 ff.

————, "Inaugural Address as President of Confederacy, Feb. 18, 1861," *Messages and Papers of the Confederacy,* edited by James D. Richardson, 2 vols. (Nashville, 1905), Vol. I, pp. 32-36.

Davis, Jefferson, *Jefferson Davis, Constitutionalist: His Letters, Papers, and Speeches,* edited by Dunbar Rowland, 10 vols. (Jackson, Mississippi, 1923).

————, *The Rise and Fall of the Confederate Government,* 2 vols. (New York, 1881).

Dew, Thomas R., "Review of the Debate in the Virginia

Legislature, 1831-'32," *Political Register* (Washington), Oct. 16, 1833.

Elliot, Jonathan, ed., *Debates in the Several State Conventions on the Adoption of the Federal Constitution,* 2nd ed., 5 vols. (Philadelphia, 1888).

Farrand, Max, ed., *The Records of the Federal Convention of 1787,* 3 vols. (New Haven, 1911).

Fielder, Herbert, *The DisUnionist* (Georgia, 1858).

Fitzhugh, George, *Cannibals All! or, Slaves Without Masters* (Richmond, 1857).

——————, *Sociology for the South, or the Failure of Free Society* (Richmond, 1854).

Fouche, Simpson, *Address on the Sovereignty of the States, delivered before the State Rights Association of Wilkes County, Georgia, June* 3, 1834, pamphlet (Washington, Georgia, 1834).

Garnett, M. R. H., *The Union, Past and Future: How it Works and How to Save It.* By a Citizen of Virginia. pamphlet 4th ed. (Charleston, 1850).

Georgia, *Proceedings of the Anti-Tariff Convention of the State of Georgia, held in Milledgeville,* 1832, pamphlet (Milledgeville, 1832).

Grayson, W. J., "The Dual Form of Labor," *DeBow's Review* 28 : 60 (1860).

Hamilton, James Jr., *Speech on the Operation of the Tariff on the Interests of the South, and the Constitutional Means of Resisting Its Evils, delivered at Walterborough, Oct.* 21, 1828, pamphlet (Charleston, 1828).

——————, *Speech on the Tariff Bill in the House of Representatives, April* 6, 1824, pamphlet (Washington, 1824).

Hammond, James H., "Hammond's Eulogy on John C. Calhoun," *Southern Quarterly* 20 : 107.

Hammond, James H., "Letters on Slavery," *Pro-Slavery Argument* (Philadelphia, 1853), pp. 99-174.

——————, *Selections from the Letters and Speeches of James H. Hammond* (New York, 1866).

—————, "Speech in the Senate, Mar. 4, 1858, on the Lecompton Constitution for Kansas," *Congressional Globe,* 35th Congress, 1st session, Vol. XXVI Pt. I, pp. 959-962.

Hammond, J. D., *Letter to John C. Calhoun on the Annexation of Texas* (Cooperstown, 1844).

"Hampden," *Genuine Book of Nullification,* pamphlet (Charleston, 1831).

Harper, William, "Memoir on Slavery," *Pro-Slavery Argument* (Philadelphia, 1853), pp. 1-98.

—————, *Speech before the Charleston State Rights and Free Trade Association, at their regular meeting, April 1, 1832, Explaining and Enforcing the Remedy of Nullification,* pamphlet (Charleston, 1832).

Hayne, Robert Y., *Fourth of July Oration at Charleston, South Carolina,* pamphlet (Charleston, 1831).

—————, *Second Speech in Reply to Mr. Webster,* pamphlet (Washington, 1830).

—————, *Speech in the Senate of the United States, Jan. 21, 1830, on Mr. Foot's Resolution,* pamphlet (Washington, 1830).

—————, "Speeches in Debate with Webster," *Register of Debates in Congress,* 21st Congress, 1st session, Vol. VI, pp. 31-35, 43-58, 82-92.

Hundley, D. R., *Social Relations in Our Southern States* (New York, 1860).

Jameson, J. F., ed., "Calendar of Letters of John C. Calhoun heretofore Printed," *American Historical Association Annual Report,* 1898 (Washington, 1899), p. 591.

Jefferson, Thomas, *Notes on the State of Virginia* (London, 1787).

—————, *The Writings of Thomas Jefferson,* Ford ed., 10 vols. (New York, 1892-1899).

McDuffie, Governor George, Remarks of McDuffie in his message to the South Carolina State Legislature in 1834, as quoted by William Slade of Vermont during speech in the House of Representatives, Jan. 18 and 20, 1840, *Niles' Register* 61 : 135-143, 154-159.

Madison, James, "Debates in the Federal Convention of 1787 as reported by James Madison," *Formation of the Union Document,* 69th Congress, 1st session, House Document 398 (Washington, 1924), pp. 109-745.

——————, Alexander Hamilton, and John Jay, *The Federalist,* University ed. (New York, 1864) ; Ford ed. (New York, 1898).

——————, *The Writings of James Madison,* 9 vols. (New York, 1900-1910).

Maxcy, Virgil, "Virgil Maxcy on Calhoun's Political Opinions and Prospects, 1823," *American Historical Review* 12 : 599-601 (April, 1907).

Mitchell, T. R., "Speech on the New Tariff Bill, Feb., 1823, in the House of Representatives," *Annals of Congress,* 17th Congress, 2nd session, pp. 1001-1012.

Phillips, U. B., ed., "The Correspondence of Robert Toombs, Alexander H. Stephens, and Howell Cobb," *Annual Report of American Historical Association* 1911, Vol. II (Washington, 1913).

Poinsett, Joel R., *Speech on the Tariff Bill in the House of Representatives,* April, 1824, pamphlet (Washington, 1824).

Pollard, Edward A., *The Lost Cause; A New Southern History of the War of the Confederates,* etc. (New York, 1866).

Randolph, John, *Speech in th House of Representatives in Debate on the Resolution . . . prohibiting the Importation of British Manufactures,* pamphlet (New Haven, 1806).

——————, *Speech on Internal Improvement in the House of Representatives, Jan.* 31, 1824, pamphlet (Washington, 1824).

Randolph-Macon College, *The John P. Branch Historical Papers,* 5 vols. (Richmond, 1901-1918).

Rhett, Robert Barnwell, "Rhett on the Biography of Calhoun, 1854," *American Historical Review* 13: 310-312 (1908).

——————, "Speech on the Veto Power," *Congressional Globe*, 27th Congress, 2nd session, Appendix, pp. 605-608 (1841-1842).

Richardson, James D., ed., *Messages and Papers of the Confederacy*, 2 vols. (Nashville, 1905).

——————, *Messages and Papers of the Presidents*, 1789-1897, 10 vols. (Washington, 1899).

Roane, Spencer, "Case of McCulloch v. Maryland by 'Amphictyon,' " *John P. Branch Historical Papers* 2: 51-76.

Roane, Spencer, "Public Letter to Governor Randolph, Feb. 13, 1788, signed 'Plain Dealer,' " *John P. Branch Historical Papers* 2: 47-51.

——————, "The Rights of the States and of the People," *John P. Branch Historical Papers* 2:71-121.

Scott, John, *The Lost Principle; or the Sectional Equilibrium; How it was created—how destroyed— how it may be restored.* By Barbarossa. (Richmond, 1860).

Simms, William Gilmore, "The Morals of Slavery," *Pro-Slavery Argument* (Philadelphia, 1853), pp. 175-285.

South Carolina, *Journal of the Convention of the People of South Carolina: Assembled at Columbia on the 19th November, 1832, and again on the 11th March, 1833,* pamphlet (Columbia, 1833).

——————, "Letters on the Nullification Movement in South Carolina, 1830-1834," *American Historical Review* 6: 736-765; 7: 92-119 (1901).

South Carolina General Assembly, *Death and Funeral Ceremonies of John C. Calhoun, containing speeches, etc.* (Columbia, 1850). A. S. Johnston, publisher.

State Rights Association, *Proceedings of the State Rights and Free Trade Convention held in Charleston, South Carolina, on the 22nd and 25th February, 1832,* pamphlet (Charleston, 1832).

Stephens, Alexander H., *A Constitutional View of the late*

War between the States, 2 vols. (Philadelphia, 1868-1870).

—————, "Inaugural Address as Vice-President of the Confederacy, Feb. 18, 1861," *Messages and Papers of the Confederacy,* edited by James D. Richardson, 2 vols. (Nashville, 1905).

—————, *The Reviewers Reviewed: a supplement to "The War between the States"* (New York, 1872).

Taylor, John, *Arrator, being a series of Agricultural Essays, practical and political, in sixty four numbers,* 6th rev. ed. (Petersburg, 1818).

—————, *Construction Construed and Constitutions Vindicated* (Richmond, 1820).

—————, *Inquiry into the Principles and Policy of the Government of the United States* (Fredericksburg, 1814).

—————, *New Views of the Constitution of the United States* (Washington, 1823).

Taylor, John, *Tyranny Unmasked* (Washington, 1822).

Trescot, William H., *Position and Course of the South,* pamphlet (Charleston, 1850).

Troup, George M., *Letter, Feb.* 10, 1833, *to a Gentleman in Georgia on the Rights of the States and the Origin and Powers of the Federal Government,* pamphlet (Milledgeville, Georgia, 1834).

[Turnbull, Robert J.] "Brutus," *The Crisis, or Essays on the Usurpations of the Federal Government,* pamphlet (Charleston, 1827).

Turnbull, Robert J., *Observations on State Sovereignty, Federal Usurpations, and State Interposition,* pamphlet (New York, 1850).

—————, *An Oration before the State Rights and Free Trade Party . . ., on July* 4, 1832, pamphlet (Charleston, 1832).

U. S. Congress, *American State Papers,* 1789-1838, 10 vols. in 38 (Washington, 1852-1861).

—————, *Annals of Congress,* debates and proceedings, 1789-1824. 42 vols.

————————, *Register of the Debates in Congress,* 13 vols. in 27 (Washington, 1825-1837).

————————, *Congressional Globe,* debates and proceedings, 1838-1873. Vols. 6-46.

————————, *Unveiling of Statue of John C. Calhoun* (Washington, 1910).

U. S. Congress—House Select Committee, *Report on Letter of John C. Calhoun asking Investigation of his Conduct while Secretary of War, Feb.* 13, 1827, pamphlet. Also in *House Report* No. 79, 19th Congress, 2nd session.

U. S. Congress—Senate, *Obituary Addresses on John C. Calhoun, April* 1, 1850, pamphlet (Washington, 1850).

Upshur, Abel P., *A Brief Enquiry into the True Nature and Character of Our Federal Government: being a Review of Judge Story's Commentaries on the Constitution of the United States* (Philadelphia, 1863).

Virginia, *Proceedings of the Virginia State Convention,* 1829-30. *To Which are subjoined the New Constitution of Virginia, and the Votes of the People* (Richmond, 1830).

Virginia and Kentucky, *The Virginia and Kentucky Resolutions of 1798-'99; Jefferson's original draft thereof; Madison's Report; Calhoun's Address; Resolutions of the Several States in Relation to States' Rights,* pamphlet (Washington, 1832).

————————, *Resolutions of Virginia and Kentucky, penned by Madison and Jefferson, in relation to the Alien and Sedition Laws: the Debates in the House of Delegates of Virginia, in December,* 1798, *on the same* (Richmond, 1832).

Von Seydel, Max, "Der Bundesstaatsbegriff," pp. 1-89; "Der Bundesgedanke und der Staatsgedanke im Deutschen Reiche," pp. 90-100; "Die neusten Gestaltungen des Bundesstaatsbegriffs," pp. 101-120. Three monographs contained in *Staatsrechtliche und politische Abhandlungen* (Freiburg and Leipzig, 1893).

————, *Commentar zur Verfassungskunde fur das deutsche Reich.* 2nd ed. (Freiburg and Leipzig, 1897).

————, "Verfassung und Verfassungsgeschichte der Vereinigten Staaten von Amerika," pp. 33-58; "Der deutsche Bundesrat," pp. 90-122. Two monographs contained in *Staatsrechtliche und politische Abhandlungen,* Neue Folge (Tubingen and Leipzig, 1902).

Wilde, Richard H., *Speech on the Tariff Bill in the House of Representatives, May* 15, 1828, pamphlet (Washington, 1828).

Wright, B. F., Jr., *A Source Book of American Political Theory* (New York, 1929).

SECONDARY MATERIALS

Adams, Charles Francis, *Studies Military and Diplomatic,* 1775-1865 (New York, 1911).

Adams, E. D., *The Power of Ideals in American History* (New Haven and London, 1913).

Ames, H. V., "John C. Calhoun and the Secession Movement of 1850," *American Antiquarian Society Proceedings* 28: 19-50 (April, 1918). Also in *University of Pennsylvania Lectures,* Vol. V.

Anonymous, "Life and Character of John C. Calhoun," *North American Review* 145: 246 ff. (1887).

Anonymous, "Nullification Movement in Georgia," *Georgia Historical Quarterly* 5: 3-39.

Ashley, J. M., "Calhoun, Seward, and Lincoln," *Magazine of Western History* 12: 599; 13: 1.

————, *Reminiscences of the Great Rebellion, Calhoun, Seward, and Lincoln* (Toledo, 1890).

Babcock, K. C., *The Rise of American Nationality,* 1811-1819 (New York and London, 1906), Vol. XIII of American Nation Series.

Bancroft, Frederick, *Calhoun and the South Carolina Nullification Movement* (Baltimore, 1928).

Bates, Mary, *Private Life of John C. Calhoun* (Charleston, 1852).

Beard, Charles A., *The Economic Basis of Politics* (New York, 1922).

Beard, Charles A. and Mary R., *The Rise of American Civilization*, 1 vol. ed. (New York, 1930).

Benton, Thomas Hart, *Thirty Years' View; or a History of the Working of the American Government for Thirty Years, from 1820 to 1850, etc.*, 2 vols. (New York, 1854-1856).

Boucher, Chauncey S., "The Ante-Bellum Attitude of South Carolina towards Manufacturing and Agriculture," *Washington University Studies*, III.

————, *The Nullification Controversy in South Carolina* (Chicago, 1916).

————, *Sectionalism, Representation, and the Electoral Question in Ante-Bellum South Carolina* (—, 1916).

Bradford, Gamaliel, *As God Made Them* (New York, 1929).

Brown, William Garrott, *The Lower South in American History* (New York, 1903).

Brownson, Orestes A., "Life and Speeches of John C. Calhoun," *Works*, 20 vols. (Detroit, 1884), Vol. XV, pp. 451-472.

————, "Mr. Calhoun and the Baltimore Convention," *Works, Vol. XV, pp.* 473-483.

Burgess, J. W., *The Middle Period, 1817-1858* (New York, 1897).

Caldwell, H. W., *Great American Legislators* (Chicago, 1900).

Carpenter, Jesse T., *The South as a Conscious Minority, 1789-1861* (New York, 1930).

Carpenter, William Seal, *The Development of American Political Thought* (Princeton, 1930).

Carroll, A. E., "John C. Calhoun and his Nullification Doctrine," *Living Age* 70: 444.

Chadwick, French Ensor, *Causes of the Civil War, 1859-1861* (New York and London, 1906). American Nation History Series.

Channing, Edward, *History of the United States,* 6 vols. (New York, 1921).

Clark, Victor S., *History of Manufactures in the United States,* 1607-1860 (Washington, 1916).

Coit, Margaret L., *John C. Calhoun: American Portrait* (Boston, 1950).

Cole, A. C., *The Irrepressible Conflict* (New York, 1934).

Curry, J. L. M., "Principles, Acts, and Utterances of John C. Calhoun Promotive of the Union," *University of Chicago Record* 3 : 93 ff.

Curti, Merle E., "John C. Calhoun and the Unification of Germany," *American Historical Review* 40 : 476 (April, 1935).

Cushman, G. F., "John C. Calhoun," *Magazine of American History* 8 :612.

Dodd, William E., *The Cotton Kingdom* (New Haven, 1921).

——————, *Expansion and Conflict* (Cambridge, Mass., 1915).

——————, *Statesmen of the Old South or from Radicalism to Conservative Revolt* (New York, 1911).

Draper, John W., *History of the American Civil War,* 3 vols. (New York, 1867-1870).

Dunning, W. A., *Essays on the Civil War and Reconstruction and Related Topics* (New York, 1898).

——————, *A History of Political Theories from Rousseau to Spencer* (New York, 1922).

Elliot, Edward, G., "Die Staatslehre John C. Calhouns," (1903), 70 pp., *Staats-und volkerrechtliche Abhandlungen,* Vol. IV, No. 2, Duncker und Humblot, Leipzig.

Fish, Carl Russell, *The Rise of the Common Man* (New York, 1927).

Fisher, G. P., "Webster and Calhoun in the Debate of 1850," *Scribners' Magazine* 37 : 578-586 (May, 1905).

Fowler, William C., *The Sectional Controversy* (New York, 1863).

Gaines, Francis Pendleton, *The Southern Plantation, a*

Study in the Development and the Accuracy of a Tra-dition (New York, 1924).

Garner, James W., and others, *Studies in Southern History and Politics*. A symposium by the former students of W. A. Dunning to whom the book is "inscribed." (New York, 1914).

Gazley, J. G., *American Opinion of German Unification, 1848-1871*. Columbia University Studies, CXXI.

Gettell, Raymond G., *History of American Political Thought* (New York and London, 1928).

Gray, Lewis C., *History of Agriculture in the Southern United States to 1860*, 2 vols. (Washington, 1933).

Green, W., "John C. Calhoun and the Memphis Memorial," *American Whig Review* 7 : 15.

Hamer, P. M., *Secession Movement in South Carolina, 1847-1852*, University of Pennsylvania Thesis, 1918.

Hart, A. B., "American Triumvirate; Clay, Webster, Calhoun," *Mentor* 5 : 1-11 (March, 1917).

Heckscher, G., "Calhoun's Idea of the Concurrent Majority and the Constitutional Theory of Hegel," *American Political Science Review* 33 : 585-590 (August, 1939).

Henry, R., *Eulogy on the Late John C. Calhoun* (Columbia, 1850).

Hollis, Christopher, *The American Heresy* (London, 1927).

Houston, Davis F., *A Critical Study of Nullification in South Carolina* (New York, 1908).

Hunt, Gaillard, *John C. Calhoun* (Philadelphia, 1908).

Jacobson, J. Mark, *The Development of American Political Thought* (New York and London, 1932).

Jenkins, John S., *The Life of John Caldwell Calhoun* (Auburn and Buffalo, 1850).

Jenkins, W. S., *Pro-Slavery Thought in the Old South* (Chapel Hill, 1935).

Jervey, Theodore D., *Robert Y. Hayne and His Times* (New York, 1909).

Johnson, Zachary T., *The Political Policies of Howell Cobb* (Nashville, 1929).

Kendrick, Benjamin Burks, and Alex Mathews Arnott, *The South Looks At Its Past* (Chapel Hill, N. C., 1935).

Ladies' Calhoun Monument Association, *History of the Calhoun Monument at Charleston* (Charleston, 1888).

Lalor, John J., ed., *Cyclopedia of Political Science, Political Economy, and of the Political History of the United States,* 3 vols. (Chicago, 1883).

Lamb, M. J., "John C. Calhoun as Candidate for the Presidency," *Magazine of American History* 12: 385.

Lodge, Henry C., *Democracy of the Constitution* (New York, 1915).

——————, *Speech on the Acceptance of the Statue of John C. Calhoun, delivered in the Senate March* 12, 1910, pamphlet.

Lovat-Fraser, J. A., "John C. Calhoun: Another Study in Disappointment," *London Quarterly Review* 151: 227-238 (April, 1929).

McLaughlin, A. C., "Background of American Federalism," *American Political Science Review* 12: 215-240.

——————, *A Constitutional History of the United States* (New York, 1935).

——————, *The Courts, the Constitution, and Parties* (Chicago, 1912).

——————, "Social Compact and Constitutional Construction," *American Historical Review* 5: 467-490 (April, 1900).

Magoon, E. L., *Living Orators in America* (New York, 1850).

Malone, Dumas, *Public Life of Thomas Cooper* (New Haven, 1926).

Meigs, William Montgomery, *Life of John C. Calhoun,* 2 vols. (New York, 1917).

Merriam, Charles E., *A History of American Political Theories* (New York, 1903).

——————, *History of the Theory of Sovereignty since Rousseau* (New York, 1900).

——————, "The Political Philosophy of John C. Calhoun," *Studies in Southern History and Politics* (New York, 1914), pp. 319-338.

——————, "Political Theory of John C. Calhoun," *American Journal of Sociology* 7: 577-594 (March, 1902).

Merritt, Elizabeth, *James Henry Hammond, 1807-1864* (Baltimore, 1923).

Meyers, Gustavus, *The History of American Idealism* (New York, 1925).

Miles, J. W., *Discourse on the Occasion of the Funeral of John C. Calhoun* (Charleston, 1850).

Miller, Marion Mills, ed., *Great Debates in American History* 14 vols. (New York, 1913).

Miller, W. L., "John C. Calhoun as Lawyer and Statesman," *Green Bag* 11: 197, 269, 326, 371, 419.

——————, "John C. Calhoun as Orator and Writer," *American Law Review* 33: 531.

Myres, S. D., Jr., "Politics in the South," *Arnold Foundation Studies in Public Affairs*, Vol. III, No. 1, Summer, 1934.

Nixon, Herman Clarence, "Changing Political Philosophy in the South," *Annals of the American Academy of Political and Social Science* 153: 246-250 (1931).

Parrington, V. L., *Main Currents in American Thought*, 3 vols. (New York, 1927-1930).

Parton, James, *Famous Americans of Recent Times* (Boston, 1869).

Phillips, U. B., "Economic and Political Essays in the Ante-Bellum South," Vol. VII, ch. 8, of *The South in the Building of the Nation*, 13 vols. (Richmond, 1909-1913).

——————, "Georgia and State Rights," *American Historical Association Annual Report*, 1901 (Washington, 1902), Vol. II.

——————, "John Caldwell Calhoun," *Dictionary of American Biography*, III, 411-419.

——————, *Life and Labor in the Old South* (Boston, 1929).

—————————, *Life of Robert Toombs* (New York, 1913).

Pinkney, Gustavus M., *Life of John C. Calhoun, being a view of the principal events of his career and an account of his contributions to economic and political science* (Charleston, 1903).

Powell, Edward Payson, *Nullification and Secession in the United States, a history of the six attempts during the first century of the Republic* (New York and London, 1897).

Robinson, E. V., "Nature of the Federal State," *Annals of the American Academy of Political and Soical Science* 3:785-809 (1893).

Russel, Robert R., *Economic Aspects of Southern Sectionalism, 1840-1861* (Urbana, 1924).

Salley, A. S., *The Calhoun Family of South Carolina* (Columbia, 1906).

Schlesinger, Arthur M., *New Viewpoints in American History,* 1928 ed. (New York, 1922).

Sicussat, St. George L., "John C. Calhoun, Secretary of State, March 6, 1844 to March 6, 1845," *American Secretaries of State and Their Diplomacy,* edited by S. F. Bemis, 10 vols. (New York, 1927-1929), Vol. V, pp. 125-233.

Smith, Goldwin, "John C. Calhoun," *Nineteenth Century* 24:266 (1888).

Smith, H. H., "John C. Calhoun: Some Personal Characteristics," *Methodist Quarterly Review* 78:692-695 (October, 1929).

Stephenson, W. W., "Calhoun, 1812, and After," *American Historical Review* 31:701-707 (July, 1926).

Styron, Arthur, *The Cast-Iron Man: Calhoun and American Democracy* (New York, 1935).

Thatcher, H. W., "Calhoun and Federal Reinforcement of State Laws," *American Political Science Review* 36:875-880 (October, 1942).

Thomas, J. P., ed., *The Carolina Tribute to Calhoun* (Columbia, 1857).

Thornwill, J. H., *Thought Suited To The Present Crisis,*

a Sermon On The Death of John C. Calhoun, pamphlet (Columbia, 1850).

Trent, W. P., Southern Statesmen Of The Old Regime (———, 1897).

Tucker, John Randolph, The Constitution of the United States, 2 vols. (Chicago, 1899).

Turner, Frederick J., The Significance of Sections in American History (New York, 1932).

————, The United States 1830-1850, the Nation and Its Sections (New York, 1935).

Van Deusen, J. G., Economic Bases of Disunion in South Carolina (New York, 1928).

Von Holst, Hermann E., The Constitutional and Political History of the United States 8 vols. (Chicago, 1881-1892).

————, John C. Calhoun (Boston, 1883). American Statesmen Series.

Wagstaff, Henry M., State Rights and Political Parties in North Carolina 1776-1861 (Baltimore, 1906).

Walker, J. H., "John C. Calhoun On Government," Southern Quarterly 26 : 121 ; Putnam's 7 : 90.

Walmesley, J. E., "Return of John C. Calhoun to the Senate in 1845," American Historical Annual Report, 1913, (Washington, 1915), Vol. I, pp. 159-165.

Warren, Charles, The Making of the Constitution (Boston, 1928).

————, The Supreme Court in United States History, 3 vols, (Boston, 1922).

Whelpey, J. D., "John C. Calhoun in the Mexican War," American Whig Review 7 :217.

Williams, John Mason, Nullification and Compromise: A Retrospective View (New York, 1863).

Willoughby, Westel W., The Fundamental Concepts of Public Law (New York, 1924).

————, The Nature of the State, 1928 ed. (New York, 1896).

Wiltse, Charles M., John C. Calhoun, Nationalist (Indianapolis, 1944).

————, *John C. Calhoun, Nullifier* (Indianapolis, 1949).

Wise, Henry A., *Seven Decades of Union. The Humanities and Materialism, illustrated by a Memoir of John Tyler, with Reminiscences of Some of His great Contemporaries. The Transition State of This Nation— Its Dangers and Their Remedy* (Philadelphia, 1876).

Wright, B. F., Jr., *American Interpretations of Natural Law* (Cambridge, 1931).

Index

Abolition, 28, 39, 190, 254, 257
Abolitionists, 21, 22, 148, 225
Abolition petitions, 21-22
Adams, John, 71-72
Adams, John Quincy, 36, 42, 54
Adams, Samuel, 48
Admission of new States to Union, 196-97, 253; of California, 23-24, 146
Agrarianism, 50, 66, 70-71, 263; as agricultural capitalism, 32-33, 189-90, 251-54; *see also* Plantocracy
"Agrarianism," 91
Agrarians, 20th century Southern, 270-75
Alien and Sedition Acts, 46, 48
Altruism in human nature, 79
Amending power, the Constitutional, 149-50, 176, 196, 204
American nationalism, 60-61, 190, 192-3
American Revolution, 84, 86, 107
"American system," 18, 37
Analytical jurists, 165, 175
Anarchy, fear of, 82, 90, 151, 154
Annexation of Texas, 22-23
Archer, William Segar, 119
Aristocracy, 52, 139, 155-56; Southern concept of, 104, 114, 124, 237-39, 271-72
Aristotle, 35, 41, 78, 82; on the good life, 94; on organic relation of state to individual, 105; on economic basis of politics, 134; on slavery, 227, 230, 263
Articles of Confederation, 140, 191
Athens, 158, 163
Austin, John, 165
Authority, abuse of, 105-21

Balance of interests in politics, 55, 147-48
Balance of power, *see* Sectional equilibrium
Balanced economy, 274
Baldwin, Henry, 35
Bank of the United States, 20, 39, 73, 190
Barnes, Gilbert H., 39
Beard, Charles A., 50, 260, 275
Bentham, Jeremy, 92, 165-66
Benton, Thomas Hart, 38-39, 40
Blackstone, William, on sovereignty, 165-66
Bledsoe, Albert T., 86-87, 96-97, 123
Bodin, Jean, 105, 134; on sovereignty, 164-65
Bolingbroke, Henry St. John, 142
Bowie, George, 34
Brown, A. V., on sectional equilibrium, 146
Brownson, Orestes A., 125
Bryan, E. B., 127
Bundesstaat, 208-9, 213
Bureaucracy, 112, 138
Burke, Edmund, 35, 41, 90; as opposed to divine right of majority, 121; as philosophical conservative, 264
Burlamaqui, J. J., 177, 179, 195
Business interests, the business community in politics, 20, 64-65, 66-67; as industrial and commercial capitalism, 13, 25-26, 146, 189-90, 252, 262; as the "money power," 29, 112
Butler, Pierce, 114

Calhoun, Floride Bonneau, 15